T0374511

THE LIFE OF ALCIBIADES

A volume in the series
CORNELL STUDIES IN CLASSICAL PHILOLOGY

Published in association with the Cornell University
Department of Classics

Edited by Frederick M. Ahl, Annetta Alexandridis,
Benjamin Anderson, Caitlín Eilís Barrett, Tad Brennan,
Charles Francis Brittain, Michael Fontaine, Rachana Kamtekar,
Sturt Manning, Alan Jeffrey Nussbaum, Hayden Pelliccia,
Verity Platt, Éric Rebillard, Courtney Ann Roby,
Jeffrey S. Rusten, Barry S. Strauss, Michael L. Weiss

A list of titles in this series is available at cornellpress.cornell.edu.

VOLUME LXVIII
*The Life of Alcibiades: Dangerous Ambition and
the Betrayal of Athens*

By Jacqueline de Romilly
Translated by Elizabeth Trapnell Rawlings

The Life of Alcibiades

Dangerous Ambition and the Betrayal of Athens

Jacqueline de Romilly

Translated by
Elizabeth Trapnell Rawlings

Cornell University Press
Ithaca and London

Original French edition, *Alcibiade, ou, Les dangers de l'ambition*.
Copyright © Éditions de Fallois, 1995.

English-language translation and translator's preface copyright © 2019
by Cornell University

All rights reserved. Except for brief quotations in a review, this book, or
parts thereof, must not be reproduced in any form without permission in
writing from the publisher. For information, address Cornell University
Press, Sage House, 512 East State Street, Ithaca, New York 14850. Visit
our website at cornellpress.cornell.edu.

First published 2019 by Cornell University Press

Library of Congress Cataloging-in-Publication Data

Names: Romilly, Jacqueline de, author. | Rawlings, Elizabeth, translator.
Title: The life of Alcibiades : dangerous ambition and the betrayal
    of Athens / Jacqueline de Romilly ; translated by Elizabeth Trapnell
    Rawlings.
Other titles: Alcibiade. English
Description: Ithaca : Cornell University Press, 2019. | Series: Cornell
    studies in classical philology | Includes bibliographical references and
    indexes.
Identifiers: LCCN 2018059296 (print) | LCCN 2018060257 (ebook) |
    ISBN 9781501739965 (pdf) | ISBN 9781501739972 (epub/mobi) |
    ISBN 9781501719752 | ISBN 9781501719752 (cloth)
Subjects: LCSH: Alcibiades. | Statesmen—Greece—Athens—Biography. |
    Generals—Greece—Athens—Biography. | Greece—Foreign relations—
    To 146 B.C. | Greece—History—Peloponnesian War, 431–404 B.C.
Classification: LCC DF230.A4 (ebook) | LCC DF230.A4 R6613 2019
    (print) | DDC 938.05/092 [B]—dc23
LC record available at https://lccn.loc.gov/2018059296

For Bernard de Fallois, as a token of gratitude and friendship

CONTENTS

Translator's Preface

Jacqueline de Romilly's lifelong contributions to ancient Greek literature and history made her a major figure in French culture. In 1973 she became chair of Greek at the Collège de France, the first woman nominated to this distinguished institution. In 1988, she was elected to the Académie Française as its second female member. In her later years she became famous in France for her ardent advocacy of classical education for all. Romilly (1913–2010) was well known on both sides of the Atlantic as an intellectual and cultural critic and served as A. D. White Professor-at-Large at Cornell University from 1974 to1980.

I was drawn to Romilly's work in 2010, when I undertook the translation of her seminal book *Histoire et raison chez Thucydide*, first published in Paris in 1956. That study altered the course of scholarship on Thucydides's history of the Peloponnesian War by revealing the author's rhetorical and literary artfulness, the means by which he refined and shaped the "facts" of history. The title chosen for my translation, *The Mind of Thucydides* (Cornell University Press, 2012), aptly captures Romilly's purpose and achievement.

Alcibiades is a quite different kind of work, a biography of the meteoric career of the egomaniacal figure who dominated Greek politics and the Peloponnesian War from 416 to 404 BCE. It is a product of Romilly's superb scholarship and of her lifelong effort to acquaint the public with the pertinence of the ancient world to contemporary political and cultural life. To appeal to a wider audience, Romilly composed this book, which was published in Paris in 1995, in an informal style that would arrest attention and enable her readers to see Alcibiades's charismatic personality in full. She wanted her contemporaries to appreciate the dangers his singular character posed to Athens, Sparta, and Persia, all of which fell under his spell and granted him authoritative roles in their policymaking. Although this is a work of history, it often reads like a novel.

But Romilly evinces her usual acumen and care in the research she conducted for this book. She plumbs and critiques the sources for Alcibiades's life, including Thucydides, Plato, Andocides, Lysias, Xenophon, Isocrates, Plutarch, Athenaeus, and Diodorus. On the one hand, she reproduces from the later biographers numerous anecdotes from Alcibiades's youth in order to paint his character, while acknowledging their historical unreliability; on the other hand, she critically evaluates the contemporary and more authentic portraits drawn by Thucydides and Plato, and accords them respect, but not complete credibility. Numerous footnotes disclose her sources to the reader, thus making her biography an unusual blend of erudition and accessibility.

Romilly's treatment of Alcibiades's youthful insolence and arrogant disregard for social norms, and of his later athletic, financial, and religious scandals, was informed by her perception of events in her native France in the mid-1990s. Several times she refers to contemporary scandals in French politics that mirror Alcibiades's outrages in fifth-century Greece. Her central lesson is that a charismatic, amoral, and narcissistic leader imposes enormous risks on a democratic state. Few commentators are as well qualified as Romilly to warn of the public dangers inherent in such reckless individuals. To say that twenty-first-century readers of this biography are likely to find in it parallels to today's political environment is to understate the case.

AUTHOR'S PREFACE

The life of Alcibiades is one of astonishing journeys and adventures. As a young man, he was adopted by Pericles and beloved by Socrates. He was at the center of all political activity at the end of the fifth century BCE. Driven by ambition and endowed with uncommon abilities, he dominated politics first in Athens, then in Sparta, then in the Persian satrapies. He experienced highs and lows worthy of a Greek tragedy. From a position of power over all of Athens, he was suddenly forced to flee from the city that had condemned him to death. He returned as a savior, honored and acclaimed, only to be exiled once again, and ultimately assassinated, by order of the state, in a village in upper Phrygia. Following him everywhere, from city to city, from Sicily to Lydia, from one campaign to another, was the persistent whiff of scandal.

Moreover, a colorful adventurer, he did not live in ordinary times. The Peloponnesian War, in which he played a leading role, was one of the most important turning points in Greek history. It had begun at a moment when Athens was at the very peak of power and influence. It ended in utter defeat. Athens lost both its empire and fleet, thus ending a century of tragic greatness and glory. Alcibiades had presided over all the important decisions, on both sides. He therefore bore, undeniably, responsibility for the disastrous results. And he died in the same year as Athens' defeat. It is as if, from every angle, his personal experience was interwoven with the crucial moments in Athenian history. It is for this reason, then, that he held the attention of and inspired contemplation by the greatest minds of his time. The names of Pericles and Socrates appear above in the opening lines for good reason: Pericles gave his name to the century, and Socrates was the founder of Western philosophy. Moreover, Alcibiades figures in the work of the greatest historian of the time, Thucydides, as well as works of Plato and Xenophon, the historical works and the memoirs on Socrates. Other authors contain allusions or references to Alcibiades, including Aristophanes and Euripides. Even after his death, the orators Isocrates and Lysias argued about the role and character of Alcibiades.

There was, in fact, an Alcibiades problem. An orphan and the ward of Pericles, he seems to have pursued a political path contrary to that of his teacher. Over twenty-five years, that change could be seen to correspond to the ruin of Athens. Was there a connection? And if so, what was it? Was it simply a generational issue of personality and temperament? Or was there a broader decline in civic purpose and morality in political affairs? And did this decline reflect, or cause, a crisis in the democracy and its workings? If the latter hypothesis is correct, as was thought at the time, then it is of paramount interest to us and to all those who hold dear the idea of democracy.

We might say that the life of Alcibiades brought out two political problems that were apparent as early as the fifth century and are still current in today's world.

First, his life embodied Athenian imperialism, in its most extreme and dominant form and in the lack of prudence that led to its ruin. Any reflection on the mentality of conquest benefits from considering his example, which the analyses of Thucydides clarify.

In addition, Alcibiades embodied, and carried to its extreme, the very picture of personal ambition overtaking the public interest. In this he illustrated Thucydides's analysis showing how the successors of Pericles, failing to succeed on their merits as he had done, were led to flatter the people and resort to personal schemes, harmful to the public interest.

Thus, anyone thinking about the problems of democracy in general will profit by looking at the improbable adventures of Alcibiades in light of the assessment of Thucydides or the fourth-century philosophers.

Alcibiades is a unique case, and well beyond the ordinary. But he is also an exemplar for every age, a living example. For this reason, we find so many details in common with our own time. In the life of Alcibiades, we recognize the ambition and the power struggles; the athletic victories that contributed to the popularity of leaders, and that led to financial misconduct. We recognize the "affairs" by which all celebrities are compromised. And we recognize popular reversals of one kind or another. At times, we almost have the impression that the famous text in which Thucydides contrasts Pericles with his successors could apply equally to a contrast between General de Gaulle and his successors.

It is important to guard against such comparisons, for they are always false. One senses, however, that the case of Alcibiades assumes greater value in the degree to which it relates to crises hitting very close to home. That is why I was moved to write this book.

Alcibiades—I feel I have always known him. One cannot study fifth-century Athens, as I have all my life, without encountering him at every turn. One cannot return year after year to Thucydides and Athenian imperialism without growing attached to the man who was a major character in Thucydides's history and who personified the most ambitious aspect of Athenian imperialism. In addition, I was a student of Jean Hatzfeld at the École des Hautes Études at the time when he devoted himself, year after year, to elucidating, for the benefit of a few advanced students, each of the great issues of the period. That is true erudition. For two or three years, I chose to devote myself, at the École Normale Supérieure de Sèvres, to explication of the texts on Alcibiades. It was always Alcibiades. But I would never have started writing this book had I not been struck one day, to my surprise, by the overwhelming sense of contemporary relevance attached to these texts. I began writing at that moment.

These unusual circumstances explain the tone I have adopted in this book.

First, this is not a fictional biography. All words spoken by the characters are taken from the texts. There are no dialogues, reconstructed encounters, or inner thoughts attributed to anyone. My work is that of a Hellenist, trained to respect the sources, and it is therefore based on rigorous scholarship. In citing, and saying whom I cite, I intend to inject an element of authenticity. Besides, I admire these texts, and I love citing them, not only as a sort of validation, but for the pleasure of doing so, and also in order to have them admired, appreciated for their subtlety and depth. I have allowed Plutarch, Thucydides, and Plato to speak for themselves. One may be surprised at times by the foreignness of their style, but these texts bear the mark of authenticity; and we can know the real Alcibiades only through these texts.

In general, I have indicated the problems resulting from disparities among these texts and from the uncertainty they create for scholars. That is all part of the search for the truth. And it seems to me that sometimes the research itself is an adventure, one that adds to our fascination with the political adventure—that of Alcibiades.

So, one asks, is this another "Greek" book, intended for Hellenists? Not at all.

Most Hellenists know all about Alcibiades. I have written this book for those who don't know anything about him, or only very little. And I have tried not to disappoint them.

I have been selective; I have edited and condensed.

Moreover, I have eliminated all details of interest only to scholars; these can be readily found in the works of experts. I have also eliminated a lot of proper names. I know, from experience with Russian novels, how distracting unfamiliar names can be. And they present an aspect of technicality to untrained eyes that can be discouraging. As often as possible I have said "an adversary," or "the Lacedaemonian general," or "a friend of Alcibiades," rather than naming the individual. I know their names of course. They are known to many Hellenists. Again, for anyone who wants to know, these can be found and filled in. And I hope the reader will benefit from these omissions.

Conversely, I have sought, whenever referring to institutions or political situations, to give some word of explanation about them: this may involve a position, like that of general, or a particular custom, like ostracism, or something else, the name of which may be familiar but not the precise meaning.

Although the author of this book may be a professor, she has the benefit of introducing a unique individual, through whom the texts, and the culture to which he belonged, become all the more vivid.

It is normal for the author of a biography to cite the sources from which she drew. And since, as in this work, the texts are Greek ones, as are the names that will be cited frequently, I want to offer a glimpse of the authors I will reference and situate them in the context of Alcibiades's life.

First, among historians, in chronological order, we find the following authors:

THUCYDIDES was about twenty years older than Alcibiades and had certainly met him. He wrote a history of the Peloponnesian War, and though he lived to the war's end, his history stopped in 411. Alcibiades enters the work starting in book 5, and his involvement continues to the end, so from 420 to 411 BCE.

XENOPHON was younger. He wrote the sequel to the unfinished history of Thucydides: his work is called *Hellenica*. Alcibiades enters the story for the years 411 to 404. Xenophon also wrote about Alcibiades in his memoir on Socrates, *Memorabilia*.

With DIODORUS SICULUS we move forward several centuries. He was born around 90 BCE. He wrote a large work entitled *Bibliotheca historica*. Its importance for the story of Alcibiades comes from his use of EPHORUS, a fourth-century BCE historian whose work has been lost.

PLUTARCH lived in the first century CE. He consulted numerous sources for his *Parallel Lives*. There exists a very valuable *Life of Alcibiades*[i] that is completed by the *Life of Lysander* (the Spartan who defeated Alcibiades).

CORNELIUS NEPOS, a Roman, also belongs to the first century CE, and is the author of *Lives of Famous Men*. His testimony may occasionally be cited as a reference. Among the philosophers, besides Xenophon, PLATO is quoted. Although he was considerably younger (by more than twenty years), he could still have known Alcibiades. He names him, or places him, in the scene of several dialogues: principally the first *Alcibiades* and the *Symposium*.

Various disciples of Socrates, less well known, will be cited in chapter 12.

Last, the following orators are mentioned:

ANDOCIDES was a bit younger than Alcibiades. He is included primarily because he had an important role in the events that led to the

---

i. Unless otherwise noted, this is the source for all references to the work of Plutarch.

exile of Alcibiades. He relates the facts in his speech *On His Return*.
An unauthenticated speech that bears on the ostracism in which Alcibiades was implicated is called *Against Alcibiades* and is merely a
school exercise and a series of more or less gratuitous charges.[ii]

ISOCRATES was a master of rhetoric and author of speeches, never delivered, offering political advice. He, too, might have known Alcibiades. He was about fifteen years younger. He wrote a speech on
behalf of Alcibiades's son, in which he praised the father.

LYSIAS was a bit younger than Alcibiades but wrote only after the latter's death. His work includes two speeches: *Against Alcibiades*,
numbers 14 and 15. They attack the son of Alcibiades, and the first
of the two attacks the father. Questions about their authenticity
have been raised, but some scholars accept them.

Of all these authors, only the historians Diodorus, Plutarch, and Cornelius Nepos could not have known Alcibiades. But even they could have
drawn, from the remains of all those texts, directly or indirectly, entirely
authentic testimony of the time.[iii]

Apart from these sources, I will not cite modern works on Alcibiades;
they will, as needed, be referred to in the notes. But I want to mention at
least the large book, very detailed, by Jean Hatzfeld, entitled *Alcibiade*
and published in 1940 by the Presses Universitaires de France. Since that
time, there have been various offerings in various languages.[iv] Those discussions usually concern matters of detail—when scholars aren't clashing
over the question of whether or not Alcibiades had a child with the wife
of the king of Sparta, a type of question that is never easy to resolve even
without the difficulty of seeing through a veil of twenty-five centuries!

---

ii. In citations, it is customary to place square brackets around the name of the author when the work is thought not to be his. Thus "[Andocides]" means "pseudo-
Andocides," i.e., a dialogue erroneously attributed to Andocides.

iii. There are also a few documents on papyrus. The fragment of a biography of Alcibiades (Grenfell and Hunt, 3, 411) does not contain anything new. But new fragments
of *Hellenica of Oxyrhynchus* (a fourth-century work, by a historian writing a continu-
ation of Thucydides) contain an account of the battle of Notium (Papyrus of Florence,
C, published in 1949).

iv. One of the best, and most reliable, is in English: Walter M. Ellis, *Alcibiades*
(London and New York: Routledge, 1989), 141. For a lively and novelistic adapta-
tion, I would mention, in Greek, the book of A. Vlachos, *My Master Alcibiades*, which
has been reprinted numerous times since 1990. There is also, in German, H. Bengtson,
Griechische Staatsmänner (1983).

There is more to be gained from the commentaries on the authors, starting with the great historical commentary on Thucydides, in English, in five enormous volumes, published by Oxford from 1945 to 1981; the work was begun by A. W. Gomme and finished by A. Andrewes and K. Dover.[v]

It is also useful for our understanding of the historical figure Alcibiades to return to those luminous literary texts that never grow old. These make the life of Alcibiades unforgettable and give it a context that relates to our own time.

v. The same can be said for the annotated editions of other authors, to which, for someone like Alcibiades, one should always refer in a systematic way. This is also true for works about these authors.

CHRONOLOGY

508 BCE	Beginning of Athenian democracy.
490–480	Persian Wars, victory of Greece over the barbarians.
480–430	Expansion of the Athenian Empire.
461	Beginning of Pericles's political power
450	Approximate date of Alcibiades's birth; adoption by Pericles in 447.
447–432	Construction of the Parthenon.
443–429	Pericles as general (death in 429).
431–404	Peloponnesian War.
421	Peace of Nicias.
420	Alcibiades enters public life.
415–413	Sicilian expedition.
415 (summer)	Scandals involving the herms and mysteries; Alcibiades goes to Sparta to avoid prosecution.
412 (summer)	Alcibiades goes to Ionia with the Peloponnesian fleet.

411	Political unrest in Athens. Athenian fleet in Samos remains loyal to the democracy and welcomes Alcibiades (who had been at the court of Tissaphernes).
411–410 (winter)	Victory at Cyzicus.
407	Alcibiades returns to Athens.
407–406	Defeat at Notium; Alcibiades leaves Athens permanently.
404	Battle of Aegospotami; the war ends with Athens' defeat. Death of Alcibiades.
399	Trial and death of Socrates.

THE LIFE OF ALCIBIADES

1

Richly Endowed

Alcibiades needs no introduction: Plato has already provided that, on one unforgettable page. In the *Symposium*, he imagines a meeting of famous men who, over dinner, are discussing love. There are a lot of people there. They are talking, listening, the dialogue progresses. But then, after some time, a new guest arrives, after all the others. This arrival is intentionally reserved for the end, when its impact is greatest; suddenly everything is livelier. A knock on the door, and the sound is accompanied by the noise of merrymaking and a flute player. Who is coming at this hour? It is Alcibiades, completely drunk and supported by the flute player.

He stands at the door, "crowned with a bushy wreath of ivy and violets and wearing a great array of ribbons on his head."

Immediately he is welcomed and seated next to the host. On his other side is Socrates, whom he hasn't seen at first. A conversation ensues between the ivy-crowned youth and the philosopher: the rest of the dialogue is entirely between these two.

Such is the appearance, both triumphal and disturbing, of this individual. It contains the seed of his great appeal as well as of his scandalous failings.

They love him; they welcome him. Why? Who is he? Those at the banquet knew; but twenty-five centuries later, we need to describe him. In a word, he has everything one could want.

Beauty

One quality is immediately apparent: Alcibiades is gorgeous, exceptionally so. All the sources speak of his beauty and describe all the love affairs in which he figures. This is the quality that Xenophon, in his *Memorabilia*, points to first, stating with characteristic naivete that "because of his beauty, Alcibiades was pursued by many well-known women."[1] People spoke of "the beautiful Alcibiades." At the beginning of Plato's *Protagoras*, when Socrates is teased about his great admiration for Alcibiades and seems to be a bit confused, they asked: "What could have brought *this* about? Has anything happened between you and him? For surely you can't have found anyone more beautiful, at least not in this city."[2]

There was no one more beautiful than he. But there might be another kind of beauty besides physical beauty, and that is what Socrates meant when he said that he had met Protagoras, the wisest of all living men; it is a distinction he will make frequently.[3]

It should be remembered that at that time beauty was a virtue, widely recognized and celebrated. It was linked to other qualities of a moral nature that formed an ideal human condition, called in ancient Greek *kalos kagathos*. Beauty also attracted less virtuous admirers, and they were not secretive—such as those on many painted vases celebrating some young man by the single word *beautiful*. And at times, as was the custom, we find an almost lyrical evocation of the frenzy inspired by the beauty of someone or other: we see it in the *Symposium* of Xenophon, where this theme occurs several times, in particular in the excitement aroused by

---

1. Xenophon, *Memorabilia* 1.2.24.
2. The Benjamin Jowett translation, revised by Hayden Pelliccia, in *Selected Dialogues of Plato* (New York: Modern Library, 2000).
3. Plato, *Symposium* 218–19.

young Critobulus, who extols his own beauty and that of his friend Cleinias: "I would rather be blind to all things else than to Cleinias alone."[4]
Young Cleinias was Alcibiades's first cousin.

Returning to Alcibiades, we wish we could imagine his beauty, but
we must be satisfied with the opinion of his contemporaries in assessing
his perfection. They never precisely describe Alcibiades, and we have no
image with any authenticity at all. We are told[5] that after his victories in
the Olympic Games he had his portrait painted while receiving the crown;
but the two paintings have been lost. There were various statues in which
he is shown driving a chariot, but these were generally produced posthu-
mously. We allow ourselves to imagine his countenance, a classic face,
proud silhouette: that would be him.

We do know that along with beauty, he had charm and the power
of seduction. Plutarch marvels at this power very early in his biography:
"As regards the beauty of Alcibiades, it is perhaps unnecessary to say
aught, except that it flowered out with each successive season of his bodily
growth, and made him, alike in boyhood, youth and manhood, lovely and
pleasant. The saying of Euripides, that 'beauty's autumn, too, is beautiful,' is not always true. But it was certainly the case with Alcibiades, as
with few besides, because of his excellent natural parts. Even the lisp in
his speech became him, they say, and made his talk persuasive and full of
charm" (Plutarch, *Alcibiades* 1.3).[6]

He could cajole even those he had offended. In another important text
by Plutarch, he is shown to have seduced a Persian satrap (governor) to
do his bidding.[7]

He was of course conscious of his ability to seduce and took pleasure in
it. One anecdote relates that when he was learning everything a well-bred
young man needed to know, he refused to learn the flute: it would distort

4. 4.12. See also 1.9, on the beauty of Autolycus, accompanied by modesty and reserve:
"For in the first place, just as the sudden glow of a light at night draws all eyes to itself, so now
the beauty of Autolycus compelled everyone to look at him. And again, there was not one of
the onlookers who did not feel his soul strangely stirred by the boy; some of them grew quieter
than before, others even assumed some kind of a pose."

5. Athenaeus 12.534d. For the statues, see Pliny, *Naturalis historia* 24.80, 88; the detail
is discussed elsewhere.

6. Throughout the book, Plutarch passages are based on Robin Waterfield's translation in
Plutarch: Greek Lives (Oxford: Oxford University Press, 1998).

7. See below, chapter 7.

his mouth and prevent him from using his voice. The impudent refusal of this beautiful boy became famous, and, according to legend, the flute was removed from the course of liberal studies.

With a taste for the dramatic and for provocation, the handsome Alcibiades would sometimes walk around the agora in a long, purple robe. He was a celebrity, the spoiled child of Athens, allowed to do whatever he pleased and admired for everything he did.

Movie and television stars today are for us what Alcibiades was for Athens—with the difference that, in that small city, everyone encountered him, everyone knew him.

Aristocracy

They knew him for the very good reason that he was not just anyone—far from it.

He came from an aristocratic family, a fact not to be ignored even in the egalitarian democracy that governed Athens at the time. Around the middle of the fifth century BCE, powerful families were highly regarded and enjoyed considerable authority. Alcibiades came from the two largest of these families. His father, Cleinias, was from the Eupatrid family, whose lineage, according to legend, went all the way back to the hero Ajax; and one family member, also called Alcibiades, had been a political associate of Cleisthenes, the founder of Athenian democracy. In this way, Cleinias, through marriage, became part of the most famous family in Athens, the Alcmeonids. He married the daughter of one Megacles, a political figure important enough to have been ostracized, a measure that was intended to remove an individual who was attracting too much attention. And was that all? Oh no! This same Megacles, Alcibiades's grandfather, had a sister who was Pericles's mother, the very Pericles who was for so long the most important man in Athenian democracy and who gave his name to the century.[8] So many titles, such glory! Our own newspapers, so fond of the

---

8. Alcibiades's genealogy is the subject of much discussion, and we will not go into the details of that here. For example, some scholars hold that Pericles was not Alcibiades's uncle but rather his cousin (W. E. Thompson, 1970). See also P. Bicknell, who reconstructed the family tree in 1975 (*Museum Philologum Londiniense* 1 (1975): 51–64). That Alcibiades belonged to both great families is not disputed.

fates of princesses and famous families, give us some idea of the awe that was attached to such a pedigree, even at the height of the democracy. In addition, such status constituted a valuable asset and useful preparation for political life.

Moreover, for Alcibiades, the dazzling pedigree was not all: on the death of his father, in 447, while he was still a child, our Alcibiades was adopted by his guardian, none other than Pericles himself. There was no greater attainment than that.

All these great names were like a brilliant halo around his head.

Such promise! On all sides, there were men around him who were used to leading Athenian politics, who were themselves from the aristocracy, yet who had often taken the side of democracy. There could be no inheritance better suited to start a young man on a life of political engagement.

And this heritage could be an advantage even outside Athens. Important families like his had relationships in other cities. Sometimes the ties were official. One would be named *proxenos* for a foreign city—in other words would be responsible for representing interests as well as the citizens—rather like a consul today with the important difference that the role did not make those individuals bureaucrats. At other times, this office might involve offering hospitality, something that held a strong element of obligation in the fifth century. In some cases, these relationships might be quite personal—just as, in the modern world, aristocrats or business leaders feel connected to their counterparts in foreign countries. Alcibiades, through his family, found himself possessed of numerous ties of this kind. One example: at the time Athens concluded the peace with Sparta, in 421, Alcibiades was offended that the Spartans did not go through him as intermediary and, according to Thucydides, had not shown the respect owed him based on a former *proxeny*: his grandfather had given it up, but he himself dreamed of renewing it by taking charge of the Spartan prisoners (5.43.2). These ties were not insignificant. The grandfather in question, Alcibiades the elder, had given up these functions during earlier proceedings between Sparta and Athens. One of the most important men of Sparta—on whom Alcibiades depended greatly, a man named Endius— was the son of another Alcibiades, in Sparta! This Endius would later welcome the exiled Alcibiades in Sparta.

It was much the same everywhere. Wishing to turn to Argos, Alcibiades sent "a private message" there. We will meet, in the story, "the hosts

Alcibiades had in Argos," and we will also learn that he "was related to the leaders of the Milesians as well."[9] Foreign affairs were often conducted through personal relationships, and the family of Alcibiades had no lack of these . . .

In a word, his family lacked nothing.

Wealth

Actually—and do not think this is unimportant—we are talking about wealth on both sides. On the paternal side, we note that Cleinias provided, at his own expense, a warship for the state. On the Alcmeonids' side, we know that they were related, after being exiled following a sacrilege, to the priest of Delphi and had contributed heavily to the reconstruction of the sanctuary there. Pericles himself was clearly in possession of significant resources: at the beginning of the Peloponnesian War, the king of Sparta who led the invasion and sacking of Attica intended to spare Pericles's property. Because there were social obligations between them, such an exception would have aroused suspicion against Pericles. Pericles deflected this danger by declaring that if that were to happen, he would make a gift to the city of all his property.

Alcibiades was born with every advantage, everything money could buy to advance his career, from an excellent education among the greatest minds to the means of achieving fame throughout the democracy.

What's more, Alcibiades did not have to settle for his own inheritance. Later, he would marry (in 422). And whom did he marry? A daughter of Hipponicus, who was also from an important family, one especially famous for its wealth. Whenever a member of this family is named, it is with the adjective *rich*: rich Hipponicus, or wealthy Callias. It was at the home of this wealthy Callias (Alcibiades's brother-in-law) that Plato's dialogue *Protagoras* took place, because Callias was rich enough to invite every sophist around: Protagoras, Hippias, Prodicus, as well as all the fashionable men who came to hear them. Plato names a dozen, and Alcibiades, of

---

9. Thucydides 6.61.3, 8.17.2. If the cities of Chios, Ephesus, and Lesbos participated in the festivals in his honor (see below), it was no doubt because he had friends there.

course, is among them. In fact, we never really leave this milieu: Pericles's wife had been married first to Hipponicus; she was Callias's mother. With ancient Athens, we soon get the impression that we are in a country where everyone knows everyone else, for it is a small world. And that is also true for the aristocracy in general. And the aristocracy still maintained a very privileged place in the most democratic of cities.

There is another aspect to the wealth of Alcibiades. Because he spent so much, he always needed a lot of money. He had a stable of racehorses, a huge luxury. And he always wanted to show off. He made large public contributions sponsoring triremes (warships) and choruses for dramatic productions. They were still talking about him in the next century, and Plutarch will cite "his voluntary contributions of money, his support of public exhibitions, his unsurpassed munificence towards the city."[10] In addition to this there were occasional gifts here and there. It is said that Phaedo—the philosopher who gives his name to a dialogue of Plato—was taken captive and sold into slavery. Socrates had Alcibiades buy his freedom, according to some accounts at least.[11] Our man, as a true nobleman, loved grand deeds as well as opulence.

Some people thought that, in these moments of extravagance, he spent too much; that happens in every age. And it may be that worry about his financial solvency weighed on his conduct. The very sober Thucydides says so: "His tastes exceeded his means, for maintaining his stable as well as other expenses" (6.15.3).[12]

Nevertheless, the difficulties caused by his extravagance have been exaggerated. When he was exiled, there was a public sale of all his confiscated assets. Stone fragments from this auction have been found. At first it was believed that the sale was very small. As a result, some thought that he had been bankrupt, or that he had managed, before the seizure, to conceal and keep some of his wealth (something that still happens today, as we know). However, new fragments have been found and rest assured: there were still beds and bedding, coats and chests, and the

10. See Isocrates 16.35; [Andocides] 4.20; Plutarch, *Alcibiades* 16.
11. These also mention Crito: see Diogenes Laertius 2.105.
12. Throughout the book, passages from Thucydides's *History* are Richard Crawley's translation in Robert B. Strassler, ed., *The Landmark Thucydides: A Comprehensive Guide to the Peloponnesian War* (New York: The Free Press, 1996).

like.[13] Furthermore, the city would compensate him for this sale by offering a gold crown and an estate. Though Alcibiades may have lost a fortune, he was never poor.

Clearly, this man was a prince.

Now we can see exactly what that meant. Athenian politics had long been in the hands of this cultured and aristocratic group. But that tradition was changing because many Athenians resented it. The rights of citizenship had expanded, as had elementary education: the new social classes were gaining importance. As long as Pericles lived, things were fine; but after his death, power passed to Cleon, a rich tanner, and all our sources commented on his vulgarity, brutishness, and lack of culture. Apparently, ordinary people in every democracy are vulnerable to a vulgarity that feels familiar and optimistic. Aristophanes wrote a comedy, five years after Pericles's death, denouncing this rule by merchants. In the play, the followers of Demos, the People, cite an invented oracle according to which there would come a ruler of the city who was a seller of hemp, until another came who was a sheep dealer, and finally another individual, the worst of all, a sausage seller *(Knights* 126–45). Naturally, he would not have any education: "I know my letters, and then actually, very little, and very badly." "Your only fault is knowing anything, even 'a little, even badly.' Leading the people is not the work of an educated man of good character, but demands an ignoramus, a jerk" (188–94). We won't go further into this social development that always runs the risk of leading, as it did in Athens, to the emergence of a terrible demagogue. This degeneracy was denounced by everyone, from the comedians and tragedians to Thucydides and Aristotle. Such a judgment demonstrates the superior wealth, class, and appeal that the young descendant of two famous families had in contrast to these new demagogues. Alcibiades was supposed to be the next Pericles for Athens.

And now let's acknowledge that Alcibiades's advantages were not limited to the material and the practical.

---

13. See chapter 5 regarding this sale. The steles were published in 1953. See articles by W. K. Pritchett and Anne Pippin in *Hesperia*, 1956, pp. 178, 317, and 318, 328. Even following the exile and return of Alcibiades, authors were still disputing the size of his fortune and his losses: see Lysias 14.37, 19.52

Intellectual Superiority

Just imagine the early education of young Alcibiades, the ward of Pericles. From childhood, he had heard political discussion among well-informed men. According to them, his mind was sharp. In Pericles's home he met, first as a child and then in adolescence, the most distinguished thinkers of his time. He had undoubtedly learned rhetoric, for his mentor was a friend of the greatest sophists. And we know the affection that Socrates always showed him. How could such teachers and role models not have kindled the dazzling intelligence that had so often been a mark of that family?

Moreover, no one ever questioned his keen eye for politics, the rapidity and breadth of his grasp. Thucydides, whose praise of Alcibiades is always reserved, says that the city lost a great deal in sending him away because "publicly his conduct of the war was as good as could be expected."[14] And in every case, when faced with a problem, Alcibiades found a solution, the right combination of the necessary steps to take.

He was also able to persuade others. Ah! How well he did this. He could convince crowds with his eloquence; and he could do the same one on one, arguing with a combination of promises and charm. Even the authorities on such matters, Demosthenes and Theophrastus, said that he spoke admirably. Theophrastus stated, according to Plutarch (10.4), that of all men Alcibiades was "most capable of finding or inventing whatever the circumstances demanded." He sometimes paused in his effort to find just the right words (a slight mispronunciation lending charm to his words . . .). In short, he approached politics with a social superiority that matched his undeniable intellectual superiority, each facilitating the other.

Even apart from these qualities, it was apparent that everything was leading him into politics. He had the means and the talent. He also had the desire. Accustomed from an early age to being first in everything, he strongly desired a political role. This is how he is portrayed in the dialogues of Plato where he appears, particularly in the dialogue called *Alcibiades* (sometimes called *First Alcibiades* to distinguish it from another dialogue of the same name). We will return to this *Alcibiades*.[15] For now

14. Thucydides 6.15.4. On this expression, see below, chapters 2 and 5.
15. See below, "First Interlude" and chapter 12.

we must bear in mind the ambition propelling this young man to political triumphs that Socrates boldly explains: "What is the hope that fills you? I will tell you. You think that if one day you address the people—and you intend to do so very soon—Athenians will immediately be persuaded that you merit even more respect than Pericles or anyone before him, and you will say to yourself that henceforth you will be the most powerful man in this city. And if you are the most powerful man among us, you will be the same among all Greeks; no, not just among Greeks, but also among the barbarians who inhabit this continent" (105a–c). Naturally, this ambition doesn't stop with a continent: true ambition knows no limits. And this text says exactly what is driving him.

And before long that ambition will move him to act. We see him first in war—he was very brave—and soon he will make his appearance in politics. He will assume the highest offices that his age will allow.

Socrates's name has already been mentioned on two occasions. In this picture of all the gifts accorded the young Alcibiades, it would be an odd omission to leave out one very unusual advantage, unlike all the others and not derived from his family: it was his access to the philosophical ideal and influence of Socrates.

Socrates's Friendship

The friendship between the young man and the philosopher is seen best in the dialogue that opened this chapter, Plato's *Symposium*. But the ties they shared are confirmed in many quarters, in both dialogues and biographies. It is true that Socrates loved Alcibiades and Alcibiades loved Socrates. Even if we put aside the erotic aspect of their relationship, it suggests Alcibiades's deep comprehension, at least temporarily or sporadically, of another Socratic ideal, the desire to follow the path of goodness, which reveals an exceptional understanding and admiration. After all, it was to Alcibiades, the failed disciple, that Plato assigned the task of describing his master.[16]

In the *Symposium* a handsome young man enters and sits next to his host. Once there, he notices with awe that his neighbor on the other side

16. On his reasons for this choice, see chapter 12.

is Socrates. They exchange coy remarks. Alcibiades learns what the diners were talking about and decides that he himself will give a toast to Socrates. He begins, and it is these famous pictures of Socrates that have moved generations of readers. In all of Plato's works, no text is more personal, or more profound, on the subject of the master.

In other words, Alcibiades could depict, in the liveliest way, the personality of Socrates; and, by his own account, he was also touched, moved, and inspired.

He begins with a comparison to the statues of the Sileni. Like them, but without the flute, Socrates charmed all who heard him, and Alcibiades described the effect of his words: "They strike us, trouble us, and we are possessed."[17] And then he says, speaking only for himself: "When I hear him speak, my heart beats faster than any Corybantes in a trance; his words make my tears flow; and I see great numbers of other people who feel the same emotions." After listening to Socrates, "it didn't seem possible to go on living as I had before . . . ; he forced me to promise myself that, when I was lacking so much, I should persist in thinking not of myself but of the affairs of Athens."

In other words, Socrates was like these statuettes (Sileni) in that inside he holds the most precious wisdom: "When he grows serious and the Silenus is exposed, has anyone else ever seen the figurines enclosed inside? I don't know. But I have. And I found them to be so divine, so precious, of such complete beauty, so extraordinary, that I would have done on the spot whatever Socrates asked me to do."

There followed a long speech on Socrates's temperance,[18] on his independence from external things, and on his courage.

The speech describes Socrates admirably, but it also shows something about Alcibiades. It shows him impassioned in the evocation of a moral idealism, moved by the idea of the good, ready to change his life, a disciple more sensitive, more moved, more passionate than any other.

The beautiful youth, inebriated from the beginning, could also be drunk with exaltation for the discovery of the good: "I myself have seen it . . ."

---

17. 215d. Subsequent quotations are all in the pages that follow this one. The translation is that of Benjamin Jowett.

18. See chapter 2.

That is quite a gift Plato has given him. None of the previous speakers and none of the disciples who appear in the dialogues have had such royal treatment. Whatever the reasons for this choice, which will not become clear until the end of the book, we must admit that it reflects a real relationship that left a deep impression. Alcibiades may have been influenced by a charm that affected him deeply.

We will return to this charm in the next chapter, and to an implied amorous context. What mattered here, in a chapter that opened with Plato's *Symposium*, was to add that extra spark, unlike anything else, that further enhanced the individual and his reputation. From the beginning, this young man is not just the archetypal "golden boy."

The very phrase "young man" calls for an additional comment. We think of Alcibiades as a young man. And it is partly Plato's fault if this label has stayed with him and added to his charm.

Youth

Alcibiades was never old: he wasn't fifty years old when he died. However, at the time of the *Symposium* he was no longer a young man. He was probably born between 452 and 450 BCE. When the Peloponnesian War began, he had just left the tutelage of Pericles. He had his own house, his own slaves. He would soon assume political responsibilities. But his character was still that of an adolescent—brilliant, bold, a little irresponsible, the way he would always be seen. The events in the *Symposium* are thought to have occurred in 416, when Alcibiades was thirty-five years old. But he was still seen as a "boyfriend," someone other men pursued,[19] and as a spoiled child, one who could say anything and was forgiven everything. This adolescent view has, in some way, permeated our image of him, and is imprinted there forever.

In 416, it should be said, Plato was twelve years old. He never knew the young Alcibiades. There was a generation between them. But the legend of Alcibiades is etched in our minds. And in relation to Socrates he is always

---

19. The story he tells of a failed seduction, which we will return to in the next chapter, is obviously prior to the supposed date of the banquet; but it is not presented as an old story.

seen as an adolescent. Plato, who was never very faithful to chronology, portrays him thus, at the expense of realism.

It should be added that Alcibiades, even while remaining very handsome as he aged, eagerly projected youthfulness.

He assumed major political roles as soon as his age permitted, and he made a strength of his youth. When opposing Nicias, in that very same year of 416, he spoke for youth and claimed the right of young people to speak and offer advice.

That claim occurred during the debate about the Sicilian expedition. Nicias, who opposed the expedition, viciously attacked the ambitious young Alcibiades. Nicias was himself more than fifty years old. He did not mince words: "And if there be any man here, overjoyed at being chosen to command, who urges you to make the expedition, merely for ends of his own—especially if he is still too young to command . . ." And he summarized: "When I see such a person now sitting here at the side of that same individual and summoned by him, alarm seizes me; and I, in my turn, summon any of the older men."[20] There it is, in fifth-century Athens, the contrast between old and young that we know well. The same theme occurs in the theater fairly often. It is something we might call a social phenomenon. But Alcibiades was not to be intimidated. Yes, he was young. He points to his success and declares: "Thus did my youth and so-called monstrous folly find fitting arguments to deal with the power of the Peloponnesians, and by its ardor win their confidence and prevail. And do not be afraid of my youth now, but while I am still in its flower and Nicias appears fortunate, avail yourselves to the utmost of the services of us both."[21]

Later in his speech he repeats scornfully: "Do not let the passive policy which Nicias advocates, or his setting of the young against the old, turn you from your purpose, but in the good old fashion by which our fathers, old and young together, by their united counsels brought our affairs to their present height. . .; neither youth nor old age can do anything the one without the other."

As in the *Symposium*, youth will continue symbolizing the young man of thirty-five. And in his hands, his youth became an advantage, another

---

20. 6.12.2, 6.13.1.
21. 6.17.1; the following quote is at 6.18.6.

means of persuading individuals and mobs, another means of making everything about himself.

He had everything. He had too much. Why would he not think that he was more important than anyone else? He became a symbol worthy of reflection for all time, and the most dazzling symbol of all. In every era there are brilliant boys whose youth seems a golden age. There are many gifted young men with talent for political life. But Alcibiades had all these qualities and more. His nobility, his beauty, his boldness were incomparable; what is more, his country had attained the highest degree of power and culture. His ambition was boundless. Moreover, the teacher who was drawing him to the good demanded absolute truth and justice. Thus, the life of Alcibiades represents an ideal and an unforgettable symbol. It has meaning for every era. And perhaps more than in any other age, it has meaning in ours. Alcibiades, as a figure of selfish ambition in a democracy in crisis, reveals, through the betrayals and scandals of his own time, crises of our times—even though there would seem to be no discernible Alcibiades among modern politicians.

Actually, as in a blueprint, we see his destiny leading him and Athens. It began with small scandals of an insolent selfishness and grew into plots of political audacity—up to the day when the scandals swept violently over him. In a democracy, scandal is and always has been dangerous.

Alcibiades's scandals began early and continued for a very long time.

2

INSULTS AND SCANDALS

A gilded youth is no friend of self-discipline, and the young Alcibiades was too gifted not to become spoiled by success. Insolence was part of his nature, and it conformed to circumstances. He was confident and was not going to let anyone get in his way.

These are traits that were no doubt less threatening for the future than his ambition but, when combined with ambition, first encouraged it and then, owing to scandals, thwarted it, and led to failure.

He was no more moderate in his flaws than in his talents. So while the self-control, reserve, and piety of an Alexander were extolled, posterity would remember Alcibiades with a litany of the most exaggerated reproaches. Cornelius Nepos exclaimed, in a Latin phrase that even today needs no translation: *"Luxuriosus, dissolutus, libidinosus, intemperans!"* (1.1).

We will not go that far, but let the reader decide. The anecdotes collected by Plutarch are sufficient to suggest Alcibiades's character—and all the dangers therein.

Plutarch recounts anecdotes randomly; and he has retained those that lack any grounds: a person like Alcibiades excited passions, myths, and tall tales. But the anecdotes agree among themselves, and the individual is unmistakable.

Admittedly, the stories are entertaining. We read them with the indulgence an older generation often shows toward youthful pranks, for they express a certain courage, gaiety, and freedom. But we should be wary because, little by little, the stories go from cheerful insolence to real affronts to people and disdain for rules. Indulgence has no place when you realize that the slope can be slippery: it certainly was for Alcibiades.

His character can be detected as early as the description in Plato's *Symposium*. Was he drunk, this fellow Alcibiades? Was he not yelling at the top of his lungs? Should he not have been subdued by the flute player? Oh, but it was his charmed youth. Oh well, everyone admired him. But they should have recognized in the beautiful Alcibiades what could already be seen, his inseparable other side, the intolerable Alcibiades.

His insolence went very far back, to childhood and early adolescence.

One of Plutarch's first anecdotes tells us about an incident in a busy street. It is the kind of thing one can imagine in any small city of our own time. Alcibiades is a small child (*mikros*); he is playing with little bones in the street when a vehicle arrives loaded with merchandise. "First, he ordered the driver to stop because his little bones had dropped in the path of the vehicle. The man, who was a bit boorish, didn't listen and kept going. The other children scattered." What did Alcibiades do? He lay down in front of the truck and yelled: "You can continue now if you want." At that, the driver withdrew, frightened, and the bystanders ran, crying in fear, toward the child (2.4).

Of course, he should have allowed the truck to pass. That was obvious. But what presence of mind. What courage. Alcibiades never lacked courage. He was always taking risks—in war and in politics, even at the moment of his death. But this early view illustrates his almost reckless valor; and perhaps readers today are thinking, in the backs of their minds, about a young man all alone in front of a tank, on the great square in China. In any case, the heart of all the Athenians who were present that day went out to that child, despite his arrogance and foolhardiness.

And then we see him, a very young man, learning to wrestle. He bit his opponent, who let go, yelling: "You bite like a girl, Alcibiades!" Was he ashamed? Not at all. Proudly, he retorted "No! Like a lion" (2.3). Plutarch quotes it as one of Alcibiades's famous sayings, one worthy of a Spartan.[1] In any case, it suited him. Obviously, Alcibiades should not have bitten the boy, but the boldness of his reply was admired. So what if he was violent? Alcibiades's "words" would often become famous. Intelligence helped, but so did the total lack of timidity and consideration for others.

With such a temperament, young Alcibiades was bound for a lifetime of insolence. And in fact, it is clear that the many assets he enjoyed gave rise to increasingly serious faults in his day-to-day life.

Handsome, rich, noble, he took no account of others and felt entitled to everything.

This attitude appeared first in his manners. As noted already, there were the long, purple robes. But that wasn't all. We know that he was the first to wear a new shoe style known as the "Alcibiades."[2] People say that he raised fighting cocks; he enjoyed leading the life of a spoiled youth.

In relations with others, this meant an attitude of deliberate arrogance. From this came a series of small insults, at times friendly, and at other times hateful, revealing a total contempt for others.

Once, for example, he met a schoolteacher and asked for a book of Homer. The man didn't have one. What did Alcibiades do then? Apologize and say thank you? No, he simply slapped the man.[3] Not everyone can defend the study of Homer in this way, even if sometimes tempted to do so. The difference is that Alcibiades never resisted temptation: he was quick to strike a blow.

At another time, it was a *choregos* who was a competitor of Alcibiades: another slap (16.5).

And then there was an artist—a painter—whom he kept sequestered until he finished his work (again, one might wish to do the same, without claiming that such behavior is acceptable . . .).

1. *Apophthegms* 186d, 234d.
2. Athenaeus 12.534 c.
3. Plutarch, *Life of Alcibiades* 7.1. Someone else, meriting a reprimand in the form of a smack, received compliments full of irony (7.2). Montaigne, noting the first anecdote (2.36), related it very nicely, calling Alcibiades "that silly man," and compared the gesture to that of someone calling out "a priest without a prayer book."

He criticized, he insulted. It was said[4] he was so sure of himself that he would have criticized even the twelve gods . . .

What's more, he could, out of pure insolence, ridicule the very rules of the city. One anecdote—frankly a rather dubious one—relates how he supposedly tore up and destroyed a bill of accusation against one of his protégés.[5] Even if it is made up, the story is still symbolic of what it meant to feel so free to do as one pleased.

At the very least we can understand the ferocity of the words of his adversaries. The author of *Against Alcibiades*, which is falsely attributed to Andocides, exaggerated: "Some he robbed, others he beat, or locked up and held for ransom. He showed that democracy was nothing, for he spoke like an advocate for the people and acted like a tyrant" (27).

This refusal to respect the rules was emboldened by the two great advantages of wealth and beauty. With the first came the outrageous behavior, and with the second, moral scandals.

Alcibiades was rich. Because he enjoyed being talked about, he was also a big spender. As a result, he always needed money; and perhaps at times he counted on his fame and notoriety to excuse his lack of scruples.

Three anecdotes bring vividly to life this love of ostentation and this lack of scruples, either admitted or demonstrated.

The first is innocent and almost endearing. According to Plutarch, his entry into public life came during an assembly where the people collected gifts and acclaimed public donors. Ah! Such a beautiful noise, all this acclamation. Alcibiades hastened to an official and offered his contribution. It must have been large, because "the people applauded and shouted cries of joy."[6] Alcibiades, delighted, released a quail he was carrying under his coat. And with that the Athenians scrambled to catch the bird of the stylish young man. The quail suggested levity, the gift implied generosity, while the acclamations are a reminder of Alcibiades's appetite for popularity and attention.

Very quickly though, we turn to something more serious. One day when he went to see his mentor, Alcibiades was told that he was busy;

---

4. Aeschines of Sphettos: about him, see below, chapter 12.

5. This anecdote comes from a certain Chamaileon; for a critical view of this and other cases, see Hatzfeld, 132.

6. Plutarch, *Life of Alcibiades* 10.1. See later in this chapter and below, chapter 10.

he was trying to prepare his account for the people of Athens. (The magistrates had to do this at the end of each year, and some people claimed that Pericles had taken certain liberties.) Alcibiades is said to have replied: "Better to find a way to avoid giving an account!"[7] How promising in the future politician! In fact, throughout his life, Alcibiades showed a disturbing unwillingness to be accountable—diplomatic lies or financial trickery, the pleasant youth had some unpleasant ways.

And then the third and most famous of the anecdotes on this subject is equally revealing. It concerns the dog with its tail cut off. Alcibiades had a valuable dog with a very beautiful tail, which he cut off. An appalling and reprehensible act. But he was delighted: "It is exactly what I wanted, for the Athenians to blabber about it." Why? Because he liked to be talked about? Because he liked to attract attention? Of course, but not only for that reason. Alcibiades always had a plan, and there was also always something he wanted to be forgotten; he went on: "I want the Athenians to blabber about this so that they won't say something worse about my accounts" (9.1).

The scandal pleased him because it satisfied his vanity; it also pleased him because it provided a smoke screen to distract from other aspects of his ambition or misbehavior.

Are we any better now, in the twentieth century?

In any case, the rumors continued, rightly or wrongly. Plutarch, comparing Alcibiades and Coriolanus, wrote: "As for money, there are reports that Alcibiades often took money, illegally, from people seeking to corrupt him and that he used the money to line his pockets and pay for his debaucheries" (3). Just slander? Have we never heard such charges against other statesmen? Even the Athenian democracy let itself be tainted by corruption. In this, we are hardly unique.

We know where this extravagance and the desire for fame would lead Alcibiades: just as in other epochs, he sought fame in athletic success; he maintained a stable of racehorses and ran into legal trouble over the money invested in this operation. We will return to this later, but the meaning of it all is clear.

7. Plutarch, *Life of Alcibiades* 7.3. These words appear in Diodorus and recall an old view that Pericles might have taken the advice of his ward in starting the war (12.38). This is still cited in Plutarch in *Apophthegms* 186e.

But first, we come to the area most scandalous of all, relating not to Alcibiades's wealth, but to his beauty: his love life.

The stories multiply. They may not all be true, of course; but together they leave an unmistakable impression. Not surprising, either, that his good looks would lead to scandal: he was involved with both men and women. It was said that even here he always wanted to win.

And winning was easy for him.

Normally, relationships with women caused little gossip in Athens. Marriage demanded that women submit to their husbands, living in the home, seeing no one. And relationships with prostitutes were ignored. They were talked about only in the case of Alcibiades because of the number of liaisons and the rumors that flew about them.

But our man went further: he managed to inject scandal into his own marriage.

First, some gossip: while still young, he had been to Abydos, on the Hellespont, with his uncle. There, the uncle and nephew were said to have married the same woman; a daughter was born, but which one was the father? Later, both would enjoy her favors, a case of possible incest. The story is outrageous and defies belief.[8] But again, he was rich. Later, people would even say that Alcibiades was guilty of incest with his mother, his daughter, and his sister.[9] The vile charges transmitted under the name of Antiphon say that he went to the women of Abydos to learn things that met his inclinations for vice and debauchery.[10]

Nevertheless, he had a real marriage. The choice was an honorable one, for he married the intelligent and well-raised daughter of a very rich and famous man. But there was such behavior . . .

First, he slapped his future father-in-law, following a bet. The next day he invited this man to punish him with a whipping. But . . . he was pardoned.

---

8. The primary source is a fragment of a speech attributed to Lysias. It is found again in an anecdote in Athenaeus, among other references to hetaeras known to have had ties to Alcibiades.

9. See chapter 12.

10. Fragment 4 Budé. This is all that remains of this text; hence it is not cited among the sources in our preface.

He received a very nice dowry, but before long the young groom demanded more, alleging that it had been agreed to in case there were children. His wife's family feared they were being robbed.

Was he a good husband? Of course not. His wife knew that Alcibiades was "frequenting both foreign and Athenian courtesans, so she left his home and repaired to the house of her brother. Alcibiades did not care and continued his debaucheries."[11] She sued for divorce. Divorce by a woman was rare and looked on with disapproval, but it did exist. On the day of the decree, according to Plutarch, Alcibiades "ran, grabbed her, and led her home across the public square as bystanders watched without daring to save her" (8.5). It was useless to argue, according to Plutarch, that this was absolutely against the law. Such was the audacity of Alcibiades.

There were other women in his life. After the capture of Melos by the Athenians in 416, all the men on the island were killed and the women were taken as slaves. Alcibiades took one as a partner and raised the child he had with her (16.6). Plutarch might say that is human nature; one could say that a master suits himself and serves his passions at the expense of the helpless people whose fate has been a constant source of shame for Athens. It appears that Alcibiades supported the decree that called for the harsh repression of the island—at least the proposal to enslave the women.[12] After that, to have a child with one of them was low behavior.

Having now slipped into the political realm, led there by his amorous adventures, we might as well continue. Two episodes in his political career show vividly the role his relationships with women of all sorts and from all countries would play over the course of time.

As an exile in Sparta, Alcibiades owed his new friends everything. What did he do? According to the texts, he took advantage of the king's absence when he was off on a campaign to seduce his wife and father a child (yes, another one). The queen, overcome with passion, is reported to have named the child, from day one, Alcibiades. Scandalous! As for our hero, he was as proud as he could be, bragging that he did it so that one day his descendants could be kings of Sparta. The husband was less proud, calculations confirming his bad luck; an earthquake,

11. Plutarch 8.4–5.
12. Thucydides does not report it, but see [Andocides] 20.

easy to date, had forced the handsome Athenian to flee from the queen's bedroom.[13]

Is there more, you ask? Oh yes. But this act resulted in Alcibiades's breaking with Sparta and approaching Persia, which from then on was going to control the action. The outcome of the war was altered by his behavior. Athens profited from it. But, indirectly perhaps, the fate of Europe vis-à-vis Asia was affected. The actions of a seducer in the midst of powerful people influences politics whether he wants to or not.

We will skip over these years: we reach the finale. Alcibiades is again an exile. He finds himself in a village of Phrygia with a courtesan named Timandra.[14] There he was assassinated. Our final view of the young god of Athens is a body riddled with arrows and spears, a body that a courtesan covered with her own clothes to improvise for him there, so far away, the best burial possible. This woman was the mother of another very famous courtesan, Laïs.

These women were faithful to Alcibiades. But he was never faithful. Even up to this final episode that concludes Plutarch's written account and shows how legends are born, starting with certain well-known traits. Assassins would not have been hired by his political enemies, but by the victims of a different scandal: "He had seduced and was holding a young woman from a good family, and it was her brothers who, tired of his outrageous behavior," ended, in the middle of the night, the life of the seducer.

How fitting that would be! An ending worthy of reflection. Plutarch does not quite believe it. But he leaves us to wonder, inconclusively, and without commentary. So we have a choice of these two types of women surrounding the death of Alcibiades.

Alcibiades was a ladies' man, and his female conquests were well known throughout Greece. But, as was quite common in Greece, he also knew the other kind of love. It was his good looks that attracted many admirers, who courted him with differing degrees of success.

Plutarch shows that he could be hard and insolent. And he certainly was with Anytus. Later Anytus would be Socrates's accuser; but at this time he was one of the whole Socratic group; and he was quite taken with

13. For more about this event, see below, chapter 6.
14. And probably another one, Theodotia of Athens (according to Athenaeus 13.574). See below, chapter 11.

Alcibiades. One evening, he gave a dinner to which he invited his beloved. Alcibiades refused, got drunk at home, and then marched with a rowdy band on Anytus's house, where he ordered his slaves to take half of all the gold and silver. Anytus's guests were appalled, but the lover did not complain, observing on the contrary: "Rather say . . . that he treated me with consideration and kindness, because, free to take it all, he left me something" (4.5). The anecdote is well known. It may reveal the submissiveness that love may impose, but it also reveals the insolent manners Alcibiades might adopt toward those enthralled by his beauty.

By contrast, he was at times generous—not with his favors but with money. He did not give it away, no. He did more. A certain metic (resident alien) was smitten with Alcibiades; he sold all his goods to offer the profit to Alcibiades. The latter, amused, invited him to dinner, gave him back his gold, and advised him to go the next day to pursue a certain office. He himself went to stand with the metic. The men who held this office were uneasy about their accounts and offered the metic money to drop the case. Alcibiades pushed him to bargain, and the metic left one talent richer—which was a lot more than he had offered Alcibiades in the first place.

Quite an operator, the handsome young man, as clever and irritating as you could wish. The sharp eye, the pleasure in playing a trick—both give us a sense that he was mocking it all, his own ability to attract and those shady types who would pay to have him.

Clearly, he did not always say no. And in this too he was never bothered by scandal. A story is told that as a child one day he disappeared. People worried and wanted to organize a search; Pericles declined, knowing that the child was with Democrates, one of his *erastai*, or lovers. The great man thought it was better to avoid drawing attention that would compromise the boy (3.1). Alcibiades himself had no such qualms.

The texts contain frequent allusions to these relationships. People talked about the lovers of Alcibiades. And it seems that as a young man he was immersed in an atmosphere of pleasure and its pursuit. We mentioned earlier the incident of Alcibiades's debut in the Assembly and the quail that flew away. To be presented to an official, one had to be an adult; but everyone knew that common birds, cocks and quails, were often gifts between lovers. In the *Birds* (line 707), Aristophanes cites the handsome boys who "won over or ceded to lovers when they received a quail, a waterfowl, a goose, or a cock." The flight of the bird could be a clear sign (to those) around the young donor of the amorous relations in which he took pleasure.

All the stories and all the profiles of the lovers taken or rejected are enough to show that Alcibiades was no more discreet or moderate in this domain than in others. We will see how they explain the relationship between Socrates and Alcibiades. But from now on, added together, all those anecdotes, true or false, are enough to explain the harsh opinions many held of the beautiful Alcibiades. Xenophon, in his *Memorabilia* (1.2.12), awards him the prize for the three flaws particularly offensive to Greek morality: he, more than anyone else, lacking all self-control (*akratestatos*), was guilty of excesses and crimes (*hubristotatos*), as well as violence (*biaiotatos*). With self-discipline he might have resisted the temptations of amorous pleasures, popularity, extravagance; the insolence that he showed so readily came from *hubris* and aggressiveness.

The record would be overwhelming if we could forget that for all his excesses, Alcibiades was charming. The devilish man was charming. He could raise eyebrows in his financial dealings and then dazzle with his generosity. He could pursue, provocatively, lovers of all kinds, and remain the nice boy everyone loved anyway. He could offend, strike, insult, and be forgiven because he always did it with grace and good humor. As Plutarch said, "Even his flaws were met with indulgence and favor." He also noted that "he was not despised by his fellow citizens, even those he had wronged," whereas Coriolanus, "as admirable as he was, was never well-liked."

All the damning superlatives that Alcibiades unquestionably deserved were softened by the indulgence that for so long attached to him and that all of us today continue to feel a bit, even as we censure unreservedly his indisputable faults.

This very fact leads us to pause a moment to conclude with two final incidents that drew attention in antiquity, and in which the reputation of the man and his moral failings came together. The first concerns his relationship with Socrates, which is colored by the romantic mores of the time; the other leads us right into his role as a leader involved in politics.

Socrates is widely regarded as one of Alcibiades's suitors. Plutarch speaks of Socrates's love for Alcibiades (*erōs*, several times) and of his rivals. The *First Alcibiades* begins with a speech by Socrates, who calls himself the first to have loved (*erastēs*) Alcibiades, and the only one who remained faithful to him. The first words of *Protagoras* are addressed to Socrates: "Where do you come from, Socrates? I wager that you have been chasing after handsome Alcibiades?" In *Gorgias,* Socrates says he has two loves: Alcibiades, son of Cleinias, and philosophy. In all cases, and Alcibiades's arrival in the *Symposium* proves the point, the relationship between the two men is presented to us in the light of pursuit and flirtation, with a hint of homosexual tenderness openly expressed, perhaps slightly in jest and also treated with irony, perhaps because it was serious.

There would be no point here in trying, as so many others have done and without the slightest bit of evidence, to determine Socrates's actual feelings. But one fact emerges from all the evidence: whatever his feelings were, Socrates did not seek a physical union but a spiritual one. In this case, as in those mentioned in the *Symposium*, his firmness (his *karteria*) was legendary. He withstood temptations just as he resisted cold, fatigue, and sleep. Moreover, he expressed indignation about making sexual demands of a loved one.[15] Several texts show Socrates contrasting love of the body with that of the soul, physical beauty versus internal beauty. Confusion occurred easily because of the vocabulary used. This has sometimes led critics to misunderstand a very beautiful text by Aeschines of Sphettos in which Socrates compares the feelings he experienced toward Alcibiades with those of the bacchants. There was a rush to proclaim ecstasy and passion. But if you read the sentence to the end, you see that his meaning is just the opposite. Why then, the bacchants? "Because the bacchants, when they were possessed by the god, drew milk and honey from wells where others could not even find water. In the same way, having no knowledge the teaching of which would make me useful to him, I still believed that by spending time with him, my love would improve him."[16] Drawing milk and honey from so unlikely a soul—that is how Socrates was comparable to the bacchants.

While scholars may have been mistaken, the first to be mistaken was Alcibiades himself. Not that he, savvy as he was, was foolish enough to regard Socrates as an ordinary lover. He was troubled, and surprised. He

15. Xenophon, *Memorabilia* 1.2.29, relates how he considered Critias a pig for having wanted to demand sexual favors from young Euthydemus.
16. Fragment 11; see the excellent commentary of G. Vlastos, *Socrate: Ironie et philosophie morale*, 340–41, of the French translation.

felt that Socrates had something that he himself lacked. But he believed that all he had to do was to offer himself as he would to someone else. That, at least, is what Plato has him say with self-awareness and irony and inimitable charm.

Alcibiades finds himself with Socrates; he has sent his servants away; he is anticipating an advance to which he wants to yield. But nothing happens. Next, he invites Socrates to exercise with him, alone. Again, nothing. "So I invite him to have dinner with me, in the very friendly way of a lover who wants to attempt something with his beloved." Socrates is reluctant to accept and then wants to leave right after dinner. Alcibiades insists, obliges him to stay . . . The story is delightful, the outcome almost obvious. But the result is that Socrates and Alcibiades are finally stretched out under a blanket while nothing happens except a lofty discussion about inner and outer beauty. Socrates's inner beauty won.

After that, the roles may have reversed. In the *Symposium*, Alcibiades frankly admits to feeling drunk when he listens to Socrates: "My heart beats harder than the Corybants in their frenzy; his words make my tears flow" (215e). The feelings have changed sides, and love has changed its very nature.

To admit all this, one had to have the boldness of Alcibiades. The story implies overtures that made him look ridiculous when they failed. This was a venture to suppress. But Plato saw it clearly: Alcibiades's audacity, reinforced by wine, was in telling all, making fun of himself; his amorous successes protected him from any shame about this—and he was not a man to be easily embarrassed.

Moreover, the story is a nice one: it shows the discovery of another meaning of love. I cite it here only because it also shows how unprepared for this he was, given his usual behavior.

Besides, it was undoubtedly too late to change his behavior. Whatever may have been the date of the night with Socrates, the *Symposium*, where Alcibiades tells the story, is thought to have taken place in 416. He was already involved in political life, actively in pursuit of glory.

The second incident, the final one, took place at the beginning of that brilliant career. It combines great glory with the absence of scruples for which we have seen ample evidence.

Whenever someone wanted to be talked about, to draw attention, to get ahead, one of the best ways to do so was to win victories in the

Panhellenic Games. The contests that were properly called "athletic" were obviously the domain of specialists. However, one could, and often did, own a stable of racehorses and compete in the chariot races. Doing so won great notoriety: a bit like someone who, today, manages and trains a football team to compete in the major competitions. This was a sure way of getting oneself into the spotlight and earning the acclaim of the city that would celebrate the victories. Add a bit more hype in the fifth century BCE and a bit more of a populist chord in the current era, and the similarity is even more striking.

In the family of the Alcmeonids to which Alcibiades belonged there was a tradition of greatness in victories at the Panhellenic Games. He wanted to resume that tradition. In 416 he was victorious in not one but in several events, an incomparable achievement.

As Plutarch said soberly, "He gained great notoriety from his stable of racehorses and from the number of chariots. No one, either private citizen or nobleman, had ever, in the history of the Olympics, entered seven chariots at once. He alone did it" (11.1).

By itself this was awe-inspiring. But the result was no less so: Alcibiades took three prizes, including first and second place.

As for the third prize Alcibiades won, history is ambivalent: Thucydides says that he won fourth, Isocrates says third, a point also made in an ode Plutarch attributes to Euripides.[17] It is a nice example of how stories are always simplified for emphasis. Today, if someone wins first prize in Latin and second prize in Greek in the general exams, the press will say she won first prize in both; I know from experience.

It was in any case a triumph. Thucydides, Plutarch, Isocrates all mention it, all agree on that point. The celebrations that followed were unforgettable. The ode Plutarch attributes to Euripides sets the tone: "Of you I wish to sing, son of Cleinias. It is wonderful to win; but what is more wonderful is something that no other Greek has done: that is to take first, second, and third prizes in the chariot races and to return twice, with ease, as the object of the herald's proclamation."[18] Many Greek cities showered him with honors: Ephesus offered him a magnificently decorated tent,

17. Thucydides 6.16.2; Isocrates, *On the Team of Horses* 34; Euripides, in Plutarch 11.3.
18. Plutarch 11.3; the *Life of Demosthenes* mentions this ode, noting that he is unsure it is by Euripides, and no one today would attribute the ode to Euripides.

Chios gave him food for his horses, and Lesbos gave him wine and food for his own table and for the receptions he hosted at Olympia.

He himself celebrated his victory with all the pomp one would expect. Among the events he sponsored was a parade in Olympia, for which the city allowed him to borrow gold vases; according to *Against Alcibiades,* falsely attributed to Andocides, Alcibiades used the vases for a private party. But he kept them for a procession that took place the next day; it was a procession he organized, distinct from the official procession that followed. The result: strangers believed the vases belonged to Alcibiades. Many of them, seeing the ways in which he acted on his own, "laughed at us when they saw that a single man was more powerful than the entire city" (29).

The brilliance of the victories and celebrations was long remembered. All the authors refer to it. We know that there were paintings (cited by Athenaeus) and a third-century sculpture mentioned by Pliny. Alcibiades is sometimes represented by a quadriga (four-horse chariot). And the lack of scruples? It is there, of course, and not only in the incident involving the borrowed vases. As usual with this character, shameless carelessness was combined with glowing success. In sports, in our own time as well, financial affairs are not always strictly proper.

Alcibiades had a friend, an honest man named Diomedes. Diomedes, who also wanted to enter chariot races, heard that there was a fine chariot in Argos that belonged to the state and was available for sale; he asked the very influential Alcibiades (who was especially influential at Argos, for reasons we shall soon learn) to buy the chariot "on his own, Diomedes's, account." Very well! What did Alcibiades do? He bought the chariot . . . and kept it! Diomedes was furious, sued, went to court. The speech *Against Alcibiades* that has come down to us in the name of Andocides mentions a "stolen" team and a race entered "with horses belonging to someone else" (26–27). Indeed, we have seen that Isocrates's speech about Alcibiades is called *On the Team of Horses.* This is the team involved. The case went on a long time. Diomedes's suit over this incident in 416 was halted with Alcibiades's exile; despite efforts by Diomedes in 408, the case was not heard until 396, twenty years after the event. The charge was brought by a certain Tisias, who was unaware of Diomedes's case,[19] and was directed against Alcibiades's son, who had just attained majority. The improprieties

---

19. On this trial, see below, chapter 12.

linked to the pursuit of athletic victories can lead to a lot of problems. Alcibiades's son argued, we can be sure, that the race was entirely proper and that the suit was an awful conspiracy.

Nevertheless, a moment of glory unique in the entire fifth century was dulled by shadows that had accumulated consistently in the life of this man.

All the insolence and scandalous behavior was diverting and amusing. But from the moment the man entered politics, they acquired some weight and played a role—one that historians have not failed to reflect on, beginning with Thucydides.

Causing a fuss around oneself could be useful. Prestige leads to power. It could even be a benefit to the city. On Alcibiades, Thucydides devotes a brilliant analysis of this possibility that is not to be overlooked.

Nicias made the Athenians suspicious of Alcibiades's excessive ambition: the man "may astonish you with his extravagant racehorses and find in the exercise of his duty the means of covering his enormous expenses." To which Alcibiades responded by saying:

> The Hellenes, after expecting to see our city ruined by the war, concluded it to be even greater than it really is by reason of the magnificence with which I represented it at the Olympic Games, when I sent into the lists seven chariots, a number never before entered by any private person, and won the first prize, and was second and fourth, and took care to have everything else in a style worthy of my victory. Custom regards such displays as honorable, and they cannot be made without leaving behind them an impression of power. Again, any splendor that I may have exhibited at home, in providing choruses or otherwise, is naturally envied by my fellow citizens, but in the eyes of foreigners has an air of strength as in the other instance. And this is no useless folly, when a man, at his own private cost, benefits not himself only, but his city. (6.16.2–3)

We do not need to drown this powerful text in commentary. The elaborate boasts about prestige, extravagant banquets, noisy celebrations that Alcibiades makes in this argument are familiar to every age.

20. Quoted in my earlier discussion, which constitutes an anticipation of Thucydides 6.15.

But wait: there is another side to it. This attitude has a political cost; it sows jealousy. And when scandals are added, defiance and enmity grow. Alcibiades's argument might have been excellent; it might have succeeded; but it was weakened, very quickly, by the bitterness and anger it had sown. It was not so much his arguments that led to failure as it was the memory of his refusal to respect the laws, the liberty he took in speech and behavior, that *paranomia*, as Thucydides called it.[20]

Thucydides explains this in another important passage that gives meaning to the whole series of misdeeds and misdemeanors that we have just examined. It provides a passage of general reflection. Thucydides recalls Alcibiades's keeping of a stable and other expenses, all of which were beyond his means, and he adds:

> And later on this had not a little to do with the ruin of the Athenian state. Alarmed at the greatness of the license in his own life and habits, and at the ambition he showed in all things whatsoever that he undertook, the mass of the people marked him as aspiring to tyranny and became his enemies; and although in public life his conduct of the war was as good as could be desired, in his private life his habits gave offense to everyone and caused them to commit affairs to other hands, and thus before long to ruin the city. (6.15.3–4)

This passage has been heavily debated, for it seems to telescope two different periods. Thucydides was writing about 416 and the hostilities that led to Alcibiades's first exile; but it slips right into the final disaster, following the second exile.[21] This slip, though it need not be taken up here, is nevertheless revealing: it shows how, in the life of Alcibiades and in the history of the war, things repeat themselves. In fact, Alcibiades's entire public life can be read as a dialogue in which the talents and the defects compete, each as vivid as the other.

There is a lesson here, and it interests us still today because it shows the formidable interaction between private scandals and public works—or, as we might say, between morality and politics.

---

21. One wonders whether the part of the phrase "his conduct of the war was as good as could be desired" refers to his brief command of the Sicilian expedition or to later events. Here, let us preserve the double possibility.

First Interlude

Alcibiades between Two Lifestyles

These scandals involving Alcibiades have led me, by way of random anecdotes, to a point late in his life. But as Thucydides's work makes clear, the scandals did not become a serious issue until the day they became mixed up with politics.

Could that combination have been avoided? One might have hoped that before entering politics Alcibiades would have calmed down, reflected on the real purpose of politics, and understood at a deep level the lessons of the man he admired most and whose words he found profoundly moving. Was it possible that the failed seduction, in the scene with Socrates, might have eventually opened his eyes?

These are strictly hypothetical questions since we know that Alcibiades never allowed himself to pause, that he ran from intrigue to success, from success to scandal, from betrayal to rehabilitation, without ever thinking about the lessons of his teacher. But Plato, perhaps for the purpose of justifying Socrates,[1] demands that we stop this line of thinking and ask

---

1. See below, chapter 12.

ourselves about that moment when, between the two paths before him—
that of philosophy and that of immediate success—Alcibiades not only
failed to choose, but he was not even aware there was a choice.

There are two dialogues among the works of Plato called *Alcibiades*.
We distinguish between them by referring to *First Alcibiades* and *Second
Alcibiades*, the latter a dialogue on prayer. This second is definitely not an
authentic work of Plato. Although the authenticity of the first dialogue
has also been questioned, it would sadden me to deny Plato's authorship.
And it does admirably address the issue of Alcibiades's failure to make a
choice between the two paths.

The problem is similar to the one Prodicus describes when he sets
Hercules at the crossroads, one path leading to justice and the other to
pleasure. This quandary is what confronts anyone who is about to take
action. From the very beginning, Socrates confronts Alcibiades (still a
young man,[2] and unfamiliar with politics) about the choice before him.
What Alcibiades wants is immediate success. In a phrase previously noted,
Socrates describes Alcibiades's ambition as extending from Athens to all
of Greece and beyond (105a–c).

To serve that ambition, Alcibiades needs Socrates. Otherwise, what
would he know? Where has he learned the meaning of the just? And
how can he enter politics without knowing what it is? Only knowledge
of the just is useful. He must aim high. Alcibiades's true rivals, the only
rivals worthy of him, are the kings of Sparta and Persia; such a rivalry
demands application and a serious apprenticeship, in the course of which
he can acquire self-knowledge. The conclusion: "And if you are to manage the city's affairs properly and honorably, you must impart virtue
to the citizens" (134b). Alcibiades then agrees, and makes a resolution:
"Well, it is decided, I shall begin here and now to focus my attention on
justice" (135e).

Socrates expressed his doubts, doubts that would be borne out by
subsequent events. When this dialogue was written, Plato (or someone else after him, if we do not believe it to be authentic) knew perfectly well that Alcibiades never applied himself to virtue; that he threw

---

2. Not yet twenty years old, according to the text (123d, and also 118e). Another passage
is ambiguous about his age but still gives the impression of youth.

himself into politics and used every means to advance his personal objectives; and that after many highs and lows, he ended up a failure, entirely alone.

First Alcibiades is written, clearly, to show that Socrates's teaching was useless, since Alcibiades never applied it. The dialogue also shows that this remarkable young man might have taken a different course had he listened more to his teacher, had he paused and reflected. Just before describing the launch of his political career, this momentary pause Plato evokes helps us to assess the gravity of the situation. The disasters in Alcibiades's life and the disasters in the history of Athens for which he bears responsibility all began with this failure of the student to listen to his teacher, and with the grievous separation between morality and politics.

This same idea reappears in a variety of dialogues, authentic or not. The *Second Alcibiades* presents a young Alcibiades who knows nothing of the good, an ignorance that invalidates his piety: he cannot make a sacrifice until he dispels his ignorance. And there again, Alcibiades promises to apply himself and to learn. He never does so, and was eventually, as we know, condemned to death for sacrilege.

At the end of this book we will reflect again on the subject of Alcibiades's character and life as inspiration for Plato. For now, having mentioned the opportunity offered to this ambitious young man, the moment when something we might call the temptation of the good occurs, it is touching to reflect on one final image. It comes by way of a disciple of Socrates, one very close to the teacher, named Aeschines of Sphettos. We cannot be certain of its authenticity, but no one can dismiss its symbolic value. As in Plato's *Alcibiades*, Aeschines of Sphettos shows Socrates shaming Alcibiades: he compares him to Themistocles and shows how unworthy he is by comparison, how ignorant he is. According to the author, Alcibiades was then "forced to lay his head on Socrates' knee and weep."[3] Alcibiades weeps with regret because he fears that he lacks the necessary preparation for the career he desires.

His discouragement, if it ever really existed, was not to last long. But at the threshold of a political career full of great hopes and great disappointments, it offers a brief hint of what might have been.

3. We have the text from the rhetorician Aelius Aristides.

What might have been never was. Alcibiades's entry into politics, with its long train of scandals, was where the waters divided; the current was henceforth to carry Alcibiades to his fate, and far from the lessons of his teacher.

Now we must leave Socrates and Plato. The historians take the stage, primarily Thucydides. Alcibiades begins to act.

3

POLITICAL DEBUT

The Argive Alliance

The first mention of Alcibiades in Thucydides's work (5.43)—in history, in other words—refers to the year 420 BCE. Thucydides's introduction lacks the personal charm found in Plato, but it goes straight to the heart of the man's character.

Leaving aside, for the moment, the context for this introduction, the following conveys the spirit of the passage.

"Foremost amongst these was Alcibiades son of Clinias, a man still young in years for any other Hellenic city, distinguished by the splendor of his ancestry. Alcibiades thought the Argive alliance really preferable, not that personal pique had not also a great deal to do with his opposition" (5.43.2). The explanation, both clear and concise, continues, but what we retain from this passage is the characteristic pride and ambition, conveyed from the very first mention of his name, and the emergence of two kinds of themes, the rational ones, and the self-centered ones. Compounding the problem, it is the latter that are dominant, the former being little more than a kind of concession or acknowledgment of fortuitous coincidence.

The word "ambition" is a highly charged one when we recall Thucydides's assessment of Pericles, in which he describes Pericles's successors as being more or less equals: "And each grasping at supremacy, they ended by committing even the conduct of state affairs to the whim of the multitude" (2.65.10).

This juxtaposition of contrasting motives—the future of Athens versus the promotion of self-interest—is found throughout the work of Thucydides whenever Alcibiades is involved: in the Sicilian expedition and later during the action in Asia Minor. We will have occasion to return to this theme: Alcibiades acted solely out of self-interest. This is a point that has already been made emphatically, and all that follows will serve to repeat it.

Let me add that Plutarch himself (who obviously had read Thucydides) also adopts this interpretation. After he refers to Alcibiades's messy private life, he states: "Nevertheless, it was actually by pandering to his ambitious longing for recognition that his corrupters set him prematurely on the road of high endeavor; they convinced him that as soon as he took up politics, he would not merely eclipse all the other military commanders and popular leaders, but would gain more power and prestige among the Greeks than even Pericles enjoyed" (*Life of Alcibiades* 6.4).

Once the subject of politics was brought up, all the flaws and insults were erased as compared with the ambition that would lead him to the pinnacle of success and the depths of disaster.

How would he use that ambition? And to what purpose?

First, he had to strengthen his position in Athens and take power. How does one do that?

Athens functioned as a direct democracy. All citizens had the right to speak in the Assembly. For someone from one of the great families, like Alcibiades, this was particularly easy and normal. He had to do it. We know that he spoke up to offer a gift of money to the city (on the occasion when he released his quail): he was applauded and earned popular approval. We also know that he supported Cleon's effort that increased the tribute paid by the cities of the empire.

But what could be expected to result from these endeavors? If one really wanted to play a role, he had to hold an office. It should be remembered that all public offices in Athens were determined by lottery, were collegial, and were nonrenewable. No democracy has ever taken such care to avoid control by individuals and the establishment (as is apparently the case today) of the "politics of personality." No office, no administrative position, could lead to the slightest influence.

There was one exception. The highest leadership position, because it entailed military responsibility, was elective and renewable. These were the offices of the ten generals, elected by vote, once a year. There were also a few fiscal offices, but they had little weight. The generals were the true leaders of the democracy: Pericles had led the city as a general; he had been reelected to the post fifteen times. Moreover, among the ten generals (each of whom had slightly different charges) one ranked higher than the others. As Thucydides often remarked, "Pericles was general, with nine others." Often a famous or well-liked individual succeeded in getting his friends elected. But that was not always the case.

Alcibiades intended to become general, and without delay. In fact, he was elected in the same year, 420 BCE.

In these elections, as in the workings of the Assembly, nothing was done according to party affiliation: there were no parties. There were, however, political friendships, as well as dominant political tendencies. There were also, during the course of this democratic regime, secret enemies who remained loyal to the oligarchy and hoped to see it reestablished someday. These would come to play a particular role a few years hence. It was known that some people belonged to clubs, or *hetaereiai*, around important people. However, anyone who expected to participate in politics was a supporter of democracy: the difference was mainly between extreme and moderate democrats. Alcibiades oscillated between these inclinations. Athenian politicians cared little about policies and general principles. Alcibiades, as his later conduct would prove, cared even less: he preferred opportunity to principle.

In politics, personal rivalries were consequential. Thucydides knew this very well. At this time, many people talked about Nicias, who became a natural rival of Alcibiades. Their views about internal politics differed very little; but they took altogether opposing positions on the most important question of the day, namely, external relations and the war with Sparta.

Athens and her allies had been at war with Sparta and the Peloponnesian League since 431. The war had begun under the rule of Pericles. It dominated Alcibiades's entire youth.

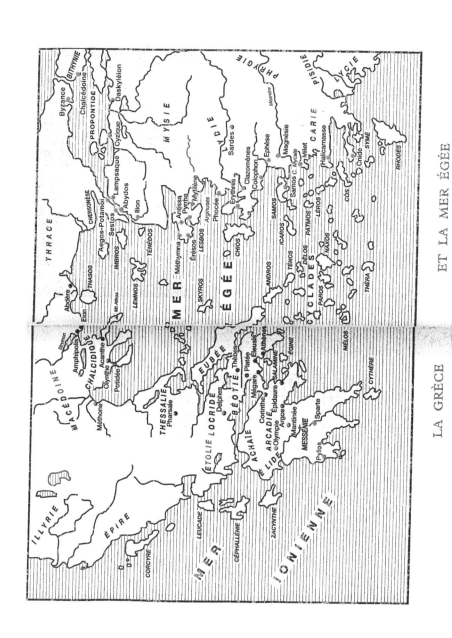

LA GRÈCE   ET LA MER ÉGÉE

Map 1. Greece and the Aegean Sea

It provided an opportunity to make his name and he did not let the opportunity escape him. In the *Symposium* he tells, or Plato has him tell, how he and Socrates had fought in the battle of Potideia, in the far northern Aegean, in Chalcidice. It was the year before the war with Sparta began. Alcibiades was wounded there and saved by Socrates. Alcibiades demanded that Socrates should receive a medal of honor, but because of Socrates's entreaties, Alcibiades received it. The young aristocrat had served in that battle as a foot soldier. Just a little later, in 424, he fought at Delion, this time in the cavalry. Both battles enabled him to stand out.

However, the war was more than an occasion of brilliant conduct for a young man like Alcibiades; it led him to make some critical decisions about the conduct of his affairs.

It is important to see the entire Greek world then as divided into two blocks: on one side, Athens, with its democracy and maritime empire; on the other, Sparta, with its oligarchy and continental allies.

The conflict had grown slowly in the middle of the fifth century, following the shared victory of the Greeks in the Persian Wars. Fifty years later, Athens had added to its authority by transforming allies into subjects, and by developing its fleet thanks to the money they provided in the form of an annual tribute. The reputation of Pericles's Athens, her power, the construction of the Acropolis, were all linked directly to this maritime empire. And the Peloponnesian War resulted, specifically, from the fear sown by her growing power in Sparta.

The two sides had been fighting for ten years: on one side was Athens, ruling almost all the islands, and busy at home working to maintain the regime of the democracy. On the other side was Sparta, a city-state ruled by oligarchy, that led the Peloponnesian League and defended oligarchy as much as possible. The league included all the peoples of the Peloponnese except for two: the Argives and the Achaeans had been allies of both sides.

For ten years these two blocs waged war throughout most of the Greek world. The Peloponnesians regularly invaded Attica, and the Athenians had won, in a pitched battle, a bridgehead at Pylos, in the Peloponnese. Both sides also engaged in the affairs of their respective allied cities where civil wars had broken out. The Athenians supported the partisans of democracy and the Lacedaemonians supported oligarchies. Their involvement prolonged the conflicts and intensified the violence.

Finally, on both sides, there arose a desire for peace, and in 421 peace was concluded. Both sides had reasons to want to come to terms. The Athenians had managed to capture a certain number of Spartiates at Pylos (that is, true Spartans, the elite, as opposed to Lacedaemonians, referring to a wider population), while on their side, the Lacedaemonians had procured the defection of several allies of Athens, from the Chalcidian peninsula. Having already crushed several defections, Athens feared they would continue to grow. The peacemakers got to work in both cities: in Athens, it was Nicias, and historians today call the peace of 421 "the Peace of Nicias."

Nicias's importance among the supporters of the peace would only encourage Alcibiades to throw himself into opposition. From beginning to end throughout his career, he would stand for Athenian ambition and imperialism; first he opposed Sparta, but later he would take up other ideas for conquest, always opposing Nicias.

Initially, he was able to exploit the fragility and ambiguities of the peace. These were real. Naturally there were issues of reciprocal restitutions, giving rise to arguments and delays; there were issues of the date and order of restitution. But the biggest complications arose from the unhappiness on the part of Sparta's allies. Some had refused to vote for the peace. Moreover, the terms had allowed for possible modifications if they were agreeable to both Sparta and Athens; there was no mention here of the allies, and they took offense.[1] There were two main consequences of this: first, it multiplied the delays and refusals of the restitutions, and second, they considered unifying against Sparta.

That would have been a serious problem at any time; it was especially serious in 421, because of Argos.

As has been noted, Argos had not joined the war with the Peloponnesian League; in 451 it had concluded a thirty-year peace agreement with Sparta, which was about to expire. It found itself free and could join either Athens or Sparta, or even play a role in combining around itself the Spartan allies who were not happy about the treaties.

All eyes were now on Argos. After the conclusion of the peace, the Corinthians began negotiations with certain leaders of the city: Argos, they

---

1. Thucydides 5.29.2.

told them, should "look after the safety of the Peloponnese." To that end, Argos should announce that "every city that is independent and values its rights could, if it wished, ally with the Argives in a defensive pact." And it should designate leaders empowered to negotiate with these cities. The Corinthians were hoping that many cities would rally out of hostility toward Sparta.[2]

What should Athens do? Nicias thought Athens should embrace peace and come to an agreement with Sparta. He had set an example by returning to Sparta its famous prisoners, those it had sought so strenuously. In doing so, he had brought on himself the anger of many Athenians.[3] For his part, Alcibiades took the other side. He declared, from the beginning, that Sparta "was not reliable." It was seeking to take advantage of the treaty in order to be finished with Argos and to oppose Athens again. Once his course of action was fixed, he would play the Argive alliance card with determination.

The Argive alliance was a grand idea and could claim illustrious antecedents. Themistocles, when he was ostracized, took refuge in Argos at the beginning of the century. Perhaps influenced by him, Argos and Mantinea became democracies. A little later, when the political alliance with Sparta had failed, Athens had turned to an alliance with Argos. This was an ally that could resist Sparta in the middle of the Peloponnese.

However, turning to Argos was a choice fraught with consequences. Whereas Pericles had grasped the superiority of naval power, and whereas the Athenian tradition, ever since the Persian Wars and Themistocles, had been "to stick to the sea" (Thucydides 1.93.4), now comes Alcibiades seeking to gain a foothold in the Peloponnese. Going even further, he decides to "stick to the land" (Plutarch, *Life of Alcibiades* 15.) It represented a break with tradition, an innovation, a bold stroke.

Plutarch adds that Alcibiades based his plan on the "oath of the ephebes," which vowed to make the borders of Attica grain and crops, as if the agricultural lands belonged to them. It sounded good, but it was not true. The actual text of the "oath of the ephebes," carved in stone, was discovered several decades ago; it says nothing of the kind.[4] Was this

2. Thucydides 5.27.2.
3. 5.35.4.
4. See L. Robert, *Études épigraphiques et philologiques* (Bibliothèque de l'École des Hautes Études, 272), 296–307.

a problem of communication? An intentional misunderstanding on Alcibiades's part, always mindful of providing sources for his policies? Who knows? One thing only is certain: the Argive alliance, by rejecting the important distinction between maritime and continental power, represented a new direction that demanded an aggressive propaganda campaign. Alcibiades lost no time.

The first among the Spartan allies to manifest their discontent and to approach Argos were the cities of Mantinea and Elis. These cities had caused problems between Athens and Sparta over the restitutions required by the Peace of Nicias. This was Alcibiades's opportunity.

It was at this point that Thucydides named Alcibiades for the first time and introduced him in the passage quoted at the beginning of this chapter. He did so for the very good reason that Alcibiades was just then beginning to make his diplomatic moves.

Alcibiades had friends in various cities, particularly in Argos, and he sent a private message there inviting the people of Argos, Mantinea, and Elis to come as quickly as possible to Athens to conclude an alliance. The moment, he said, was right, and he himself would advance their cause with all his might. He convinced them.

The people of Argos, persuaded by Alcibiades, bent to Athens' side, telling themselves that "the longstanding friendship of a city like Athens, living like themselves in a democracy and possessing a powerful navy, would be on their side in the case of hostilities" (Thucydides 5.44.1). They sent their representatives: the business was going to work.

Alcibiades's entry into politics was thus both bold and resolute. It seemed he was bound to succeed. One will note that he had acted on his own and, thanks to his friends in Argos, very privately. Thucydides is categorical on this point.

The following actions of Alcibiades will show him using tactics still more dubious, to the point that they perplex historians even today.

It is quite an extraordinary episode. Thucydides has left a detailed, but perplexing, account. One is left with a sense of intrigues so subtle that they make it difficult to distinguish truth from falsehood.

The people of Argos had sent their representatives. At the same time, an embassy arrived from Sparta composed of friends of Athens. They were sent in haste with a twofold mission: to prevent any alliance between

Argos and Athens, and to do their best to resolve the problems of the restitutions important to Athens. They were received by the Council of Five
Hundred and declared that they were authorized to settle the restitutions
once and for all. Thucydides tells us that Alcibiades, fearing a settlement,
devised a strategy. This was no small thing: "He persuaded the Spartans
by a solemn assurance that if they would say nothing of their full powers
in the Assembly, he would give back Pylos to them (himself, the present
opponent of its restitution, engaging to obtain this from the Athenians)
and would settle the other points at issue."[5]

This was a bizarre arrangement. Even more bizarre was the meekness
of the Spartans who agreed to it. Before the people in the Assembly, they
contradicted what they had said in the Council, and in so doing lost all
credibility. The people lost patience; and when Alcibiades bitterly attacked
Sparta, the Assembly was all set to conclude an alliance with Argos.

But as luck would have it, there was an earthquake. Even in that enlightened century, Athenians always respected what they took to be divine signs
(at times someone might allege a dubious earthquake to cause the suspen-
sion of the Assembly); the Assembly was adjourned until the next day.

With that, Nicias took the matter into his own hands and tried to convince the Assembly that ambassadors should be sent to Sparta (Nicias
among them) and that the Spartans then needed to clarify their intentions, remembering that Athens had not (or not yet) made an alliance
with Argos.

It was a last resort and it failed. Nicias managed to get some of what
he wanted but not enough. The result: the Athenian people, furious, concluded without delay two peace treaties and an alliance with Argos and
its allies, Elis and Mantinea. Corinth did not join. But this was quite a triumph for Alcibiades. A personal triumph. In the following spring he was
a general and led a military expedition to the Peloponnese, organizing the
alliance and having fortifications built wherever he could.

These are the facts as related by Thucydides. However, the report has
been the source of some misgivings. There are good historians who have
wondered if Thucydides has misrepresented the facts and perhaps rushed
to judge Alcibiades's actions too harshly. In addition, some have cited the
unfinished state of book 5 of his work.

5. Thucydides 5.45.2.

What to believe? Alcibiades gives the Spartans this ridiculous advice and they listen to him? Don't they realize they will lose all credibility by one day saying one thing and something else the next? What do they expect? They know that Alcibiades did not like them, that he had never wanted peace or an alliance with them. How did they not mistrust him? Not only did they not suspect him, but after being duped completely, they held no grudge against him. Later, when he had to flee Athens, he went to Sparta! Better still, he was welcomed there by a certain Endios, with whom he was united by strict bonds of hospitality between their two families.[6]

And Endios was one of those very same ambassadors who were duped by Alcibiades's ploy to secure the alliance with Argos. How could the man have forgiven such cruel treachery? No, this story is not plausible.

There have been efforts to correct Thucydides.[7] Some have suggested that the Spartans never really had full authority (later, Nicias too failed to reach agreement) and that Alcibiades had simply forced them to admit that publicly. We acknowledge that here Thucydides casually adopted a version of the events unfavorable to Alcibiades and incoherent as well.

The problem is that this kind of unfairness on the part of Thucydides and this hostility toward Alcibiades are not found elsewhere in the work—nor, for that matter, is such a casual approach. This anomaly would require positing an evolution of his feelings about Alcibiades that does not match any reconstruction of the development of this work.

It is true that book 5 is not one of Thucydides's best, far from it. There is confusion about the years when the war is interrupted or when the story moves faster than in other sections of the work. There are problems with his depiction of conspiracies, and his refusal to deal with internal politics creates real difficulties. That is all true. But these explanations for the weaknesses and ambiguities in the text do not mean we should reject his version of the facts for the sake of psychological rationalism. Rather, the very ambiguity we feel reading this account may reveal something about the character of Alcibiades.

Let us take a closer look at these ambiguities that might allow us to correct the most accurate of historians. We say that it is implausible that the Spartans would have been persuaded by Alcibiades to change their

6. Thucydides 8.6.3. See chapter 1.
7. J. Hatzfeld, *Alcibiade*, 89–95.

declaration; and that it was not realistic for them later to forgive his treachery. But are we confident that Alcibiades should have been judged according to the norms of the time?

No one can claim that Alcibiades, as persuasive, attractive, brilliant, daring, and deceptive as one could be, was incapable of pulling the wool over the eyes of the Spartans. Who would claim that, even after the Spartans' failure in Athens, he could not blame circumstances, say that his advice was good but that he had some bad luck or awkwardness, that he had done everything possible, etc.? The Spartans badly wanted to get Pylos back, territory that Athens still held and had used for years to foment uprisings against Sparta. Whenever someone wants something badly enough, he will follow risky advice and allow himself to be fooled. Alcibiades told the Spartans, as reported in Plutarch 14.8–10 (and as is generally accepted), that the Assembly would be more demanding and impassioned than the Council if they acknowledged that they had full authority. He also told the Spartans that if they were to resolve their other issues, that would compromise the return of Pylos. And he could always find other arguments. Don't forget, after all, the Athenian talent for the art of persuasion—and don't forget that adversary of Pericles who claimed that if Pericles were defeated in battle, he could convince the Athenians that he had actually won. Alcibiades had far fewer scruples and far greater audacity than his famous mentor . . .

Often in textual or literary criticism, an unjustified accusation draws attention to an original feature that is ultimately revealing. The same may be true for historical criticism that rests only on plausibility; it draws attention to what the narrative presents as implausible but true, to the extraordinary and unique. It is entirely possible that Thucydides, who did not like going into anecdotal detail involving individual actions, allowed himself this carefully wrought account to highlight, from the start, the amazing methods Alcibiades used for successfully deceiving everyone around him. Incredible? Oh yes. Alcibiades was unlike anyone else.

Moreover, his ties with Endios were very tight: remember that Endios's father was named Alcibiades. It is not necessary to imagine, as one scholar does,[8] some kind of secret pact between the two men; ties such as theirs could pass as the surest guarantee. Of course Endios could trust this

8. R. B. Kebrick, in *Mnemosyne*, 1976.

young man: his family's relationships alone would have been as convincing as Alcibiades's well-known verbal skills.

We need not conclude that the story lacks credibility, that we should therefore dismiss it; we should rather conclude that the story, while not widely known, shows just what Alcibiades was able to do.

And it is so very revealing! His first public act led straight to the heart of conspiracy and manipulation, where the double game is king. Alcibiades's early success in politics was amazing, based on a lack of scruples that would remain his trademark to the end.

The result of these events would first confirm Alcibiades's success, then quickly reveal its weakness.

The Argive alliance had the problem of involving Athens in the upheavals in the Peloponnese. Argos had a dispute with Epidaurus (which Alcibiades may have imagined adding to the newly formed group): there were troop movements, expeditions, and diplomatic campaigns; Athens risked finding itself again fighting Sparta, with nothing to gain from it. Then, as the quarrels dragged on, it became evident that the situation was not at all stable, either in Athens or in Argos.

Athenians were soon unhappy to see events in the Peloponnese going nowhere and changing abruptly: in 418, Alcibiades was not reelected general, whereas Nicias was. Alcibiades was not entirely moved aside. Thucydides tells us that he became an ambassador (5.61.2), but his popularity declined. This sequence shows just how damaging such shifts in direction are. Any policy needs to be allowed some continuity and goodwill. Nicias felt no need to support allies he had never sought and who opposed those with whom he had worked to build good relations. In the course of these campaigns, the Athenian troops are too few in number, and too slow. In the battle at Mantinea, the one great battle of those years, the Athenian contingent comprised just a thousand hoplites and three hundred cavalry, while Thucydides calls the overall forces "by far the finest Hellenic army ever yet brought together" (5.60.3). The Athenians must have realized this because a new contingent of one thousand men came, after the battle, to join those already gathered (75.5). The quarrel between Nicias and Alcibiades, and the Athenian hesitations, following first one leader and then the other, had become a source of weakness. There may also have been a price to pay for an alliance just barely concluded through manipulations and misunderstandings.

Still more serious was the fact that Argos was neither more stable nor more secure. Again, there had been vacillation, and divisions remained. During one of the first Spartan attacks, two Argives (one of whom was a *proxenus* of Sparta) acting privately went to King Agis, who was commanding the Lacedaemonian army, and convinced him to withdraw. Their initiative did initially turn out well for them. But then others furthered their effort, and soon Argos seemed ready to surrender to Sparta. When the aforementioned Athenian reinforcements arrived, the Argives refused to allow them into the city, fearing that doing so would cause a break with Sparta. According to Thucydides, "their plan was to make a treaty with the Spartans first, follow it with an alliance, and after this to fall on the popular party" (5.76.2). Sparta offered proposals for agreement. Discussions followed (which included Alcibiades, who just happened to be there). In a nice reversal, the friends of Sparta prevailed. The Argives dropped their alliance with Elis and Mantinea. They dropped their alliance with Athens. They concluded a peace treaty and an alliance with Sparta. And voilà, there they are hand in hand with Sparta. The democracy was immediately overthrown and an oligarchy favorable to the Spartans was established in Argos.

It is easy to see just how fragile the situation was, and how uncertain its success.

Was it then a failure? Not really. The specifics matter for understanding Alcibiades's life. Democracy was soon reestablished in Argos and a new treaty was concluded between Athens and Argos at the end of the summer of 417. There were various maneuvers on one side and another, including a small naval expedition from Athens to Argos, leading to the deportation of a certain number of oligarchs. In short, order was reestablished. Argos remained a faithful ally of Athens to the end. It sent contingents for the Sicilian expedition, as did Mantinea.[9] The presence of those troops greatly enhanced Alcibiades's prestige, and his enemies dared not attack him, fearing, as Thucydides says, that the people might protect him "because it was thanks to him that the Argives and some of the Mantineans joined the expedition."[10] Still later, while Alcibiades was at the head of the Athenian

9. Thucydides 6.43.1, 7.26.1: 500 Argives, plus 250 Mantineans and mercenaries.
10. 6.29.3. For the offer of service to the democrats at Samos, see 8.86.8–9. Argos will offer temporary asylum to Alcibiades (Isocrates 16.8–9).

forces installed at Samos, which maintained a democratic regime, Argive delegates came to offer assistance to that democracy. Despite a few close calls,[11] the Argive alliance and the Argive democracy endured.

However, this success, though it matters, was not the success Alcibiades had hoped for. The Argive alliance had not served as the lever for an action against Sparta in the Peloponnese. And throughout the period when hope for such action was at play, the alliance proved to be fragile, shaky, and of little use.

Alcibiades was not entirely responsible for this problem. Divisions within Athens and Argos rendered political activity incoherent and uncertain. This is one of those cases that reveal the extent to which any state, divided internally, proves itself weak and insecure in all external political efforts. Contemporary European politics offers similar examples.

Overall, this great project and its disturbances shed light on two facts about the literary and political history of the time: the first concerns Thucydides's history; the second, events that followed in Athens and led to a verdict of ostracism.

Today, when we speak of the "Peloponnesian War" we are talking about Thucydides's account of the war between Athens and its allies and Sparta and its allies, between 431 and 404 BCE. It ended in the total defeat of Athens: it lost its empire, was occupied, and saw its walls destroyed. But there had been a peace in 421, that famous "Peace of Nicias," just described. So people often speak of a first war, sometimes called "the war of Archidamus" or the "ten-year war" (431–421). Separately, there followed Athens' Sicilian expedition, and then a new war between Sparta and Athens. Thucydides's originality lies in his having perceived that in fact there had been a single war and that the years following the Peace of Nicias—years of clashes, conflicts, contests—had really been just a parenthesis. He explains his view in his "second preface" in book 5, chapters 25 and 26: "Only a mistake in judgment can object to including the interval of treaty in the war. Looked at in the light of the facts, it cannot, it will be found, be rationally considered a state of peace, as neither

---

11. At one time there was talk of an antidemocratic plot at Argos fomented by friends of Alcibiades (6.61.3). Was that true? Probably not. For a harsh judgment of Argive politics, see E. F. Bloedow, in *Klio* (1991): 49–65.

party either gave or got back all that they had agreed" (5.26.2). His analysis continues: solid, clear, original. The thesis has been widely accepted ever since: the Peace of Nicias was not a true peace. Had the interval been shorter, others might have been able to group together the two wars. However, given a seven-year break, Thucydides's insight is original and penetrating.

The picture we have just drawn of the vagaries and reversals in the Argive alliance clearly shows the artificial and unstable nature of the peace that prevailed at that time. From this perspective, we see clearly both the optimism in the Argive alliance and its precariousness. Nowhere does Thucydides say that lasting peace would have been possible if Nicias had been given a chance and there had been more support for a true alliance with Sparta; nor does he say that peace would have been better assured if Athens had let Alcibiades act and had taken bases in the Peloponnese capable of checking Sparta. Thucydides is not one to adopt unverifiable hypotheses or a priori reconstructions. But divisions and indecisiveness were harmful. Thucydides makes that clear. And Athenians of the time did not deceive themselves. Which led to the business of ostracism.

Ostracism was a uniquely Athenian practice. It meant the exile of a politician for ten years. But this form of exile was not dishonorable, nor was it a punishment. Cleisthenes, the founder of the democracy, was said to have initiated this practice to remove the friends of tyrants. The practice actually began even earlier, but the purpose was always to remove anyone who disturbed and opposed Athenian politics, either because he had become too important or because there was a conflict between two leaders and two policies. In this respect, in our own time, we acknowledge the wisdom of an institution that seems harsh or risky but would not endure otherwise. Every year the people voted, by a show of hands, whether or not to proceed with an ostracism vote. If the response was positive, another vote, requiring a full quorum, was held to decide whom to ostracize. Some of the leading men of Athens had been struck with ostracism, including Themistocles and Aristides, as had two illustrious ancestors of Alcibiades.

We must admit that the circumstances just described, including the vacillations and plotting between Nicias and Alcibiades, represented a typical occasion for ostracism. It would remove one of them and leave the other with a free hand. In the spring of 417, apparently,[12] a certain Hyperbolus succeeded in setting in motion the idea of an ostracism. The popular vote was to take place in March.

Hyperbolus was a democrat. Thucydides speaks of him scornfully, treating him as dishonest and contemptible (8.73.3); the comedians were no kinder. In the *Knights*, Aristophanes calls him "a bad citizen, Hyperbolus—a scoundrel."[13] The harsh judgment is both moral and social—a bit like that of Cleon. Hyperbolus was a simple lamp peddler.

The question then arises: Who would be banished? Nicias? Or Alcibiades? The episode had a surprise ending, with supreme irony.

Alcibiades had few arguments for persuading Athens against Nicias. It seems that in the beginning another individual was the target of his efforts: this was someone named Phaeax, an aristocrat who had held some political office and was involved in various political cases. And several witnesses say that he was caught up in this ostracism effort.[14] However, we know nothing about it. Was he at first supported by Alcibiades? Or was he the straw man for Nicias? It is a mystery. Actually, we have one speech, transmitted in the works of the orator Andocides, entitled *Against Alcibiades,* that deals with an ostracism. However, based on all the evidence, this speech is a fiction and could not have been written at that time or by Andocides. It appears to have been a school exercise in which Phaeax was supposed to have spoken. It is a violent attack and relates to both the public and private life of Alcibiades. Maybe this was someone Alcibiades had at one time wanted to go after. But he was neither well known nor dangerous enough; so Alcibiades had another idea.

There is no doubt about Alcibiades's diplomatic talents. He and Nicias came to an agreement. If we can believe Plutarch, in the *Life of Alcibiades,* 13, the idea was his: "Once it became clear that . . . one . . . would suffer the effects of the ostracism vote, Alcibiades combined the disparate factions and, after holding talks with Nicias, arranged things so that the

12. One inscription suggests a later date (A. G. Woodhead, *Hesperia,* 1949); but the text is not decisive.

13. 1304. See also *Clouds* 1065; *Wasps* 1007; *Peace* 681–82.

14. In Plutarch, see *Aristides* 7.3–4; *Nicias* 11; and *Alcibiades* 13. For other theories, see Gomme, Andrewes, and Dover, *A Historical Commentary on Thucydides, ad* 8.73.3.

ostracism backfired."[15] What does he do? He convinces Nicias. Both men
worked with their supporters and, on the day of the vote, the designated
victim was none other than . . . Hyperbolus, the very one who set in motion the ostracism. He was banished by more than six thousand votes.

He would never return to Athens. He reappears in Thucydides's history
when he was assassinated in Samos by the enemies of the democracy.[16]

The ostracism of Hyperbolus is one of the great surprises of the popular vote. It is also an illustration of Alcibiades's extraordinary ability. The
two principal figures remained face to face; they would soon be seen confronting each other over what was the most important episode in Athenian history of the time: the Sicilian expedition.

15. In *Life of Nicias* 11, he doesn't say it, but he doesn't deny it either.
16. Thucydides 8.73.3. This is where the historian's harshest judgment is found. He recalls that Hyperbolus was not ostracized "for fear of his influence and prestige," but was despised for his faults. The same idea is found in the comic Plato, frag. 187 ("It was not for
people like him that ostracism had been invented").

4

THE GRAND DESIGN

In the spring of 417, Alcibiades succeeded in his scheme to avoid the risk of ostracism. He entered a period of glory and good fortune, and it was during this period that he drew Athens into his major undertaking.

Everything was going well for him.

The Argive policy, following a number of setbacks, was finally bearing fruit: a new agreement between Argos and Athens[1] would be finalized the following spring.[2]

Additionally, in 416, Athens seized the little island of Melos, near the Peloponnese; although Alcibiades's role in this affair is not well known, its audacity would have pleased him, as it was aimed indirectly at Sparta,

1. A part of the inscription has been recovered.
2. See above, chapter 3.

whose inhabitants had once colonized Melos. It was also the first indication of the imperialist goals he would advance.

The idea of an expedition against Melos had little justification. As Thucydides reports, the inhabitants "would not submit to the Athenians like other islanders and at first remained neutral." But that did not satisfy the Athenians, who returned with thirty-eight ships to attack the island.[3]

Thucydides chose to emphasize this episode. In his account he includes a dialogue between the representatives of Athens and of Melos, the former explaining to the latter the reasons why they should yield immediately, since no one was coming to help them, neither the Spartans among men nor the gods who, they said, recognized the law of the strongest; "by a necessary law of their nature they rule wherever they can" (5.105). And to the Melians who wonder why they cannot remain neutral, the Athenians respond that such a stance is not possible: "For your hostility cannot so much hurt us as your friendship will be an argument to our subjects of our weakness, and your enmity of our power" (5.95). The dialogue continues over several pages, the retorts tight, dense, and abstract: never has the right of the strongest, henceforth the foundation of Athenian imperialism, been more forcefully expressed and denounced.

We cannot help thinking that it is not by mere chance that this analysis comes as prelude just before the ambitious undertaking of the Sicilian expedition.

Moreover, the harshness of the repression of the Melians came to amplify the vanity of the effort. The island was conquered. All the men old enough to bear arms were executed. The women and children were reduced to slavery. And the Athenians themselves colonized the country.

3. Some believe that Thucydides characterized the attack against Melos as gratuitous because the island was inscribed on the list of tributes prior to the attack. But that inscription on the list may have corresponded to demands that were never met. When would the island have been taken or won over?

The severity of this decision was not without precedent. Earlier there had been analogous repressive measures in the case of Torone (5.3.4) as well as in Scione (5.32.1). Before that, equivalent measures had been envisioned for Mytilene, but that decision was revoked. Imperialist measures had worsened, no doubt owing to anger about the revolts. But Melos had not been a city in revolt.

Here, the situation involves our friend Alcibiades. Not for the undertaking in Melos! No, we do not know anything about his role. Thucydides chose to judge the event as characteristic of Athenian imperialism generally, and never names him. However, in regard to the measures of repression, other historians have.

The speech falsely attributed to Andocides declares, in a passage of great eloquence, that it was Alcibiades who had "proposed enslaving the population" (Plutarch, *Life of Alcibiades* 21); and Plutarch affirms that he "had spoken out in support of the decree" (16.6). Plutarch even says that he was "primarily responsible" for the massacre of the Melians. As I have already reported, Alcibiades took a Melian woman as a slave, with whom he had a child.[4] While it is not at all clear that he had a part in the decision about the expedition, he could still have encouraged a tight hold on the island. And he must have been proud of such a harsh policy as confirming Athenian power and Spartan apathy.

But that is not all! He had more reasons to feel proud of these private successes. It is almost certainly in this same year of 416 that he won the brilliant Olympic victories and caused a sensation in Greece.[5] The memory of that would have been very fresh when, in the summer of 415, Nicias is seen in Thucydides's work as fiercely critical of these successes and the arrogance they produced: "He wants to dazzle us with the luxury of his stable."

In every respect, at the end of 416 Alcibiades has good reason to be content with his life and confident about his future.

Too content, maybe? Too confident?

In any case, out of all this grew his great ambition. And to begin, he threw himself into the Athenian effort to conquer Sicily.

4. See above, chapter 2.
5. See above, chapter 2.

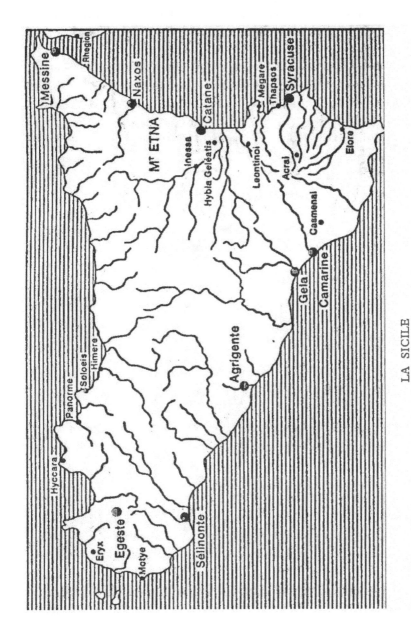

LA SICILE

Map 2. Sicily

To us, the idea seems almost incredible. This little city of Athens, with its resources at the time, seeking to subjugate a large and distant island? The thought of such an undertaking reveals Athens' maritime strength at that time as well as its authority in the Greek world.

In fact, Athens' interest in the large island was not new. We should remember that Sicily was occupied at the time by numerous Greek colonies from different cities and belonging to different ethnicities; they quarreled among themselves frequently. A city like Athens, mistress of the sea, could hardly disregard these quarrels since the island was at the time the largest producer of wheat in the Greek world. Even if Athenian imperialism were not primarily based on her economic needs, those feuds could not be ignored.

At the beginning of the fifth century, Themistocles, who launched the policy of Athenian maritime expansion, had also turned his eyes to Sicily. Not to conquer it, certainly, but to get involved there and to develop ties. There he is, yet another individual who serves as precedent and model for Alcibiades. Two of Themistocles's daughters bore the eloquent names of Sybaris and Italy. He seems to have been in a fight with the tyrant of Syracuse and considered, when he was forced to leave Athens, taking refuge in Sicily. Later, Pericles showed renewed interest and established alliances in Sicily, while also presiding over the founding of a vast Panhellenic colony at Thourioi in southern Italy.

This interest did not end with Pericles's death. Athens had allies in Sicily, like Segesta (or Egesta, near Palermo) and Leontini (between Catania and Syracuse). These allies appealed to Athens, furnishing a pretext. Moreover, Athens was wary of Syracuse, the large city in the eastern part of Sicily, founded long ago by the Corinthians. At the same time Athens was defeating the Persians at Salamis, Gelon, tyrant of Syracuse, defeated the Carthaginians at Himera. The tyrants of that city had kept a brilliant court, visited by Pindar and Aeschylus. The tyrants were gone but the city was still powerful. And Athens was suspicious of its ambitions.

Even during the war, Athens had not neglected Sicily. The first expedition to Sicily was a model, one that prefigured the opportunities and risks of Athenian ambition in 415.

That was in 427,[6] and Athens sent twenty ships to Sicily. The Leontines, who were Ionians, found themselves in difficulty in Syracuse and

6. Thucydides 3.86–88.

appealed to Athens for help. Thucydides is specific: "The Athenians sent it upon the plea of their common descent, but in reality to prevent the exportation of Sicilian corn to the Peloponnese and to test the possibility of bringing Sicily into subjection."

It is clear what happened; we can understand this opportunism, born of the combination of local conflicts and ambition, always present in Athenian hearts.

We also recognize the risks inherent in this type of undertaking.

Initially, everything went quite well in the first expedition. The Athenians established themselves at Rhegium, opposite Sicily, and worked locally, rallying Messina to their side (3.90)[7] and removing from Syracuse the Sicels, a non-Greek people (3.103). At the end of the next winter, Athens, at the request of its allies, even decided to send reinforcements, with forty ships. These ships were delayed, and the Syracusans took advantage of that time to resume their offensive (4.24). Several attempts were made in the straits of Messina, and later to the north, near Naxos. But nothing decisive occurred, until the summer of 424. This ended the first Athenian attempt, in a noteworthy way. Thucydides devoted a major account and even a speech to the event.

Syracuse had not neglected diplomacy. Soon all the Sicilian cities that had been at war with each other held an important congress at Gela, at the southern end of the island, at which the delegate from Syracuse, Hermocrates, spoke to an attentive gathering. Hermocrates was to preside over the future of Syracuse for many years and would become one of Athens' most resolute and effective enemies. At the congress of Gela (one is tempted to write "the Gela summit"), Hermocrates spoke on behalf of unity. He condemned wars in which Sicilian cities tore each other apart and showed that their divisions were playing into the hands of Athens: the presence of Athens should encourage all the cities to unite.

His theme was clear, emphatic, and brief: "There is also the question whether we have still time to save Sicily, the whole of which in my opinion is menaced by Athenian ambition; and we ought to find in the name of that people more imperious arguments for peace than any which I can advance, when we see the first power in Hellas watching our mistakes

---

7. Messina would revert to Syracuse the next year, following a Syracusan expedition (4.1).

with the few ships that she has at present in our waters, and under the fair
name of alliance speciously seeking to exploit the natural hostility that
exists between us."[8] And later: "The attack in question is not inspired by
hatred of one or two nationalities, but by a desire for the good things in
Sicily, the common property of us all."[9]

The common good, a united Sicily: that was his goal. He advocated for
good relations based on common interests, speaking of people who are
"neighbors, who live in the same country, are girt by the same sea, and go
by the same name of Sicilians" (4.64.3).

This shows that Athenian ambitions in Sicily were nothing new, and
the possibilities for resistance were also well grounded. Thucydides would
not have put such emphasis on this episode had he not seen it as a warning, one that went unheeded by Athens in 415.

The result? At Gela, Hermocrates was heard. The cities came to an
agreement. They informed the Athenian leaders, who could only approve,
and depart.

On their return to Athens, however, they were exiled and fined "for
having taken bribes to depart when they might have subdued Sicily. So
thoroughly had the present prosperity persuaded the Athenians that nothing could withstand them, and that they could achieve what was possible
and what was impracticable alike, with means ample or inadequate, it
mattered not. The reason for this was their general extraordinary success,
which made them confuse their strength with their hopes."[10]

This account of the first expedition ended as it began, returning to
the idea that beyond an interest in Sicily's rich agriculture, there was one
driving force always at work:[11] inherent in Athenian imperialism was the
need to expand.

At first Athens' empire emerged spontaneously and naturally. With its
fleet, Athens had played an important role in the war against the barbarians. And afterward, Athens retained prominence among its allies, many

8. 4.60.1. The "natural" hostility refers to that between races, Ionian and Dorian.
Thucydides always insists on the fact that the hostility, though real, served more as a pretext
than an actual reason, and counted for less than the interplay of fear and ambition.
9. 4.61.3.
10. 4.65.
11. Thucydides's words echoed other passages used elsewhere to characterize Athenian
ambition.

of whom preferred to pay tribute money rather than resist Athenian actions. The result: Athens grew stronger. In a short time, most of its allies became subjects. Whenever one of them sought to defect, its inferior strength forced it finally to submit; then it was reduced further. At the beginning of the Peloponnesian War Athens thus commanded, with varying degrees of obedience, almost all the islanders; and it was constantly alert to retain their respect. Pericles knew this: he had said to the Athenians, speaking of the empire, that they could never recede: "For what you hold is . . . a tyranny; to take it was perhaps wrong, but to let it go is unsafe" (2.63.2). That was just the weapon Sparta used against Athens, encouraging defections everywhere. And that is why Athens, afraid of defections, became increasingly repressive.

But Pericles was not talking about conquest. On the contrary, he had warned the Athenians, promising them victory, but on one condition: that "you can consent not to combine schemes of fresh conquest with the conduct of the war, and will abstain from willfully involving yourselves in other dangers; indeed, I am more afraid of our own blunders than of the enemy's devices" (1.144.1). He knew that temptation. He knew, as the Athenian delegates explained in book 1, that an envied power always tried to strengthen itself. And he knew the Athenian character: "addicted to innovation and their designs are characterized by swiftness," "adventurous beyond their power, and daring beyond their judgment, and in danger they are sanguine."[12] He did not trust them.

Pericles, however, had been dead for some fifteen years. During that time, Athenian imperialism, though checked somewhat by the war, had strengthened and hardened. And at that time, people thought the war was over.

What an opportunity for Alcibiades. He was the great man of the moment, with his Olympic victories. He wanted even more glory. He wanted to surpass Themistocles. He became excited about the idea of an expedition to the west, a great expedition, giving Athens a new far-off field of domination with infinite possibilities. His ideas resonated in an Athens captivated by glory and adventure. The young people joined him, but they

---

12. These passages parallel those between the Athenians and Lacedaemonians, offered by the Corinthians in 1.70.2; the preceding idea resumes the Athenians' line of argument in 1.75–76.

were not alone. Plutarch offers a vivid description of the many Athenians who, "in the wrestling schools and alcoves . . . could commonly be seen sitting and mapping out the shape of Sicily and the position of Libya and Carthage."[13] The mention of Libya and Carthage here is important, and we will come back to it. These fantasies became part of a popular daydream. For or against, everyone was talking about the possibility of an expedition and became fascinated by the distant island. In Euripides's *Trojan Women*, a play written at just this time, the poet sharply condemned offensive wars; and even in that play there is a reference to Sicily: "the land of Etna" is among the places to which the captive women imagine being sent.[14]

This curiosity implies a lot of discussion certainly; but for most people it was linked to a strong desire to go to Sicily. Thucydides says as much, and states the reasons for it, in the explanations he offers for the vote that determined the decision. It reflected the many animating desires at work: "Everyone fell in love with the enterprise. The older men thought that they would either subdue the places against which they were to sail, or at all events, with so large a force, meet with no disaster; those in the prime of life felt a longing for foreign sights and spectacles, and the soldiery was to earn wages at the moment, and make conquests that would supply a never ending fund of pay for the future" (6.24.3). For Alcibiades, beyond such material benefits was glory! The glory of bringing Athens its greatest conquest, of leading and conquering and forever eclipsing all the others.

Conquest? Oh, yes, that is the right word. It marks a departure from everything that went before. However, there are two qualifications. First, for the Greeks of that time, conquest did not have its modern meaning. Greeks never imagined making such distant territory part of their country: the idea of the city and the size of the city made that impossible. Thus, it was a matter of imposing authority, of ruling and protecting the interests of Athens, commanding respect and material assistance. But even in that form, the idea of conquest was never officially sanctioned. The goal of the expedition was, more modestly, to aid the people of Segesta who were

13. Plutarch, *Alcibiades* 17; see also *Nicias* 12. The source appears to have been the historian Timaeus (fourth century BCE).

14. Euripides, *Trojan Women* 220. This locale does not figure among the usual lists of possible places of exile.

being threatened by Selinunte, and, if possible, to reestablish the Leontines who had been forced out by Syracuse. Another goal was, according to charmingly vague wording, "to order all other matters in Sicily as they should deem best for the interests of Athens" (6.8.2).

This nice euphemism fooled no one, and Thucydides was careful to make the facts clear: his account of the expedition began by recalling the importance of the island and the history of its cities. Then he went on: "Such is the list of the peoples, Hellenic and barbarian, inhabiting Sicily, and such is the magnitude of the island which the Athenians were now bent upon invading, being ambitious in real truth of conquering the whole, although they had also the specious design of aiding their kindred and other allies on the island" (6.6.1). "Conquering the whole" (τῆς πάσης ἄρξαι): the words are clear. Later, speaking of Nicias (who opposed the expedition): he "thought that the state was not well-advised, but upon a slight and specious pretext was aspiring to the conquest of the whole of Sicily, a great matter to achieve" (6.8.4; the word he used was *ephiesthai*, "to covet a good").

That was indeed an ambitious plan. And yet beyond this one, Alcibiades was secretly planning another, even more grandiose, that he would not reveal to Athens and that became known only much later. Behind his ostensible goal was his desire to conquer the island; but behind this plan, in his cheerful ambition, floated the "greater plan." Unlike those Russian dolls that contain smaller and smaller dolls, Alcibiades's ambition revealed ever more immense intentions.

First, though, he had to obtain approval by the Assembly of the people for his expedition, the Sicilian expedition.

This was monumental: Athens was betting its future. Thucydides's work devotes two whole books to the expedition, omitting nothing in order to bring that decision to life and to make us understand the stakes.

At first, everything was simple; the project was quickly approved. The situation had been similar in 427: an ally, Segesta, had requested Athens' aid; it had offered money (managing, with a little sleight of hand, to appear richer than it was), and the Assembly had approved sending sixty ships under the command of three men given full authority: Alcibiades, Nicias, and Lamachus.

It was settled. But Nicias, seeing clearly the dangers that lay behind the overly broad and vague objectives, was appalled by the risks Athens was taking. He used a subsequent session of the Assembly, supposedly to deal with armaments, to raise the question of the whole affair once more.

This was irregular, and he knew it.[15] In a fitting final effort, he appealed to the president of the gathering in moving terms: "If you are afraid to move the question again, consider that a violation of the law cannot with so many abettors, incur any charge, that you will be the physician of your misguided city, and that the virtue of men in office is briefly this, to do their country as much good as they can, or in any case no harm that they can avoid" (6.14).

In these final words, we hear an echo of the Hippocratic oath. One can only be touched by the nobility of this appeal and by the pathos that it gives the situation. The pathos is all the more touching for the reader who knows the disastrous failure that results from the expedition, and how hard Nicias tried to prevent it. However, apart from the pathos, Nicias's appeal helps us understand two things. It shows first how skillfully Alcibiades had proceeded, taking Nicias and his friends by surprise and obtaining a vote the scope of which he never revealed. Moreover, it shows that this time Alcibiades would have the strength of his conviction; he would have to go to the heart of the matter.

Thucydides provided the two main speeches of Nicias and Alcibiades, followed by Nicias's final pitch (6.8–24). These are of course not the exact words of the actual speeches, but even so, one feels that the speakers are present, not only from the arguments that each would advance, but also from the two personalities, from their tones, their temperaments, and their aspirations.

Moreover, he included personal attacks. Nicias attacked Alcibiades for his youth and his ambition. He did not mince words: "And if there be any man here, overjoyed at being chosen to command, who urges you to make the expedition, merely for ends of his own—especially if he is still too young to command—who seeks to be admired for the stud of horses, but on account of heavy expenses hopes for some profit from his appointment, do not allow such a one to maintain his private splendor at his country's risk, but remember that such persons injure the public fortune

---

15. There was one recent precedent: in 428, Athenians voted for the brutal suppression of Mytilene; the next day, with the verdict weighing on them, the Assembly reconvened and reversed the decision. The reversal was immediate, called for by the majority of citizens (3.36.5).

while they squander their own, and that this is a matter of importance, and not for a young man to decide or hastily to take in hand" (6.12.2).

These young people are described as having come at the summons of that very individual. And as we have previously shown, Alcibiades was proud to claim to represent the young.[16] Then turning, like Nicias, to an example borrowed from medicine (in this case, a balanced diet), he spoke for a harmonious combination of young and old. He had nothing but scorn for Nicias's criticisms and his "battle between young and old"; but he allowed his scorn to come across without slipping into actual insolence.

Similarly, he acknowledged the stable of racehorses and his Olympic victories. What is more, he started with that. As shown in chapter 2, he boasted that the prestige he brought to the city had strengthened it abroad. He even provided a glimpse into that confident pride when he stated: "Nor is it unfair that he who prides himself on his position should refuse to be upon an equality with the rest. He who is badly off has his misfortunes all to himself" (6.16.4). That astonishing Alcibiades! Daring to speak in that way before the people! Yes, he admitted to being first, superior to all. And he admitted that this renown aroused jealousy one minute and admiration the next.

This is all about Alcibiades—his life, athletic victories, and awareness of his superiority. But we cannot help remarking that there is some correspondence between Alcibiades's pride and that of Athens, between the ambition of the man and the imperialism of the city.

It was Pericles who said, according to Thucydides, "Hatred and unpopularity at the moment have fallen to the lot of all who have aspired to rule others; but where odium must be incurred, true wisdom incurs it for the highest objects. Hatred also is short lived; but that which makes the splendor of the present and the glory of the future remains for ever unforgotten" (2.64.5). That was the air Alcibiades breathed, and he applied that spirit to his own life. He was, as an individual, the image of Athens.

This is clearly why, during the rest of his speech, he is the bold defender of Athenian imperialism.

16. See above, chapter 1.

Nicias of course stood for consideration of the chances of success and risks of failure. Alcibiades knew his case and argued with precision. Thus, the reader is presented with the same clear picture of the whole argument that the Assembly once had.

First the risks: Nicias emphasized them strongly. The peace was not secure; the treaty included several areas of arbitration, and all the allies of Sparta had not ratified it; Sparta herself had been humiliated and would seize the opportunity to reverse the situation. It was thus absurd to leave in Greece itself so many enemies and to go looking for others whom Athens could never truly master even if it were victorious. Syracuse's rule in Sicily was not a danger for Athens.[17] Athens should consolidate her empire in those places where it was still fragile and rebuild her strength, weakened by war and the plague. And he appealed for prudence, recalling the famous maxim about "how rarely success is gained by wishing and how often by forecast" (6.13.1).

Nicias lays out the problems and speaks as a man of experience. Alcibiades is going to answer with vigor, and he speaks with confidence.

In his analysis of the facts, he has some reasons. He recalls that, thanks to the Argive alliance and despite the Spartan victory at Mantinea, Athens has nothing to fear from the Lacedaemonians: "They have never since fully recovered confidence" (6.16.6). As for the cities in Sicily, they consist of heterogeneous and weak people who would be unable to form a real union; moreover, we can rely on the barbarians there. Then, with regard to Sparta, he returns to the theory so dear to Pericles, saying that at the very worst the Lacedaemonians could invade Attica, "but they can never hurt us with their navy, as we leave one of our own behind us that is a match for them" (6.17.8). He addresses every detail. Most of all he explains—and this is the point of the speech—that this expedition, if we can do it, is inscribed in the great tradition of Athens. There we have him, Alcibiades arguing loud and clear for imperialism. For him, imperialism means progress, action, moving ahead.

---

17. Because, he said, "one empire would scarcely attack another" (6.11.3). The point was that they would have exposed themselves to the same enmities as Athens. The argument had merit; but Syracuse as the ruler in Sicily would be a danger to Athens in other ways than as a military threat.

If we can do it, why balk when an ally appeals for help? "It is thus that empire has been won, both by us and by all others that have held it, by a constant readiness to support all, whether barbarians or Hellenes, that invite assistance" (6.18.2). That is the tradition of the origins—the tradition that inspires the patriotic plays of the first years of the war, like Euripides's *Heraclides*, and will later inspire the hymns of Athens. Like them, Alcibiades speaks of "our fathers." And recalling their past, he shames those who hesitate, reminding them that the Athenians of those days had to deal not only with the hostility of Sparta but with that of Persia as well; that did not prevent them from acting, from sending their aid wherever it was needed.

By evoking those traditions, Alcibiades was himself charged up, and he charged up his listeners. But he soon went beyond tradition with a more audacious and original argument.

He said that Athens had no choice! Resuming, and altering a bit, Pericles's theory, he held that the very existence of the empire required multiple interventions: "Moreover, we cannot fix the exact point at which our empire shall stop; we have reached a position in which we must not be content with retaining what we have but must scheme to extend it for, if we cease to rule others, we shall be in danger of being ruled ourselves" (6.18.3).

The reference to Pericles is clear. But Pericles said that they could not renounce the empire, abandon it, or let it go; he was not speaking of conquests. After him, Cleon had taken from similar circumstances the idea that it was necessary to show determination in repressions. This is a new idea: Athens cannot reject . . . conquest.

This touches on the very principle that always leads the conqueror to go farther, with all the risks that entails. From Alexander the Great to Napoleon and even Hitler, all by different means, we find the same idea. But no one ever expressed it so forcefully as did Alcibiades in Thucydides, particularly as justification and rule of conduct.

In his eyes, it is not even a question strictly about the empire: it is a rule of life with universal value. Alcibiades is the first theoretician of activism for its own sake. The clarity of his thought sparkled like a diamond: "And that, by sinking into inaction, the city, like everything else, will wear itself out, and its skill in everything decay; while each fresh struggle will give it fresh experience, and make it more used to defend itself not in word but in deed. In short, my conviction is that a city not inactive by nature could not choose a quicker way to ruin itself than by suddenly adopting such a policy, and that the safest rule of life is to take one's character and institutions for better and for worse, and to live up to them as closely as one can" (6.18.6–7).

These words are the words of Thucydides. What Alcibiades really said, we do not know. But there can be no doubt: this bold philosophy, proclaimed boldly, was his. Even if he did not put it in these words or on that day, the words express his thinking.

It is easy to imagine him expressing these thoughts with a look of scorn for the timid wisdom of Nicias. One can imagine the enthusiasm of the young people, drinking in these words, and perhaps some worry among their elders, recalling the time of Pericles and the idealism of that time.

But there must have been some who saw the weakness of the argument, for it only took a little reflection. Action, great! But what action? Going forward is good, but in what direction? And how far? The empire was being watched everywhere: the situation did not allow for weakness, but it also had to avoid failures. The conquest of Sicily could prove a failure, and a huge failure. If there were some people who had to know that, they were a minority.

The Assembly, in fact, having listened to Alcibiades, "was more committed to the expedition than ever." Nicias saw that. And then came an episode almost as comic in its irony as the ostracism.

Nicias made one last effort: he said that the enterprise would be difficult, that the cities of Sicily were strong, that they might join forces, that the distance was great, and that there would have to be a huge force . . . He was hoping to discourage the Athenians, but just the opposite resulted; everyone was excited, and the idea of a huge force reassured them. They asked Nicias how big he thought they needed. He hesitated, talked about at least one hundred ships, enumerated weapons of every kind. Nothing daunted the Athenians: if that is what it would take, that was what would be provided. They voted for everything that was wanted, and gave full authority to the generals to do their best . . .

What a meeting! Alcibiades had first called for approval of twenty ships. Nicias had protested. And now they are going to send a hundred ships. Alcibiades had never hoped for so much.

On the day of departure, there were even more forces than planned. It was an extraordinary day; Thucydides describes it with equally exceptional emphasis. Never had such a huge expedition set off for such a distant location. Everyone's excitement was great.

At dawn on the appointed day the men who were to embark went down to Piraeus. Everyone went with them. "With them also went the whole population, one may say, of the city, both citizens and foreigners, the inhabitants of the country each escorting those that belonged to them, their friends, their relatives or their sons, with hope and lamentation upon their way as they thought of the conquests which they hoped to make . . . although the strength of the armament, and the profuse provision which they observed in every department, was a sight that could not but comfort them. As for the foreigners and the rest of the crowd, they simply went to see a sight worth looking at and passing all belief" (6.30.2–31.1).

There were sixty light ships, forty troop transports. Each one had cost a lot, each competing with the others; the departure had become a kind of festival.

When everyone had boarded, the trumpet sounded for silence. And there were prayers, offered as on all ships at such times, but this time there were libations for everyone, soldiers and officers, in cups of gold and silver. When the hymn ended, the immense fleet set off, "sailing out in a column then raced each other as far as Aegina" (32.2).

Alcibiades of course was on his ship. He had armed himself splendidly.[18] This was his expedition, his plan. He was bound for glory.

Let's not think just yet about the fate of this fleet, leaving Athens with such high hopes. When he describes the splendid departure, Thucydides, though, is thinking about its fate; and he sets up the contrast that appears at the end of book 7 with the tragic end of this expeditionary force. Then the difference will be clear. Everyone will reflect on it, "especially when they contrasted the splendor and glory of their setting out with the humiliation in which it had ended. For this was by far the greatest reverse that ever befell a Hellenic army" (7.75.6–7).

---

18. Plutarch 16.1. But Plutarch doesn't mention that the bed set up for him on his trireme was made specifically for this occasion. Alcibiades did things well.

That unprecedented fleet. It was, for its day, "an invincible armada."

Alcibiades had no suspicion of this dark ending. He did have personal concerns and reasons to worry, as we will discover in the next chapter. But he must have believed that his dream was soon to be realized.

At Corcyra (today Corfu) he was supposed to join the rest of his army: when all the forces had gathered, there would be, not one hundred, but 134 triremes, plus two large ships from Rhodes as well as five thousand infantry, cavalry, archers, and supply units.

With that, he would conquer Sicily.

And perhaps even more.

Yes, even more. He had not said so, but things must have come out. Later, he would reveal the truth to the Spartans: the huge plan was part of an even larger picture that gave shape to the most extreme ambition.

It suffices for us to listen to what Thucydides has Alcibiades say at the time, giving the impression of a door opening to an unforeseen prospective:

> We sailed to Sicily first to conquer, if possible, the Sicilians, and after them the Italians also, and finally to assail the empire and city of Carthage. In the event of all or most of these schemes succeeding, we were then to attack the Peloponnesus, bringing with us the entire force of the Hellenes lately acquired in those parts, and taking a number of barbarians into our pay, such as the Iberians and others in those countries, recognized as the most warlike known, and building numerous triremes in addition to those which we had already (timber being plentiful in Italy); and with this fleet blockading the Peloponnesus from the sea and assailing it with our armies by land, and taking some of the cities by storm, and besieging others, we hoped without difficulty to defeat them completely and after this to rule the whole of the Hellenic world. (6.90.2–3)

The aspiration was majestic, coherent, and specific. Alcibiades went on to say that they would have taken silver and crops from the annexed territories in the west; everything had been foreseen. The Mediterranean would become Athenian.[19]

---

19. He said "the whole of the Hellenic world" specifically to indicate to the Spartans that they too, in turn, would have been subjugated. However, the prior subjugation of Carthage suggests that the domination was not only Hellenic.

We now understand why people were drawing on the ground the out-lines of Sicily and the position of Carthage and Libya.[20] The grand plan, mostly a secret one, was not actually an invention meant to frighten the Spartans, and a failure to take it seriously is to misunderstand Alcibiades's personality. The fact is, he was not kidding. Thucydides openly recognized by name the existence of the grand plan; it comes in book 6, chapter 15.2, when Alcibiades speaks out in favor of the expedition. He says that Alcibiades boasted that he would "reduce Sicily and Carthage." This helps us make sense of a phrase in his speech, as it has come down to us; in it, Alcibiades describes the advantages of the expedition and ends by saying, "At the same time we shall either become masters, as we very easily may, of the whole of Hellas through the accession of the Sicilian Hellenes, or in any case ruin the Syracusans, to the no small advantage of ourselves and our allies" (6.18.4). The phrase "as we very easily may" is the grand plan. While the speech says no more about it, many people must have understood it.

Can we even imagine the consequences had the plan succeeded? The unification of Greece, under the rule of Athens, the unification of the Mediterranean, having become a Greek sea. That would have changed the history of the world.

Of course, hearing these words and knowing the disaster that the expedition would become, we cannot help thinking of La Fontaine's fable "The Milkmaid and the Pot of Milk"; and we think also about the lesson there.[21] Still, it must be said, the dream was not an impossibility. Neither was starting with the conquest of Sicily. With the audacity and intelligence of Alcibiades, with all his forces . . . who knows? No one can say for certain, because nothing happened as intended. At the very moment of the triumphant and flamboyant departure, Alcibiades must have begun to worry. If not, he should have, because a dark cloud began to take shape: into the grand plan there suddenly arose the taint of scandal—that of the "affairs."

20. Mentioned earlier in this chapter.
21. You would understand if you knew La Fontaine. My apologies to young readers for this reference to knowledge so out of date.

5

THE SCANDALS

When the fleet sailed with great fanfare for Sicily, Alcibiades must have briefly forgotten his worries in the hope of future glory. But he had worries, and they were well-founded. Because two grave matters had just erupted in Athens, between when the expedition had been approved and the day of departure.

On a beautiful morning, possibly June 8 according to scholars' estimates, it was discovered that all the herms in the city (or all but one)[1] had been mutilated. Thucydides says modestly "in front," but it was clearly the phalluses adorning these rather rough images that were affected. These herms were simplified statues of the god Hermes, or rather busts placed on rectangular pillars that marked boundaries and doorways of both private homes and sanctuaries. They appealed to the god for protection; they had religious significance.

---

1. The herm of the tribe Aigeis was spared. It was claimed that Andocides was responsible (see his *On the Mysteries*, 62).

But now they had been mutilated: all of them. Emotions were high, and this was the beginning of one of the most serious and complicated incidents in Athenian history. We know a lot about it because many authors have written about it. Among them, of course, was Thucydides, but another one was directly involved in the events and was even charged with the crime: the orator Andocides, who described it all in two speeches that have been preserved.[2]

Why was this affair so upsetting? To understand that, we must remember how strong religious traditions remained in the Athenian democracy. All political activity was conducted with prayers, sacrifices, and libations. Anything that might indicate divine will was taken as a sign, from an earthquake to a mere sneeze; the rationalism of sophists and intellectuals was too recent to have penetrated to most people. This fact can be seen in the pains Pericles took to explain that a boar with only one horn was an anomaly but not a prophecy, or that an eclipse could be explained scientifically. Moreover, belief in hereditary curses continued to be an issue. Just before the Peloponnesian War, Lacedaemonians and Athenians argued about removing citizens because of hereditary curses. In such an atmosphere, it is easy to understand that a deliberate offense to a guardian spirit might terrify people, as much for its audacity as for its future consequences.

Again we ask: Why? The fact that such a blow had struck all the herms implied intention. It was too widespread for anyone to think that there were just a few overexcited or inebriated young people. There was more to it. It was the sign of a plot, one all the more alarming for having been carried out in secret. Had the conspirators sought to create a bond among themselves by committing a sacrilege together, to hide another move? But what conspirators? And what move? An air of panic swept through the city. Something sinister was believed to be threatening the democracy.

That democracy of which the Athenians were so proud had never, in spite of its greatness, lived without anxiety. It constantly feared subversive elements. And there was even a judicial procedure, specific and dubious, called *eisangelia*, allowing any citizen to bring to trial anyone suspected

---

2. The speech *On His Return* (speech 2) dates from 410 or 407, and the speech *On the Mysteries* from 399 (the incident itself took place in 415).

of acting against the democracy. The definition of such activity was very broad and these trials were held frequently.

Clearly, one of their fears was that people would band together to bring about a less democratic regime, one that was openly oligarchic. There were indeed such people. Moreover, there was a way for these groups to form. There were quite a few *hetaereiai*,[3] groups of friends or companions that brought together men with shared views, who could support one of their number and follow his advice. These might be made up of good democrats, but many of them represented reactionary leanings, and these were feared. In the affair of the herms—or as they were called, the *hermocopidai*—the *hetaereiai* were constantly blamed by their opponents. They also appear later, in the problems of 411, and in *Lysistrata* (574–81) Aristophanes has his heroine deliver a tirade against a civic union that describes everything in terms of yarn and women's work:

> Well, first as we wash dirty wool so's to cleanse it, so with a pitiless zeal we will scrub
> Through the whole city for all greasy fellows; burrs too, the parasites, off we will rub.
> That verminous plague of insensate place-seekers soon between thumb and forefinger we'll crack.[4]

The term "burrs" refers to what were for the demos a constant source of suspicion. The herms could well have been mutilated by members of any of the *hetaereiai*, as a prelude to taking political action.

And of course, it was not only reactionaries who wanted oligarchy; curiously, Athens never ceased to be haunted by the terror of a tyranny. It was, after all, in reaction to the tyranny that the democracy had been instituted. And the tragedies of the time continued to remind people of the horrors of that regime. It was Aristophanes, again, who ridiculed this constant fear. In the *Wasps*, produced in 422, a prostitute asks a man if he "wanted to re-create the tyranny of Hippias." In the *Birds* of 414, a reward is offered to "anyone who kills one of the dead tyrants." In 411, in *Lysistrata* again, the chorus says, suspiciously, "I smell the tyranny of

---

3. See chapter 3.
4. Translation by Jack Lindsay.

Hippias in particular."[5] With all these inclinations among Athenians, it is easy to imagine their reaction to a sacrilege as suspicious as the mutilation of the herms.

If there was someone considering tyranny, who was a more likely object of suspicion than Alcibiades? With all his talents and ambitions, with his scorn for the rules and his insolence? His enemies would immediately exploit these very natural fears. Accusations about him spread.

Thucydides put it clearly in the text that has been cited above, but one phrase has become significant here: "The mass of the people," convinced that Alcibiades aspired to tyranny, made themselves his enemies and deprived themselves of his talents, thereby "ruining the city."

Not only is this statement accurate: the suspicions had grown strong enough that Thucydides put here, in this context, and right after the measures taken against Alcibiades, a long digression on the end of tyranny in Athens.[6] This digression is only loosely related to the account; it repeats the ideas of book 1; but the similarity to the state of mind in 416 is striking when he returns to the account: "With these events in their minds, and recalling everything they knew by hearsay on the subject, the Athenian people grew uneasy and suspicious of the persons charged in the affair of the mysteries, and became convinced that all that had taken place was part of an oligarchic and monarchical conspiracy" (6.60.1).

This would not be the only time this suspicion was connected to the name of Alcibiades; at the moment of his return, there were those who thought he was moving in that direction.[7]

Later, in the speech *Against Alcibiades* falsely attributed to Andocides, we read that citizens who rose too high were suspect: "It is they who create tyrannies" (24). The suspicion simmered, reappearing at the least provocation. In fact, nothing ever entirely removed the idea that Alcibiades

---

5. The verses quoted are, respectively, 502, 1074, and 620. Two months later, in the *Thesmophoriazusai*, a woman pronounces a curse on several of the guilty ones, one of whom is a man who proposed being "a tyrant or helping bring back a tyrant." See my article "Il pensiero di Euripide sulla tirannia," in *Acts of the National Institute of Ancient Drama* (1969): 175–87.

6. 6.53.3–59.1.

7. See below, chapter 11. Even today, this accusation sometimes reappears among certain critics (for example, Cinzia Bearzot, in *Prometheus*, 1988).

really did aspire to tyranny. His conduct and his tone made the accusation an easy one to make.

In such an atmosphere, political suspicions added to the religious anxiety. People were afraid. That is what explains the immediate reaction of the Athenians. As Thucydides wrote: "The matter was taken up all the more seriously, as it was thought to be ominous for the expedition, and part of a conspiracy to bring about a revolution and to upset the democracy" (6.27.3).

In the midst of these doubts and suspicions, one thing at least is certain. At the very moment the city was to launch the biggest expedition it had ever seen, it felt vulnerable. And most likely that was not by chance. Whatever their previous intentions, the authors of the attack had wanted to strike a blow against the project, and also against the author of the project, and by sowing disorder, to end it.

As for sowing disorder, they succeeded. The reaction to the event was immediate. Large public rewards were offered, and it was decreed "that anyone who knew of any other act of impiety having been committed should come and give information without fear of consequences, whether he was citizen, alien, or slave" (6.27.2).

In principle, we have ceased to use denouncing and informing on fellow citizens—at least in ordinary times. But Athens felt its security at risk and the Athenian democracy was constantly mobilized for the defense of the city.

It is, in any case, easy to imagine the ensuing intrigues, legitimate and false denunciations, arrests, and all the subterfuges into which this decision would throw Athens.

Immediately, Alcibiades's problems grew.

Not because he was involved in the affair of the herms. He was not. But the decree included "any other sacrilege," and that is where things went badly for him. Did those who worded the decree that way have a specific incident in mind? It is highly likely. In any case the first denunciation that appeared had to do with another sacrilege. A slave named Andromachus was presented by his master and swore that he had been present, in a private house (the house of someone named Poulytion), for a parody of the sacred mysteries, in which Alcibiades, among others, had also participated.[8]

---

8. Thucydides is talking about the mutilations of other statues, about young people who were partying and drinking, and speaks of the parody of the mysteries "in a few private houses." But this seems to fold together several different denunciations.

This was bad business. And some people hastened to add fuel to the flames. Very soon an orator on the populist side, Androcles, tried to link the two affairs. Plutarch describes him as having been the instigator of the denunciation.[9] There were numerous allegations that this double sacrilege was a prelude to overthrowing the democracy.

It is said that libel leaves a permanent trace. The hypothetical connection Androcles tried to make between the two affairs left a trail that lasted for centuries; even the briefest reference in dictionaries of our own day continues to say that Alcibiades was involved in the affair of the herms. In this respect, Androcles was highly successful!

Whatever the case, from that time on things began to go badly for Alcibiades.

So, was he guilty?

Certainly not in the affair of the herms, and no serious denunciation ever claimed that he was. But the mysteries? Maybe. It is hard to say exactly in what way he was involved. In the aftermath, the accusations grew more serious; and it is not impossible that the charges were inflated. It is possible that everyone was guilty of insolence, of impudence; Alcibiades had a habit of both. Moreover, he loved to participate in foreign cults. One comedy presents him as joining in an orgiastic cult of the Thracian goddess Kottyto;[10] the play showed a cult with purification rites like the Mysteries of Eleusis. The play has been lost, but it was apparently very upsetting to Alcibiades who, according to one rather suspect legend, was said to have drowned the author Eupolis during the crossing to Sicily.[11] Did people, knowingly or not, confuse rites of this type with the parody? Was it simply a joke, meant for a laugh, or a true sacrilege? What we know is that Alcibiades had enemies ready to exploit anything they could use against him, and that he always showed a lack of prudence.

We would like to be less vague, and to know from whom these attacks came, or at least from which side.

---

9. *Alcibiades* 19; the role of Androcles is confirmed in Thucydides 8.65.2, where he describes the assassination of Androcles, "the man mainly responsible for the banishment of Alcibiades."

10. The comedy of Eupolis entitled the *Baptai* (that is to say, something like "The Baptized"). It was probably somewhat earlier than the "affairs." Participation in the cult was not illegal.

11. See Cicero, *Epistulae ad Att.* 6.1.17 (the source would be Duris).

This is made all the more difficult because later we find Alcibiades linked one minute with the partisans of the oligarchy and the next with those of the democracy. After his death, Alcibiades's son would confirm, in the speech Isocrates composed for him, that those who, at the time of the affairs we are concerned with, attacked his father were the same men who would later help the oligarchy triumph.[12] But Isocrates's linking of these two events stems from his rhetorical skill. Alcibiades had (or also had) many enemies among the democrats. Hadn't he had the democrat Hyperbolus ostracized? Had he not been accused by Androcles, another extreme democrat, who was finally assassinated by the oligarchs in 411?

The personal quarrels, jealousies, irritations caused by so many provocations were what seem to have mobilized opinion against him. But the hostility was strongest among those who suspected him of not supporting the democracy.

For the most part, they were right: Alcibiades—the aftermath would prove it—supported only himself.

In any case, he was in danger; and his enemies were going to do whatever they could to oppose him.

He asked to be judged immediately, before the departure of the expedition, in order to leave cleared of charges. He did not wish his command to be tarnished by unanswered rumors: "He protested against their receiving slanders against him in his absence" (6.29.2). He insisted, he pleaded, but all in vain. Thucydides said his enemies feared he would have the army on his side if he were tried immediately and that the people might relent, believing that they owed the presence of the Argives and Mantineans to him. Once he was far away, his enemies would take advantage of his absence to add to the charges against him. His appeals were in vain. Today it is easy to say that he didn't know how to manage it:[13] but that is to misinterpret the power of the tension at that time. In any case, his enemies won: they

---

12. Isocrates 16.5. According to the text, those men who later would establish the oligarchy went to Alcibiades and, when he turned them down, decided to get rid of him. We know that Pisander, one of the investigators, would establish the oligarchy in 411. But there were four years between the two events (important to the statement of the son, in ll.37: "As soon as they were rid of him, they abolished the democracy!"). And Pisander was the one who was supposed to have proposed recalling Alcibiades in 411.

13. E. F. Bloedow, "Alcibiades Reexamined," *Historia Einzelschriften* 20 (1973).

arrested the other suspects and let him depart. This was, according to some sources, the decision of Androcles.

What would happen after the fleet sailed?

Alcibiades was certainly not happy to leave in this way. But the final days had been reassuring: another denunciation came from a metic named Teucrus and concerned the affairs of both the mysteries and the herms. We know the tenor of it from Andocides (1.15): for the herms, he denounced eighteen people; for the mysteries, he said he had participated in a parody, for which he gave eleven names. Alcibiades's name was not one of them. This news must have been somewhat reassuring. And then perhaps he thought that future triumphs would silence his enemies.

That was not to be the case.

In the first place, successes were slow to come. After assembling in Corcyra, the immense fleet was to sail for the south of Italy, and it was there the disappointments began. The ships were to go to Rhegium (Reggio di Calabria); now even that city, attached to the Leontines and always loyal to Athens, did not want to receive them and declared its intention of remaining neutral. On top of that there followed another disappointment: a ship sent ahead to Segestus came back with the bad news that the silver that was counted on was not there. The inhabitants had deceived Athens. They had shown off treasures and impressed the Athenian envoys by exhibiting vases they had borrowed and that were being passed back and forth! They had been tricked. Nicias was not surprised; but it was a serious blow for Alcibiades.

What were they going to do under the circumstances? A war council was held by the three generals. Nicias advised going to Selinunte, as they had promised the people of Segestus. There they would learn what the city could or could not provide, and if it was true that they had nothing, everyone would return to Athens. Alcibiades wanted to stay, and to begin a diplomatic effort with all the cities of Sicily except Selinunte and Syracuse, and then, after winning their support, attack Syracuse. Lamachus wanted to attack Syracuse right away while the army was still fresh; but he came around and agreed with Alcibiades. The man with the big plan won again. It was hoped that his power of persuasion, demonstrated once again in the war council, would work with the Sicilians.

But it was not easy. Alcibiades went first, on his own ship, to Messina, but did not succeed in persuading the inhabitants, who refused to receive the troops. At Naxos, they would be allowed to enter. But Catania? At first Catania refused, but he tried again. Alcibiades was received with his two colleagues, and he spoke. But this was not simply a diplomatic effort. While he was speaking, while everyone was absorbed by the discussions under way, Athenian soldiers pushed into a postern gate and spread out in the city. The alliance with Athens was approved. Sometimes eloquence has to be supported by arguments of another kind!

So Catania was brought in, which was important. Then it was announced that Camarina was also in agreement. So they headed straight there. There they learned that Camarina would admit the Athenians, but only a single vessel.

There were small successes, but a lot of little steps and setbacks. Nothing, in other words, that might impress the people back in Athens, who were engaged heart and soul in the two affairs: if things were going slowly in Sicily, in Athens events were moving quickly.

It would be difficult to describe what these months in Athens had been like. Denunciations were growing. Terrified, those who had been incriminated fled. Those who remained were frequently executed without delay. These attacks fell on nearly all the most important families of Athens. There was total uncertainty. There were denunciations by people who had seen everything, who were treated with great respect; and their denunciations were soon found to be inconsistent. They had, in fact, lied. Why? Encouraged by whom? Suspicions were rampant and fear reigned. In some respects, the atmosphere was more like that of the "blacklists" than of our drawn-out affairs today.

Thucydides, who gave no names, either of the denounced or the informers, nor the number of those who were executed or who fled, did describe the atmosphere very well (he was not in Athens at the time, but we can imagine the number of stories he heard). He wrote: "Instead of testing the informers, in their suspicious temper [they] welcomed all indifferently, arresting and imprisoning the best citizens upon the evidence of rascals, and preferring to sift the matter to the bottom sooner than to let an accused person of good character pass unquestioned, owing to the rascality of the informer" (6.53.2).

In order both to provide a sense of the atmosphere and to explain what happened to Alcibiades, here are the charges of which we are aware. Two of them preceded the departure of the expedition; the others came after it. Of the first two, one came (it was said) from a slave, the other from a metic. The first concerned the mysteries and named Alcibiades; the second concerned the two affairs and did not name him. But that was not the end of it.

First there was a shocking charge about the herms. A man named Diocleides said he had seen, by the light of the moon, some three hundred people dividing into suspicious groups. He recognized forty-two of them. Catastrophic! He named two members of the Council, members of aristocratic families like Leogoras, a brother of Nicias, Critias . . . , people belonging to the ruling class who gave the appearance of a vast oligarchic conspiracy. A state of emergency was decreed, armed citizens gathered in the night in different parts of the city. There was panic: it grew stronger when the rumor, widely accepted, started to spread that troops of Boeotians were moving toward Attica, in league with Sparta.[14] The plot had become an international crisis. Important men fled; others were arrested.

Diocleides had, in fact, lied: he spoke of the light of the moon, but the sacrilege had occurred during the new moon. Questioned, he admitted that he had been urged to make this false charge by two people—one of whom was Alcibiades's cousin.[15]

However, the affair backfired. Among the accused was one Leogoras and his son Andocides. After his arrest, Andocides decided, with a promise of immunity, to confess, by way of a denunciation. He admitted that his *hetaereia* was guilty.[16] He spared his father and other people accused by Diocleides, but gave names: these were the same people whom Teucrus had denounced (his second denunciation), and four other people who were able to flee.

Andocides was supposed to enjoy immunity, but his guilt was never really erased. He was exiled by a decree relating to impiety and spent the rest of his life without ever returning to Athens; we know this from his speeches. From the same source, we also have a vivid impression of his dramatic experiences: his account remains one of the first examples of

14. 6.61.2. Andocides 1.45.

15. There is no evidence that this person (Alcibiades of Phlegonte) acted in concert with his famous cousin, but he may have wanted to save him by this ugly initiative.

16. He himself was innocent; his friend had taken advantage of the fact that he was injured (1.61–62).

conscience evinced in Greek literature. It is worth the trouble to quote passages, even though the account concerns Alcibiades only indirectly: it gives us some idea of the circumstances at the time. It might even call to mind certain situations that accused persons, from different countries, have known in our time. Andocides, with his supporters, is in prison; they weep, they lament. A cousin, or a friend[17] comes to find him and says: "I beg of you: if you have heard anything concerning this affair, disclose it. Save yourself; save your father, who must be dearer to you than anyone in the world; save your brother-in-law." And Andocides is overcome: "How unhappy I am, fallen into the worst distress, must I suffer that my relatives perish unjustly?" He describes his agonies, says how he imagines confessing, and indicates that he would feel less responsible given that among the guilty, some had already been executed and others had taken flight. He counted them: there were still four, but in danger; and he ended his night of anguish by deciding that it is his duty to save the innocent.[18]

With this confession the affair of the herms appeared to be resolved (although Thucydides remained doubtful); and the city itself, on the whole, had found immediate and palpable relief.[19]

Was that the end of it? Regarding the herms, yes, but not the mysteries. What came next was surprising: we know about two more accusations, both relating to the mysteries. The very last one did not concern Alcibiades at all, but the preceding one was enough: it proved fatal for him.

It came from a woman named Agariste, who belonged to one of the important families. Was it a simple concern for the truth that caused her, after several weeks of delay, to come forward? In any case, she did. She came to say that she knew about a parody of the mysteries held, not in the home of Poulytion, but in that of Charmides. Charmides (not to be confused with Plato's Charmides) was a member of Alcibiades's *hetaereia*. And Alcibiades was supposed to have participated, as well as his uncle Axiochus. What was worse, she said it involved the Mysteries of Eleusis, and Alcibiades had a major part in the farce; he played the hierophant, meaning the principal officiant responsible for the final initiation.

---

17. Andocides named his cousin Charmides (48), whom he also incriminated in the mysteries. Plutarch names one of his friends, Timaeus. There may be different pressures; and the advice of Timaeus, very realistic, would not have constituted a good defense for Andocides.
18. This is taken from 1.48–55.
19. Thucydides 6.60.5.

That was the last straw! Another indictment was brought charging Alcibiades. And on the belief that he should be judged immediately, an official ship, the *Salaminia*, was sent to Sicily to find him and bring him back.

As we can see, the whole business was not a credit to Athens. It was not a credit to the demos or to the city, acting in response to a wave of panic and hasty accusations. Nor was it a credit to the opposition, who appear to have fallen into a number of suspected parties. The *hetaereiai* were active. Pressures were felt on all sides. No one cared about the means, as long as they could harm their enemies and help their friends. These fights were political, certainly; but they were above all personal. And they were sordid.

We would not dare to compare this miasma with more modern times, even recent ones. But we can say that this period of Athenian history offers a reflection, in a magnifying mirror, of the problems that can arise in a democracy when the fights between factions overtake regard for the common good and the rules of simple morality.

Alcibiades had done no worse than others. He had been imprudent, even bold and provocative. He must have joined in the sacrilege. But that was all. His biggest mistake was to have made enemies. And at the moment, his enemies wanted his hide.

Would he return? How could he not return?

"Alcibiades, with his own ship and his fellow accused, accordingly sailed off with the *Salaminia* from Sicily, as though to return to Athens, and went with the ship as far as Thurii, and there they left it and disappeared, being afraid to go home for trial with such a prejudice existing against them. The crew of the *Salaminia* stayed some time looking for Alcibiades and his companions, and at length, as they were nowhere to be found, set sail and departed. Alcibiades, now an outlaw, crossed in a boat not long after from Thurii to the Peloponnesus; and the Athenians passed sentence of death by default upon him and those in his company."[20]

It is poignant to consider that a stone[21] preserves for us testimony of the sale of his property that was held one year later. In the inscription, we find tables and beds from the dining room. We cannot help thinking of the day when Alcibiades invited Socrates, planning to yield to the seduction

20. Thucydides 6.62.6–7.
21. IG I^2 325–34, with supplements. See above, chapter 1.

that never came. Plato's text enabled us to enter a domain that seemed an imaginary one, out of time: the text of the inscription brings us back to the reality, and tragic fragility, of that scene. A bed, sold among confiscated property, having belonged to a man once heaped with good fortune, today an outlaw.

At once we realize that all the fabulous stories were true, just as true as the disaster that now befell Alcibiades.

And the expedition? The grand plan?

We will never be able to gauge the consequences of Alcibiades's exile, or what might have been the outcome of the enterprise in which he believed.

Without a doubt, it was imprudent. As Nicias had said, Sicily was far away, its cities were powerful and might unite. That possibility had appeared at the time of the preceding expedition; and Hermocrates, the Syracusan, knew how to play his hand. The risk grew more real at the time of the great expedition because of Hermocrates. Thucydides leaves a very clear picture of his acts, letting us in on the negotiations at Camarina shortly after the departure of Alcibiades. Camarina was allied with Athens, and the Athenians counted on its support. Hermocrates shows up with a delegation from Syracuse at the same time as the Athenian Euphemus with his compatriots. Both spoke. Hermocrates claimed again, as he had at the congress of Gela, mentioned above, that they were in the midst of an imperialist takeover, that the help and assistance Athens claimed to be offering her allies was nothing more than a specious pretext. In brief, he brought accusations, charges, and called for a united resistance. The result: the people of Camarina, sharply divided and unsure about the future, remained allied to both sides; but once Syracuse had guaranteed its military support, Camarina sent troops to aid the city. And she was not the only one. Thucydides's entire account is filled with the troops that rallied to Syracuse; and, when Camarina did, even Gela sent reinforcements. Thucydides says: "Indeed, almost the whole of Sicily, except the Agrigentines, who were neutral, now ceased merely to watch events as it had previously been doing and actively joined Syracuse against the Athenians" (7.33.2).

But this strength of Syracuse, around which the cities gathered, came most of all from its maritime and naval initiatives. Nicias had warned the Athenians that Selinunte and Syracuse were cities with strong navies. Their experience helped them. And we know that the Athenian fleet, so large and so proudly developed, would end up blocked, and then destroyed, in the straits of Syracuse. Nicias was not wrong to warn of the danger.

He had seen the warnings confirmed on many fronts. But he had stressed the fact that they were leaving Greece itself with an unstable peace and enemies ready to take up arms at the first opportunity. What really made Syracuse succeed was Sparta's help. Shortly after the start of hostilities, Sparta would help Syracuse in two ways: by sending a capable leader and also by resuming the war in Greece, by moving to set up a base in Attica.[22]

The expedition was not prudent, that much is clear. But we must not forget that nothing had gone as Alcibiades wished: the "affairs" had arisen against him, and the consequences of his exile changed everything.

The Sicilian cities did not rally to Athens, it was true. But who was supposed to persuade them? Who had started working on that? Who was capable of being understood? Alcibiades and no one else. That was the policy he planned to lead; and he had had only a few weeks to work on it. Moreover, it was he who had wanted the expedition and who believed it would work. When Nicias was left at the head of Athenian forces, first with Lamachus and then alone, how could he have led with conviction and zeal an expedition he considered futile and bound to fail? Not to mention the fact that the prosecution of the top general as well as of other members of the expeditionary force could only have had a devastating effect on morale.

Thucydides understood perfectly this dual responsibility. He was not a man of single causes and simplistic explanations. He separated the various factors.

He said and repeated that the expedition was seriously imprudent and that Athens failed to recognize the scope of its undertakings. He had declared just that in the opening phrases of book 6: "Most of the Athenians had no idea of the size of the island and of the number of its inhabitants, Hellenic and barbarian, and they did not take into account that they were undertaking a war not much inferior to that against the Peloponnesians" (6.1.1). He also shows that Alcibiades had thrust the Athenians into this enterprise partly to oppose his adversary Nicias, and, in the best case, to

22. See chapter 6.

"gain in wealth and reputation by means of his successes" (6.15.2). The imprudence was condemned, and his motives were denounced.

But the gravity of that mistake, for which Athens was going to pay dearly, can only be seen in view of what Athens did once the decision was made. And Thucydides has left us two lines on the subject, clear and definitive. They deserve consideration.

One bears directly on Alcibiades. It analyzes the reasons that inspired the behavior of his enemies and states how serious the consequences of their conduct were: "And this later on had not a little to do with the ruin of the Athenian state" (6.15.3). Is this about the lack of prudence of the expedition? Not at all! It is about the exile of Alcibiades: "Although in his public life his conduct of the war was as good as could be desired, in his private life his habits gave offense to everyone, and caused them to commit affairs to other hands, and thus before long to ruin the city" (6.15.4). As we indicated in chapter 2, this text goes beyond the context of the Sicilian expedition and, in a bold juxtaposition, refers to the final disaster of 404. What is of interest here is the rigorous distinction drawn between Alcibiades's early imprudence and the disservice to the city by his enemies, who deprived Athens of the help he could have given her.

In his great judgment of Pericles, written after the final defeat of 404, we find exactly the same relationship, when Thucydides says: "This, as might have been expected in a great and sovereign state, produced a host of blunders, and among them the Sicilian expedition" (2.65.11). He uses the word "blunders." The condemnation is clear, as it is in book 6. But as he does there, he follows that with a qualification, and the text continues and specifies the expedition: "Though this failed not so much through a miscalculation of the power of those against whom it was sent, as through a fault in the senders in not taking the best measures afterward to assist those who had gone out, but choosing rather to occupy themselves with private cabals for the leadership of the commons, by which they not only paralyzed operations in the field, but also first introduced civil discord at home" (2.65.11). Once again this sentence can mislead us, because it condenses so tightly all the facts grouped around the Sicilian expedition and everything that followed, including the internal fighting, the start of the civil war, Alcibiades's final exploits—the entire political life of Athens from 416 to 404. But the relationship this sentence establishes regarding the expedition to Sicily is, once more, perfectly clear. The expedition was a blunder, but not the worst one: it was "less . . . than" or, to translate word for word, "not as bad as." Thucydides knows: the failures of history (or of life) rarely result from a single circumstance. He liked to distinguish the various levels of causality: they were rarely as clear as they were in this case.

He has still not specified, in either of the two passages, what would make the exile of Alcibiades so serious. It is time to state it: Alcibiades, whom we left feigning cooperation on the Athenian ship that had come to summon him to appear, may have hesitated about the direction he should take. But where did he go? He went to Sparta and gave his support to the Lacedaemonians. In other words, his exile was not simply a factor against Athens, but a factor favoring her enemies. We shall see him, like a single player playing against himself, taking the part of his opponent, sometimes playing for A and sometimes for B, taking the course of opposing his own expedition and its great plan. This became more serious than any other imprudence. But, indisputably, it was the result of the "affairs" that had torn Athens apart.

In these pages, I have had the habit of putting "affairs" in quotation marks. I would not have thought to do this as recently as just five or six years ago. Reality today brought to mind this connection to the various scandals that are breaking out all the time in our country and in Italy, England, now the United States, and Japan. And I do not do it with a wink, as a crude way of interesting readers today, at any price, in Greek history. In fact, the connection is not simplistic and the resemblance is greater than it may seem. It is instructive to see a demonstration of one of the greatest dangers that can threaten democracies, everywhere and at all times.

For that, we must return to the great analysis of Thucydides book 2, one passage of which we have just quoted. The general idea expressed there is that the successors of Pericles, too equal to each other, and each one incapable of gaining a clear superiority, reached the point where they had to flatter the people. Each aspired to the leading position, and showed himself incapable of attaining it without a serious struggle. In addition, they were willing to use whatever means necessary.

The discord linked to the affair of the herms and to that of the mysteries is one example. But the ongoing disputes between Nicias and Alcibiades regarding the Argive alliance and the plots leading to the ostracism of

Hyperbolus had been a warning sign. During these years, we have seen the effort to defeat one's adversaries by very dubious means. For Alcibiades, this ambition seems to have been matched by his concern for financial gain. Thucydides, at least, indicates this clearly on several occasions.[23] In other words, the pursuit of personal profit, at whatever level it may be, is more important than concern for the public good.

"Affairs" are simply a reflection of either power struggles or greed. They are, as they were for Athens, the warning sign of a decline in public service among politicians, leading to a decline in the state itself.

In any case, if the warnings retain their meaning today, we must also recognize that the nature of "affairs," whatever the era, differs very little. Even if Alcibiades's policies were partly inspired by the desire for profit, the scandals that led to his exile were all religious in nature: that is what moves public opinion and leads to an upheaval. The "affair" that overwhelmed the beginning of the twentieth century involved nationalism. Today, our "affairs" are most often financial, either directly or indirectly:[24] each era has the affairs that fit it.

In any case, they are a serious matter. They are all symptomatic of a profound crisis, whether the charges are legitimate or not. If they are, they expose a moral crisis in the political ranks; if they are not and are brought up in an arbitrary way, then they bring to light bitter egotistical fights that have replaced real debate about the public good. The "affairs" in 415 seem to represent the accumulation of both aspects. It may well be the same in our own time.

To return to Alcibiades, and to the enormous upheaval caused by his exile: there is another lesson to be drawn from the events of that time.

Alcibiades seems, in the final analysis, to have been, in all these events, more a victim than a guilty party. Yes, in his habitual irreverence, he may have been drawn, to some extent, into a farce mocking the mysteries. And that was imprudent. Wouldn't it have seemed imprudent, given his grand plan? At a moment when he was completely involved in this grand plan,

---

23. See 2.65.8 (judgment of Pericles); 6.12.2 (speech of Nicias: Alcibiades "seeks to use his position to help cover his enormous expenses"); 6.15.3 (Thucydides's evaluation: "His tastes exceeded his resources, for maintaining his stable as well as his other expenses").

24. This might involve stealing money or contributing it illegally by allowing something to be sold or gained in the market.

he was surely not involved in vague conspiracies (moreover, how would a private farce imply a conspiracy?). Yet it is entirely clear that people were after him. They had found a basis for accusing him. They sought a moment to combine the two affairs. They refused to let him defend himself before the departure of the expedition. They may have exaggerated the facts that incriminated him. This hostility to him was significant.

Was it, then, unjust? Probably not. This is where the tragedy that struck, so abruptly taking him from the peak of success to ruin and exile, becomes exemplary.

Why, really, all the acrimony against him? Jealousy? Maybe in part (and he did nothing to calm it or to avoid causing it). Remember all the early scandals! That wealth, that insolence, these controversial statements, the desire to shock. And then there was that vanity about his Olympic successes. And what about all the people he had deceived or betrayed—everyone from the friend who asked him to buy a chariot team to his in-laws to poor Hyperbolus, not to mention the friends among the Lacedaemonian delegation? In the end, that is what turned everything against him. He wanted too much. He did too much. Wasn't he in it only for himself? Was it perhaps true that he aspired to tyranny? And was that tolerable? Impudence may be attractive from a distance, but it breeds irritation and calls for a reaction.

Listen once more to what Thucydides says: "Alarmed at the greatness of the license in his own life and habits, and at the ambition he showed in all things whatsoever that he undertook, the mass of the people marked him as aspiring to tyranny and became his enemies." And later: "In his private life his habits gave offense to everyone and caused them to commit affairs to other hands and thus before long to ruin the city" (6.15.4). From the first, scandals marked Alcibiades's early life; they were soon used against him. In all the injustices done him, there is also a kind of justice: a justice that says scorn for the laws of morality and society will cause resentment and will, in one form or another, backfire.

This is the idea that Isocrates, in the next century, will use as the basis for his speech urging all princes and leaders to work for the good, for the devotion and support of all.

In fact, the different aspects of Alcibiades's behavior are interrelated. The same ambition that inspired his plan to conquer the Greek world was realized in his conduct by unrestrained insolence. His insolence provoked reactions that led quickly to the ruin of both the plan and the man himself. It is like a game of billiards in which one ball touches another and then by ricochet hits a third that had appeared quite distant.

Events go so quickly in this year 416 that we can almost hear the sound of these successive strikes that end in the fall of the hero. This fall leads him from summit to the abyss, like Oedipus in Sophocles:

> Hence he was called my king and hence
> was honored the highest of all
> honours; and hence he ruled
> in the great city of Thebes.
> But now whose tale is more miserable?
> Who is there lives with a savager fate?
> Whose troubles so reverse his life as his?[25]

But unlike Oedipus, Alcibiades had not said his last word. He no longer had position or property or country. We would fail to understand him if we supposed that he gave up the game. He shocked the entire Greek world by the audacity with which he now reacted.

---

25. Sophocles, *Oedipus Rex*, translated by David Grene (University of Chicago Press, 1991), lines 1202–6.

6

Exile

Defending Treason

Having broken with Athens, Alcibiades was a fugitive. His homeland had become an enemy city.

His treachery began before he even left Sicily. He revealed to Messina, the ally of Syracuse, that Athenian troops were coming to the city, expecting it to be given up to them. The plot was therefore aborted.[1]

Where was he to go? From Thourioi he traveled to Elis, then to Argos: his Argive alliance policy would have suggested this choice.[2] At the time, however, the severity of the charges to be brought against him were still unknown. He was clearly suspicious. To one who asked him if he did not trust his homeland, he replied, according to a later source quoted by Plutarch (22.2), that basically, "where my life is concerned, I would not trust

---

1. Thucydides 6.74; Plutarch, *Alcibiades* 22: "No sooner had Alcibiades sailed away than he snatched Messina from the Athenians' grasp."
2. Isocrates 16.9; Plutarch 23.

even my own mother." His suspicions were correct: very shortly came the verdict: the death penalty and the order banishing him from all of Greece.[3]

After that, Alcibiades's friends in Argos could not help him. They were already worried and weakened, suspected of antidemocratic leanings, and Athens had handed over to the Argive democrats all those it had taken hostage: he would have to find refuge elsewhere.

He did not delay: with resolute audacity, he went over to . . . Sparta!

Obviously, that would be a problem later for his defenders. We have seen how Isocrates uses the cruelty of Alcibiades's enemies who had obtained from the city a demand for extradition: he himself would have wanted nothing more than to stay "peacefully" in Argos. But could he? "Not knowing what to do amid the difficulties, banished everywhere and seeing no way out of his predicament, in the end he was forced to appeal to the Spartans for refuge."[4] This assertion of Alcibiades's innocence fooled no one; Alcibiades knew exactly what he was doing when he chose to go to Sparta.

Plutarch says clearly that Alcibiades went on his own initiative and was ready to make an offer to help Sparta. "He sent a message to Sparta, asking for asylum and promising to them the kind of service and assistance that would outweigh the harm he had done them before when they were on opposite sides" (*Alcibiades* 23). Thucydides is not so specific: he says only that Alcibiades had come "on the Spartans' own invitation, after first obtaining a safe conduct" (6.88.9). But there is no contradiction there:[5] Plutarch is considering the psychology of Alcibiades, and Thucydides the sequence of facts. The services Alcibiades promised to render are made plain enough in Thucydides's account: they are laid out clearly and are even the subject of one of his speeches.

Alcibiades was aided in Sparta by an influential person who was, at the time, ephor—a high elected magistrate, with control over the kings—and linked with Alcibiades's family through obligations of hospitality. Alcibiades had deceived him at the time of the Argive alliance, but he was able to cover his deceptions adroitly.[6] And in fact, this man Endios never stops

3. Isocrates 16.8–9.
4. Isocrates 16.9.
5. Notwithstanding Hatzfeld, 208, n. 5.
6. See chapter 3.

defending Alcibiades and helping him—perhaps because he was hoping to impose on him for influence over King Agis. The latter had no reason to like Alcibiades; he would soon have ample reason to hate him.

For now, Endios's supporters were ready to welcome Alcibiades, who was not just any refugee. And where could Alcibiades have found a place where his information had higher value and where he could get greater revenge against Athens? If Athens had become an enemy city, Sparta instantly became his ally. One phrase that Plutarch repeats several times conveys the tone of his desire for revenge: "I'll show them that I'm alive."[7]

Thus, in the winter of 415–414, he is officially welcomed in Sparta and ready to help Sparta against Athens, providing the most secret intelligence as well as his widely recognized experience. In the course of a few months, the man who had directed operations for the Athenians would now be the genius behind the war against them.

That entailed a change of sides and—let us say the word—treason such as one has rarely ever seen in history. Of course, there were occasions, even in that era, when Athenians sought refuge with enemies of Athens and were helped by Sparta, which they then praised in their works; that was true of Xenophon. He had taken part in a battle on the Spartan side against Athens and was exiled for that. But he was given some property in the Peloponnese and stayed there quietly, never claiming to direct Spartan policy, much less to direct it against Athens. Furthermore, that had not involved a long and decisive war between the two peoples.

Alcibiades, on the other hand, betrayed Athens in the middle of the war, switching from one side to the other. Moreover, in the speech given him by Thucydides, at the time of his arrival in Sparta, he is seen not only playing the part of a traitor providing Sparta with invaluable information; Thucydides has him giving a speech boldly justifying his change of sides and the morality of it. There have been traitors in history; there has probably never been one who defends treason with so much lucidity, audacity, and authority.

The speech fills paragraphs 89 to 92 of book 6. Ambassadors from Corinth and Syracuse had come to ask the Lacedaemonians for help. At first, as

7. Plutarch, *Alcibiades* 22.3; *Apophthegms* 186e6–7.

their request coincided with that of Alcibiades, Sparta told the Syracusans not to make a deal with Athens. They bought some time; and then Alcibiades came before the authorities and gave his famous speech.

He was not only made welcome and his advice taken, but he spoke publicly and freely.

It is true that the speech we read is that of Thucydides, not Alcibiades. It is probable that the historian has condensed into one striking text a whole series of revelations, justifications, and advice that were not necessarily offered at a single moment or in a public way. Thucydides may also have brought out principles that were never so clearly brought to light. It is evident, however, that he did not invent the revelations, the counsel, or the principles Alcibiades expounded, and certainly not the brilliant insolence of his tone.

Leaving aside for the moment the practical aspect of the speech, the justifications constitute a defense with three points. First there are two justifications relating to Sparta: Why would Alcibiades help Sparta when he had been against it? And how could he support an oligarchy when he had been on the side of Athenian democracy? And then followed a more general moral justification: Why would he help in a war against his homeland (6.92.204)?

The answers were not obvious.

First, help Sparta, when he had supported a policy of war against her? Absolutely!

Because it was Sparta, then, that had offended him! In the beginning, he had wanted to renew the functions of *proxenos* that had once belonged to his family. He had attempted to help the Lacedaemonians taken prisoner at Pylos. He had tried. But Sparta, instead of turning to him, turned to Nicias! Was that not cause for offense? What did he do to retaliate? He attacked Sparta in the Peloponnese . . .

This clever justification calls for two comments.

First, this is the same type of rhetorical argument that consists of erasing blame by reverting to an earlier time: "If I did this, it is because I was the first one wronged; in other words, I did not start it."[8] Our brilliant Athenian, the ward of Pericles, has experience with this kind of argument.

---

8. See, starting in book 1, the argument offered by Corcyra in 34.1, and then by Corinth in 38.2.

But at the same time, what an admission! And with what tranquil insolence he makes it! The reasoning argued here corresponds nicely with Thucydides's account and with his analysis in 5.43.2: he, too, spoke of the age-old *proxenos* and of the prisoners taken at Pylos, and he also states, speaking about Alcibiades, that his conduct had in part been dictated by an ambition stemming from pride, "because the Lacedaemonians had turned to Nicias and Laches to negotiate the treaty; they had ignored him."[9] However, though the facts coincide, their import is not the same, and depends on whether the facts are presented by Thucydides or directly by Alcibiades. As presented by Thucydides, they sound like critique; coming from Alcibiades, they become a profession of faith, bold and provocative. Alcibiades acknowledges, admits, announces that his political decisions are based on strictly personal considerations; and his selfish realism seems to ignore the possibility that he might serve the interests of his homeland.

Yet this is nothing beside what followed, when Alcibiades, just yesterday the elected leader of democratic Athens, denied having the slightest ties to the democracy.

There is, in what he says, some cleverness, but there is also reasoning. He recalled that his family had been known for its opposition to tyranny: a point that would resonate with the Lacedaemonians, who had fought tyranny everywhere, including in Athens. It was a point on which democrats and oligarchs could agree. After his death, Alcibiades's defenders would return to this argument.[10] Here Alcibiades stretches a bit in declaring: "And all who oppose arbitrary power are called the People," thereby burying the differences between the two regimes with a bit of sleight of hand. Ultimately the overall argument is both adroit and true.

To this he adds another argument that is also a fair one: after all, democracy was the regime at the time: "As democracy was the government of the city, it was necessary in most things to conform to established conditions."

He is also correct in observing that neither he nor his relatives were ever extreme democrats (like Hyperbolus or Androcles, and most of those who had earned his condemnation). "However, we endeavored to be more

---

9. See chapter 1.

10. Isocrates, *On the Horses* 16.26; "Alcibiades and Cleisthenes—the former my great-grandfather on my father's side, the latter my father's maternal great-grandfather—assuming the leadership of those in exile, restored the people to their country, and drove out the tyrants."

moderate than the licentious temper of the times; and while there were others, formerly as now, who tried to lead the multitude astray (the same who banished me)." He continued, in words worthy of Pericles, to defend the true spirit of democracy, which is not a spirit of party but a genuine civic spirit: "Our party was that of the whole people,[11] our creed being to do our part in preserving the form of government under which the city enjoyed the utmost greatness and freedom." Actually, Alcibiades is accurately describing his own political position, that of a moderate democrat; at the same time, he shows the extent to which this position was realistic and practical, rather than doctrinaire. It will not, however, surprise us at a later time to hear his defenders in Athens take a different tone and trumpet his devotion to the democracy.[12]

The argument starts to get murky when, to please Sparta, he treats democracy with a scorn he has never before shown: "As for the democracy, the men of sense among us knew what it was, and I perhaps as well as any, as I have more cause to complain of it; but there is nothing new to be said of a patent absurdity. Meanwhile, we did not think it safe to alter it under the pressure of your hostility."

"A patent absurdity." We find in many Greek texts numerous attacks against the democracy and its faults, but nowhere else do we find a statement as radical as this one.

Does this view reflect what was being said among the more enlightened people? What was said around Socrates? Such a hypothesis would be a very weak one. In the harshness of its tone, one is more tempted to see a desire to please Sparta and to speak like a Spartan. After all, we know from Plutarch that Alcibiades, the rogue, played that card with conviction. He who had been so accustomed to luxury, to all the luxuries, had instantly adopted Spartan ways, shaving his face clean, bathing in cold water, and eating very lightly that awful "foul brew," as if he had never in his life seen a cook or a perfumer![13] Plutarch actually remarks on this: "He could change more abruptly than a chameleon" (*Alcibiades* 23).

---

11. During this time of divisions, there was beginning to be an emphasis on the idea that democracy meant the power of the people "as a whole." See 6.39.1 ("I say . . . that the word *demos*, or people, includes the whole state."). This idea will save Athens during the troubles of 411. See 8.93.3.

12. See Isocrates 16.36.

13. 23.3.

Given all this, why would he not assume the tone of a confirmed oligarch by simply twisting his words a bit? So what if that meant betraying a regime that he had served and would serve again later, with apparent conviction?

In Thucydides's speeches, it is always a pleasure to see how the favorable elements and the unfavorable ones blend quite naturally, in a manner as complex as, but more ironic than, in reality. In this one, the reasonable argument is made alongside hypocritical exaggeration, realism next to cajolery. For anyone who reads the text carefully, these subtleties are striking; ultimately, they render a clearer picture of Alcibiades than the subtlest psychological analysis.

Finally, the last justification, also the most general one, bears on a serious issue; and it becomes, in the speech, even more revealing than the previous two. In it, Alcibiades must prove that he is doing nothing wrong in aiding the enemies of his homeland—in other words, in committing treason.

This text is so important and also so striking that it is worth quoting the passage (92.2–4). We see in it a reflection on the homeland as the country where one enjoys certain privileges, and that ceases to be a homeland when those rights are denied; hence, love of one's homeland means desiring to retake it with arms.

> Meanwhile I hope that none of you will think any the worse of me if after having hitherto passed as a lover of my country, I now actively join its worst enemies in attacking it, or will suspect what I say as the fruit of an outlaw's enthusiasm. I am an outlaw from the iniquity of those who drove me forth, not, if you will be guided by me, from your service; my worst enemies are not you who only harmed your foes, but they who forced their friends to become enemies;[14] and love of country is what I do not feel when I am wronged, but what I felt when secure in my rights as a citizen. Indeed I do not consider that I am attacking a country that is still mine; I am rather trying to recover one that is mine no longer; and the true lover of his country is not he who consents to lose it unjustly rather than attack it, but he who longs for it so much that he will go to all lengths to recover it.[15]

14. In this final word of the phrase, it is no longer a matter of enemies in war, but of Alcibiades having become the enemy of Athens while being its friend: he becomes an enemy in both senses of the word!

15. It will not come as a surprise to read in the book by A. Vlachos, in which a faithful servant of Alcibiades talks about his life, one part of the speech in Sparta quoted, but not this part!

Amazing Alcibiades: to hear him tell it, he is the model patriot for attacking his country.

To understand the full import of the text, of course, we should think about the eternal problem of exiles returning "in the wagons of the enemy." Every self-respecting Greek posed a problem in terms that are true for other times. But at the same time, we must go back centuries in our minds, when the Greek city was constantly confronted with the problem of exiles and their desire to come home.

During the political fighting of the sixth and fifth centuries BCE, it was normal to see a whole group of citizens sent into exile: once it was the expulsion of partisans of the oligarchy, or the rich; then it was the democrats' turn. And naturally, they immediately started plotting their return, soliciting the aid of other cities. Sparta and Athens, or Athens and Corinth, had a habit of intervening in ways that, under cover of helping the exiles, served their own prestige and power. The Peloponnesian War began by such battles between Epidamnus and Corcyra; and we read often phrases like "the last act before the war was the expulsion of those in power by the people. The exiled party joined the barbarians." (1.24.5). "The Corcyraean revolution began with the return of the prisoners taken in the sea fight off Epidamnus" (3.70.1). In fact it was in regard to the unrest in Corcyra that Thucydides begins his broad analysis of the civil wars in Greece (3.82). Similarly, we have seen how Argos went from one side to another, groups of men being displaced or brought back, and the fighting increased against this or that city "that had welcomed the banished."[16]

It is this aspect of political life in ancient Greece that in a sense justifies Alcibiades's reasoning. There is a difference, however, and it is significant. Alcibiades was the leader, the one responsible, who knew everything: his crossing over to the enemy was more serious. Moreover, he was not requesting help in returning to his country: he was offering instead to help Sparta defeat his country—his return being only a possible, but uncertain, result of that defeat. Last, he was doing this at a moment when Athens was fully engaged (thanks to him) and risked losing everything (again thanks to him). The desire to return had taken on the appearance of merciless revenge.

16. See above, chapter 3. And for the last case, 5.83.3.

In an amazing stroke, some years later the problem would again en-flame passions. Athens was defeated in 404, and Sparta installed an oli-garchy there. The democrats left in exile, then returned in glory; they fought, triumphed, and freed Athens. That would be one of the proudest moments in Athenian history, particularly as the democrats knew how to exercise moderation and civic sensibility; they achieved national reconcili-ation, one that would be respected.

Alcibiades was gone. But he had a son, who seems to have inherited his taste for scandal but not his genius. This son had trials that were, in-directly, those of his father. There we find again the whole debate about the exiled patriot.

Isocrates, in a speech pleading on behalf of the son, recalls that Alcibi-ades, in exile, had fought against his country; then right away he refers to the liberation of Athens by the democrats: they too had fought against her: "Did you not seize the Piraeus and destroy the crops in the fields and harry the land and set fire to the suburbs and finally assault the walls?"[17] This is very close to the argument Alcibiades makes in Thucydides, only in the later case there is a positive reminder of a moment of glory.

The young man's adversaries, and so those of his father also, point out the faulty reasoning and protest against it. Lysias,[18] in a speech against the younger man (for a different occasion), states:

> For he has the audacity to say that Alcibiades has done nothing outrageous in marching against his native land, since you in your exile occupied Phyle, cut down trees and assaulted the walls, and by these acts of yours, instead of bequeathing disgrace to your children, won honor in the eyes of all the world; as though there were no difference in the deserts of men who used their exile to march in the ranks of the enemy against their country and those who strove for their return while the Lacedaemonians held the city! And again, I think it must be obvious to all that these others sought to return that they might surrender the command of the sea to the Lacedaemonians and gain the command of you for themselves; whereas your democracy, on its return, expelled the enemy and liberated even those of our citizens who de-sired to be slaves.[19]

17. Isocrates, *On the Horses* 16.13.
18. Or the author of the speech passed down in his name. See the preface.
19. Lysias 14.32–34.

Of course, the comparison with the exiles of 404, appealing and flattering, helped to limit, to some degree, the difference between the two cases. This is yet another example of the way in which with the Greeks, problems are revealed and defined on the basis of experience and in the light of argument.

The speech that is found in Thucydides could not make a comparison with events that would not occur for more than ten years. This speech is assuredly characteristic of Thucydides's work. It is also characteristic of the intelligence and unscrupulous insolence of Alcibiades.

What gives his treason and the strength of his conviction in the speech such gravity is that within these diverse arguments appear certain propositions, revelations, and opinions that were going to change the course of Greek history. Whatever modern examples one might think of or imagine—spies crossing from East to West, scientists in atomic research, treasonous generals—no traitor ever brought more to an enemy.

The least one can say is that Alcibiades did not come empty-handed.

Among Alcibiades's recommendations that would come to have great weight are two that are part of his speech in Sparta. Apart from revealing the "great design" that Alcibiades had kept secret from Athens and the plans he offers to excite the Lacedaemonians, we should pause to consider these two pieces of advice that the Spartans in fact followed and that proved especially effective. First, of course, was the advice to help Syracuse, to cause the Athenian expedition to fail. But how exactly? Not by sending just any small number of troops that would be more or less helpful. No! Alcibiades wanted more and knew what would be really effective there: "Send on board ship to Syracuse troops that will be able to row their ships themselves and serve as hoplites the moment that they land; and what I consider even more important than the troops, a Spartiate as commanding officer to discipline the forces already on foot and to compel shirkers to serve. The friends you already have will thus become more confident, and the waverers will be encouraged to join you."[20]

And that is what was done. Gylippus was named to lead the troops; he was responsible for training the troops needed in agreement with the Corinthians. So it began.

20. 6.91.4.

The last chapters of book 6 of Thucydides and the first chapters of book 7 cover events between the efforts of Nicias and the arrival of Gylippus. Many peoples rallied to the cause, owing to "the energy Gylippus seems to have brought from Sparta." From the outset, Alcibiades's advice had proven sound. At last Gylippus arrived. And he arrived at the very moment that Athens was about to finish its wall around Syracuse. As the sober Thucydides notes: "The danger to Syracuse had indeed been great" (7.2.4).

From that point on, everything was going to unfold exactly as Alcibiades hoped—unfortunately for Athens. In the course of book 7 we follow a series of battles around Syracuse and in the great harbor; we also see that, once resistance to Athens solidified, many people rallied to the cause. And throughout we find Gylippus and Hermocrates together, the Spartan and the Syracusan, each one as committed as the other, supporting and complementing each other. Athens also sent reinforcements, but in vain.

We can imagine this final Athenian effort, this stubborn hope. It seems likely that Euripides is alluding to this at the end of his *Electra*, in 413, when the Dioscuri appear and announce, at the very end of the play: "We two must rush to the Sicilian seas, rescue the salt-smashed prows of the fleet."[21]

Nothing worked against the strategy organized by Alcibiades. The Athenian general Demosthenes, who commanded the reinforcing fleet (not related to the orator of the same name in the next century), saw the gravity of the situation as soon as he arrived (7.42.3–5). He wanted to attempt a hasty action. It might work: if not, he would have to re-embark and leave. We know how it ended: that rapid strike failed. Did he then re-embark? Demosthenes wanted to; but Nicias, as usual, hesitated. The result was an unprecedented defeat. Both sides had gambled everything and Athens lost. The history of this battle as told in Thucydides is full of vigor and emotion. The result was that the Athenians could not get away; they retreated in chaos and were massacred or taken prisoner, some under an agreement, others with none. Demosthenes, taken prisoner, was condemned to death. Nicias, who had once been a friend of Sparta, gave himself up to Gylippus. He met the same fate. The suffering of the Athenian prisoners in the quarries of Syracuse is well known. Of the great invasion, nothing was left. Thucydides has the last word: "This was the

---

21. Translation by R. Lattimore (New York, 1963).

greatest Hellenic achievement of any in this war, or, in my opinion, in Hellenic history; at once most glorious to the victors, and most calamitous to the conquered. They were beaten at all points and altogether; all that they suffered was great; they were destroyed, as the saying is, with a total destruction, their fleet, their army—everything was destroyed, and few out of many returned home. Such were the events in Sicily."[22]

All this time Alcibiades, who had called for the expedition and had, two years earlier, commanded it, was in Sparta, no doubt proud of the plan he had given it. "Beaten at all points and altogether." He, the mastermind, was content.

His second piece of advice also contributed to the war's outcome in no small measure, at least indirectly; its consequences extended beyond the period of the Sicilian expedition.

Back when the expedition was still being planned, Nicias had pointed out that there was danger in leaving for Sicily when peace was not yet secure in Greece itself: Alcibiades's second bit of advice had the effect of restarting the war, in a way that was particularly dangerous for Athens. Alcibiades advised the Spartans to foment war in Greece to prevent Athens from sending reinforcements to Sicily, and to seize a fort in Attica near Athens, at Decelea. Decelea was twenty kilometers north of Athens on the road to Boeotia.

> You must fortify Decelea in Attica, the blow of which the Athenians are always most afraid and the only one that they think they have not experienced in the present war: the fortification in question, while it benefits you, will create difficulties for your adversaries, many of which I shall pass over and shall only mention the chief. Whatever property there is in the country will most of it become yours, either by capture or surrender; and the Athenians will at once be deprived of their revenues from the silver mines at Laurium, of their present gains from their land and from the law courts, and above all of the revenue from their allies, which will be paid less regularly, as they lose their awe of Athens and see you addressing yourselves with vigor to this war. (6.91.6–7)

This was to conceive a direct strike against Athens; in a very modern fashion, Alcibiades was calculating all the economic and financial aspects: loss

---

22. End of book 7.87.5.

of land, of small industry and mining, revenue paid by allies. And he had chosen the most propitious strategic location.

In fact, fortifying a position within enemy territory was one of the modes of action considered in time of war. Pericles had talked about it when preparing for the war; he had reassured the Athenians on this subject by showing that an important position could only be taken with great difficulty, and that a simple position did less harm than Athens could accomplish with its navy, as the navy gave it the ability to retaliate much more effectively.[23] It was in fact Athens that, in 424, had established a fort at Pylos in the Peloponnese,[24] leading to the most serious harm to Sparta. That installation at Pylos was the object of multiple conflicts during the Peace of Nicias: Sparta demanded that the fort be returned; and Athens turned a deaf ear. Now the situation was reversed: this matter concerned a Spartan fort in the middle of Attica.

There had been some talk of this before the peace, but without specifics. Now, Alcibiades's advice would prove remarkable.

The Lacedaemonians were tempted but wary, and did not take the advice right away. But when they learned that Athens was going to send reinforcements to Sicily, they decided, under pressure from their allies, the time had come to act. They had had enough of the Athenians' threats, of their refusal to return Pylos; and since the Spartans were now fighting in Sicily, they had to follow logic. One whole winter was spent in preparations; then, in the spring of 413, they invaded Attica and began fortifying Decelea as planned.[25] The fortifications were completed during the summer; a garrison followed. This occupation would continue throughout the war that had resumed—the war that was sometimes called the "war of Decelea" (413–404).

This move was disastrous for Athens: it was exactly as Alcibiades had said it would be. Thucydides says that it "caused great harm to the Athenians."[26] He says that they were "deprived of their whole country" (7.27.5). More than twenty thousand slaves and many artisans deserted, herds were lost, and horses lamed. Crops coming from Euboea had to make costly detours. And Athens lived constantly under threat: "Instead

---

23. 1.142.4.
24. This was the whole of Navarino: the episode occupies the beginning of Thucydides's book 4.
25. 7.19.1.
26. 7.27.3.

of a city, it became a fortress. Summer and winter the Athenians were worn out by having to keep guard on the fortifications, during the day by turns, by night altogether, the cavalry excepted, at the different military posts or upon the wall. But what most oppressed them was that they had two wars at once." (7.28.1–3).

Alcibiades had aimed well and accurately. It is not surprising that bitterness against him endured. During a trial after his death, Lysias wrote: "The son of Alcibiades, who had helped the Lacedaemonians fortify Decelea . . ." Other problems would follow, with the third counsel Alcibiades gave the Spartans.[27] But this was still painful, and with reason.

We can understand, in weighing the consequences of these first two recommendations, that Alcibiades had given Sparta great service. Having once been a great man in Athens, he had become a great man in Sparta.

The Athenian disaster in Sicily had hardly ended when Alcibiades gave Sparta his third counsel, worth as much as his previous counsels combined: complete the destruction of Athens by causing the loss of the Ionian allies, the backbone of the empire.

But before tracking that course, it is useful for us to look ahead a few months: we find that the "great man" of Sparta has run into a few obstacles, just like those of the great Athenian. Another scandal! This one, despite everything else, will weaken his situation.

Had he really wanted, as a phrase quoted in Plutarch suggests, descendants who would be kings of Sparta? In any case, he seduced the wife of King Agis,[28] and gave her a child; he was seen leaving the queen's chamber during an earthquake.[29] Plutarch, having trouble understanding a text of Xenophon, is a bit unclear about this business of the nocturnal flight and the earthquake. One thing is clear, however: the scandal became public. It would matter later in the history of Sparta, for this son, named Leotychidas, would run into opposition from those who faulted his illegitimate

27. See chapter 7.
28. Despite the surveillance the ephors were supposed to exercise, if we believe what Socrates says (to Alcibiades, in fact) in Plato's *Alcibiades* 121b.
29. See Hatzfeld, *Revue des études anciennes* (1933): 387–95.

birth. Xenophon relates the whole story in *Hellenica* (beginning at 3.3.2). Leotychidas was supposed to yield to Agesilaus. Some modern historians have tried, in vain, to argue that the whole affair was simply gossip spread to remove this son from the royal succession. There has been an abundance of articles and conferences about this question of paternity in recent decades.[30] The sheer number of these proves the absence of any hard evidence. The least one can say is that the story was acknowledged by everyone in antiquity and, moreover, does not come as a surprise. Alcibiades played the perfect Spartan, but he remained Alcibiades, always as seductive and imprudent as ever and, apparently, always just as devoid of scruples.

I like the similarities that sometimes appear between the past and our own time. Here, just by being himself, Alcibiades has outdone himself.

Nevertheless, he had become such a valuable ally that at least officially, the king did not protest. Alcibiades suffered no direct consequences. Unabashed, he continued to refine his final plan—one that would dictate the new turn taken in the war.

30. See the preface. After the suspicions of Beloch and Niese, the first important critique was that of M. Luria in *Klio* (1927): 404–20. See also Westlake in 1938 and Littman in 1969. Most historians, however, accept the facts (among others, Ferguson, Ehrenberg, Glotz, and Hatzfeld).

In Asia Minor

Following the disaster of the Sicilian expedition, Athens' empire was badly shaken. The empire represented its power; now Athens had been shown to be weak. Very quickly, the effects were felt in Ionia, in the islands close to Asia Minor, and in the Greek cities of Asia Minor.

This was a key region for Greece because, in general, Asia Minor was part of Persia, and an old rivalry existed between the two peoples. The Persian Wars had started with an uprising in these countries against Persia, an uprising Athens had supported. After the Greek victory, the islands and the cities of the region were included among the allies of Athens; and among the allies, they represented some of the richest peoples. The large islands of Lesbos, Chios, Samos, the famous city of Miletus, and other cities, like Abydos to the north and Halicarnassus to the south, together constituted a symbol of the Greek presence in Asia Minor and the real power of the Athenian Empire. Just as the Persian Wars had established their independence from Persia, the defeat Athens suffered risked weakening its authority in this region. We know how strongly the Athenians had reacted to the defection of the Mytilenians, on the island of Lesbos, and how harshly they had wanted to punish them.

The risk was greater because the Persian power was close by, watching for signs of weakness. Persia was always there.

During the Peloponnesian War, Sparta had, from the beginning, thought about an alliance with that side; it knew the barbarians wanted to destroy Athens. The king of Sparta, Archidamus, had said that Sparta needed to form alliances "either Greek or barbarian." He even specified that when threatened, one could, without reproach, "for safety, seek help not only from Greeks but even barbarians." And sweeping away other considerations was the fact that Persia was rich. Moreover, at the beginning of the war, the Lacedaemonians had wanted to send an embassy into Asia, to the king, to try to persuade him to provide support and to fight at their side. The embassy never arrived, and nothing changed. But in this matter as well, one could expect to see new initiatives arise at the first opportunity presented by a weakened Athens.

The opportunity was not long in coming. As soon as the disaster in Sicily became known, defections of Greek cities took place one by one, and negotiations between Sparta and the Persian satraps began.

In Sparta there was one person who knew better than anyone else what these defections meant to Athens, and how much Athens feared an alliance between Sparta and Persia.

This person had every reason to encourage Sparta, and to show it the price of these two means for destroying Athenian power. That was, of course, Alcibiades. The strategy in Ionia was his third counsel.

Later, we will admire the perfect geographic scope of Alcibiades's movement from one end of Greece to the other. First, departing from Athens to conquer far-off Sicily to build Athens' empire. Exiled following the "affairs," he returned to Greece itself, to Sparta. From there he launched, and launched Sparta, to the extreme east of this world, into Asia Minor, in order to destroy Athens' empire. No one could have known at that time (except he himself—who knows?) that his path would lead him back to Athens, where he would return in triumph as a savior.

Every move he made along the length of this path was masterful, enhanced by a lack of scruples that surprised no one.

Things were not easy at first.

It is true that the defections of the islands and the cities of Asia Minor began quickly. No one still believed in the power of Athens. Thucydides even says that the subjects of Athens thought it could not hold for even one summer.[1] Euboea was the first to begin discussions with King Agis of Sparta (he was occupying Decelea in Attica) to prepare for joining the Spartan side. Then it was Lesbos that spoke with Agis. Chios also brought a request to Sparta. In that sphere, everything was going according to Alcibiades's wishes. The situation was less clear between Persia and Sparta because disagreements intruded.

The Persian king—"the King," as he was known—ruled through his satraps, governors of vast provinces. Two of these satraps also considered approaching Sparta. Their reasons were the same: the authority Athens exercised over the islands and cities of Asia Minor prevented them from raising tribute money for the king; but the king expected them to pay. It would therefore be profitable to help Sparta force the Athenians out. The two satraps in question who played a major role in the history of this period were Tissaphernes, satrap of Sardis, on whom Ionia depended; and Pharnabazus, satrap of Dascylium, north of Asia Minor, on whom the Hellespont depended. After the Sicilian disaster, Tissaphernes reached an agreement with the people of Chios, who wanted to defect immediately; and he sent an embassy to Sparta. Pharnabazus sent another at around the same time. Tissaphernes requested Peloponnesian assistance in his region and announced that he was ready to accept troops; Pharnabazus asked for help in the Hellespont, and his representatives had brought money. A choice had to be made!

In Sparta now there were two points of view that corresponded to a latent quarrel between the powerful King Agis and Alcibiades's faithful friend Endios, who was ephor that year. Ephors were high elected magistrates; they exercised a sovereign authority that was often superior to that of kings, whom they were responsible for overseeing. This could lead to competing for influence.

At first both parties agreed to take the side of Tissaphernes. That was also what Alcibiades wanted. He had personal relationships in Ionia. Ephesus and Chios had participated in the festivals celebrating his Olympic victories and he had, Thucydides says, "friends among the leading men

1. 8.2.2.

of the Milesians."[2] King Agis accepted this principle; the expedition was organized. Alcibiades himself would be part of it.

Therein lay the problem. The Athenians, more resolved than anyone had thought, succeeded in blocking the first ships of the Peloponnesian fleet in a small port in the vicinity of Corinth. That was a bad start. The Lacedaemonians were discouraged: ready to give up the effort, they decided not to send the ships that were to follow (the ships Alcibiades was to accompany); they even recalled the ships that had already sailed.

Then Alcibiades intervenes in earnest. Thucydides's text describes his resolve as well as his sense of intrigue:

> Alcibiades again persuaded Endios and the other ephors to persevere in the expedition, saying that the voyage would be made before the Chians heard of the fleet's misfortune, and that as soon as he set foot in Ionia, he should, by assuring them of the weakness of the Athenians and the zeal of Sparta, have no difficulty in persuading the cities to revolt as they would readily believe his testimony. He also represented to Endios himself in private that it would be glorious for him, Endios, to be the means of making Ionia revolt and the king become the ally of Sparta, instead of that honor being left to Agis (for Agis, it must be remembered was the enemy of Alcibiades).[3]

Such is the characteristic style of that man! He, the exile, now playing the two supreme authorities in Sparta against each other. He is the one advising, inspiring everything; and it is also he who will become the hero of the whole business precisely because of his treachery. Nothing can stop him in his desire for revenge against the country that could not keep him.

Moreover, what better way to get back at his old adversary King Agis, who had been the enemy opposing him in the business of the Argive alliance and at the battle of Mantinea, and who, just imagine, because of Alcibiades, was about to become the cuckolded Spartan husband!

This fine plan worked. Moreover, in a paradox reminiscent of the vote on the Sicilian expedition, Alcibiades came out of it even better than he had planned, and without difficulty. Originally, he was to have joined the expedition being organized under the patronage of Agis. Now he is leaving as the leader, at the head of a small squadron called on to settle

2. 8.17.2.
3. 8.12.1.

everything, planned solely by the very man in charge. Thucydides concludes: "Endios and his colleagues, thus persuaded, put to sea with the five ships and the Spartan Chalcideus, and made all haste upon the voyage."[4]

Everything depended on speed, on a lie of omission, and on that art of persuasion that seemed to be, everywhere and at all times, Alcibiades's signature.

He succeeded in doing everything he needed to do, and he was triumphant.

Arriving at Chios without warning, the two chiefs were received thanks to their friends and were able to convince the ruling council: the large island, with its important fleet, defected from Athens. This defection was followed by those of two cities situated opposite each other on the continent, Erythrae and Clazomenae. Neighboring Teos, despite Athens' efforts there, then joined the others. More important, Alcibiades obtained—quite justly—the defection of Miletus. Ephesus apparently then followed the movement.

To finish, an initial agreement was reached between Sparta on the one hand and "the king and Tissaphernes" on the other.

All of Alcibiades's promises were fulfilled and his advice was proven to be justified.

Still, Athens did not grow discouraged. With a resolve that we have to admire, it found the means to equip ships again and to try to stymie the enemy action by intervening everywhere. On the second try, it took the territory back. Athens incited a democratic revolution in Samos; and, for the duration of the war, it found on this important island, situated just south of Chios, a highly valuable base. Athens also took back Clazomenae, succeeded in occupying Lesbos, and briefly threatened Miletus.

Alcibiades had promised so much, and had been so confident, that the news of all these losses inclined Sparta against him. He was, for all practical purposes, the only leader, because the Lacedaemonian sent with him had been killed at Miletus. People began to suspect this all-too-brilliant adventurer (King Agis, no doubt, the first to doubt him). In some ways, the events at Athens were being repeated: Alcibiades, even when he is on your side, causes anxiety and bad feelings. As Thucydides says, soberly:

---

4. 8.12.3.

"He [was] the personal enemy of Agis and in other respects thought unworthy of confidence."[5] He was *apistos*, not credible. How could Alcibiades have been considered otherwise? All the treachery is now exposed. Added to that, the agreement reached with Tissaphernes (not by him, but conforming to his strategy) annoyed all those who valued the independence of the Ionian Greeks. Not only were these failures exposed and his personal role in the events disquieting, the very success of his strategy was cause for anger.

Now what? Let us reread the spy novels of our own time. What happens to the traitor who has worked for you and whom you come to distrust? The new commander of the Peloponnesian fleet, in the beginning of winter, received the order at Chios—quite simply—to kill Alcibiades.

This time there was no legally decided death penalty, as at Athens: this was an order to kill quickly and discreetly. Precisely as before, Alcibiades was able to escape just in time. He still had friends in Sparta to warn him: perhaps it was Endios, even if he was no longer the influential friend expecting Alcibiades to help him gain power. Or perhaps, as some historians of the time would later romantically surmise, it was Agis's wife.[6] Whoever it was, Alcibiades escaped to safety for the second time.

Where did he go? Banished from Athens and threatened in Sparta, only one solution was left to him, obvious and easy: he went to the satrap Tissaphernes!

Do not let this successful escape surprise you. The satrap welcomed him, listened, and was seduced. Here Plutarch becomes almost lyrical—showing us what the charm of Alcibiades could achieve. He writes:

> The Persian was a devious and malicious man who felt no qualms about doing wrong and he was impressed by Alcibiades's versatility and extraordinary ingenuity. No one, whatever his character or temperament, could fail to be touched and captivated by Alcibiades's charisma, if he spent time and lived with him on a daily basis; even those who feared and envied him found themselves enjoying his company and warming to him once they were with him and could actually see him. At any rate, although Tissaphernes felt as

5. 8.45.1.

6. See Justin 5.2, who is quite clear: "He was informed by the wife of King Agis, whom he had known in adultery." Cornelius Nepos says that Alcibiades was "so canny that he could not be tricked, especially when the matter affected him" (5).

savage a hatred of Greeks as any Persian, he was so won over by Alcibiades's blandishments that he outdid him in flattering him back. He declared that the most beautiful walled garden he had, which was graced with lawns and refreshing pools, and dotted with exceptional haunts and places of resort prepared in a manner fit for a king, should be named "Alcibiades"—and that is the name by which everyone continued to refer to it for a long time.[7]

The new luxury was a change from weak Spartan broth. But his new lifestyle also brought with it some difficult adjustments. Plutarch, in the text quoted above, says that Tissaphernes was cruel and hated Greeks. He was not someone next to whom a Greek could feel comfortable; the barbarian in him would appear frequently. A short time later, concerning the people of Delos, Thucydides would report that the Persian Arsaces, a lieutenant of Tissaphernes, abused some people in Delos, expelled them from their island, and moved them to Atramytteion: "On pretense of a secret quarrel, [he] invited the chief men of the Delians to undertake military service. . . . And after drawing them out from their city as his friends and allies, had laid in wait for them at dinner, and surrounded them and caused them to be shot down by his soldiers" (8.108.4). Later Alcibiades would experience this cruelty and duplicity of the Persian satraps (no longer Tissaphernes).[8] But in the meantime we can well imagine the care he took to stay in favor with his host, and to close his eyes to certain facts.

He succeeded not only in this but, beyond paying homage, he exercised real political influence on Tissaphernes. Thucydides does not hesitate to say that he became his tutor (*didaskalos*). And there he is, making decisions, advising, teaching.[9]

Moreover, the lesson, whose meaning and importance we will see, is primarily meant to denigrate Sparta and to turn the satrap against it. Obviously, Sparta had abandoned him, Alcibiades. But the day before, he had helped it. He came to Asia Minor on its ships, to serve its interests! Never mind. A second reversal, no less radical than the one that had turned him against Athens, accompanied his passage to Asia Minor. Once again, he switched sides.

7. See *Life of Alcibiades* 24.5–7.
8. See below, chapter 11.
9. Thucydides repeats the word, using the Greek verb *didaskein*, in 8.45.3.

One might well ask whether all along he had, in going over to the side of Tissaphernes, always envisioned that move as preparation for his eventual return to Athens. He must have always wanted that. His rancor must have been mixed with a desire to return. Now the possibility of returning would have taken on a more specific form. The Spartan leaders must surely have sensed that his true aim was not to help them (that is why they judged him to be "not credible"; or at least that was one reason for their doubts). In any case, he must have come to realize that the desire to destroy Athens was not as worthy a desire as managing it in order to return one day as its savior.

This is how Thucydides explains the advice he gave to Tissaphernes and the king: "Alcibiades gave this advice to Tissaphernes and the King, with whom he then was, not merely because he thought it really the best, but because he was seeking means to bring about his restoration to his country, well knowing that if he did not destroy it he might one day hope to persuade the Athenians to recall him and thinking that his best chance of persuading them lay in letting them see that he possessed the favor of Tissaphernes" (8.47.1).

Here we see Thucydides's marvelous use of double causality, the second explanation leading from objective judgment to self-interest. Thucydides seems to see this dual motivation as a constant feature of Alcibiades's actions. It was mentioned at the time of the Argive alliance, where he wrote, in 5.43.2: "Alcibiades thought the Argive alliance really preferable, not that personal pique had not also a great deal to do with his opposition." That also brought out his jealousy toward Nicias. Similarly, in 6.15.2, we see two complementary motives: the desire to defeat Nicias and the conviction that he really could accomplish his big plan. What good luck, that each time his sound judgment should match his self-interest! Maybe such a coincidence should simply be called optimism.

In any case, the advice given to Tissaphernes is emphasized in Greek by the repetition "at the same time . . . and at the same time . . ." in order to highlight his desire to return to Athens as savior and man of influence.

For this, Alcibiades proceeded in two very distinct stages, like a skillful manipulator wishing to manage the transition.

First, his advice to Tissaphernes constituted the politics of alternating between and balancing two opposing sides. Thucydides describes the perfectly realistic arguments he developed with the satrap: he should not let one of the two adversaries, Athens and Sparta, dominate on the sea and land; he should let each one exercise supremacy in his own domain. "For if the command of the sea and land were united in one hand, he would not know where to turn for help to overthrow the dominant power, unless he at last chose to stand up for himself and go through with the struggle at great expense and danger. The cheapest plan was to let the Hellenes wear each other out, at a small share of the expense and without risk to himself."[10] Further on, Thucydides concludes this calculation with the very plainest bit of advice: "Alcibiades therefore urged him to wear them both out at first, and after reducing the Athenian power as much as he could, forthwith to rid the country of the Peloponnesians." All foreign policies involving balancing two adversaries can find a model here, exposed with a realistic clarity that even Machiavelli would have admired.[11]

This was very wise advice, and Tissaphernes would adopt it once and for all.

However, the policy of alternating between Sparta and Athens represented a clear development in favor of Athens, which, only yesterday, had been the enemy.

Before stating the principle cited above, Alcibiades had, elsewhere in Thucydides's text, made other, more questionable, arguments in favor of Athens. He had suggested that he could make a deal between Athens, mistress of the sea, and the king, master on the land. Sparta, by contrast, had come as a liberator and wished to free the Greeks from the Persians as well as from the Athenians.

The rationale was subtle. It was so subtle that it confused the historian's copyists and later his commentators. But the general meaning is not in doubt. It rests on an idea Nicias had formulated to reassure Athens about the possible ambitions of the Syracusans. He had said it was not reasonable to suppose they would ever attack Athens, fighting "empire against empire."[12] There would have been solidarity among imperial powers. However, we must say the situation in Asia Minor at the time did not accord with this theory. It was Sparta that had allied itself with the king; it

10. 8.46.2. The conclusion is in 8.46.4.
11. Plutarch summarizes the analysis elsewhere (25.1).
12. 6.11.3.

was Sparta who had thought about it at the beginning of the war. And the satraps in the regions bordering Greece had not complained about Sparta, but about Athens. Besides, was it not Athens that had always been the liberating city, freeing Greeks from the barbarians? Alcibiades's view was surprising indeed. Maybe it was just another arrow in his quiver, another example of his usual powers of persuasion.

Tissaphernes, in any case, did not need to be convinced: his actions proved that.

First, he cut the pay promised to the Peloponnesian troops. He had agreed to give each man one drachma, then announced that he would give only half that (three obols). According to Plutarch as well as in all probability, that was Alcibiades's advice.[13] This move provoked some unrest, particularly with Hermocrates, who, after the victory in Sicily, had come to rejoin his Peloponnesian allies. Alcibiades had foreseen all this. On his advice (and here Thucydides is the source),[14] Tissaphernes was careful to pay the officers of the Peloponnesian army in exchange for their cooperation. That's an example of one way to "persuade" people, and it is the age-old one. Clearly, Alcibiades knew how to make these measures acceptable. Moreover, he put himself out in front. When the cities came to demand their money, it was he who turned them away, replying on Tissaphernes's behalf: he told them that Chios was rich enough to provide its own security; as for the other cities, they had previously paid a tribute to Athens. Henceforth they could pay the same amount to ensure their own security . . . With great aplomb, Alcibiades added that if the king sent subsides, then everyone would receive the amount they expected in the first place. Appeals to national pride, hopes, and promises to reward their patience—he left out nothing. And the result was achieved: the cut in pay passed without consequences.

Next there was the question of the fleet. Tissaphernes equipped the ships in Phoenicia: don't rush, said Alcibiades. His advice was followed; and his empty promises meant that the Peloponnesian fleet lost its ability to attack.

In short, Alcibiades had succeeded in sowing unrest when a group of men from Sparta arrived in Ionia; sent as advisers, they were charged

13. 6.25.1.
14. This is where he uses the verb *didaskein*; see note 9, above.

with taking measures they deemed desirable. Their leader was one Lichas. Lichas held a meeting with Tissaphernes, in which he complained about many things, but in particular about the agreement recently signed between Sparta and the king. He was outraged, saying that, as things now stood, he did not want subsidies if that was the price he had to pay. Tissaphernes got angry and the advisers left for Rhodes, which rallied to his side. In other words, as Alcibiades had wished, relations between Sparta and Tissaphernes soured; and everyone knew it.

Everyone—including the Athenians of Samos, who understood that they were in debt to Alcibiades, and also understood the price they would pay for his support.

Alcibiades led the negotiations—not with Athens, but with the Athenian force based on the island of Samos, just across from Ephesus and Miletus. This was the first sign of a characteristic of this period: there were, in a way, two Athens, and they were not always in agreement. They agreed even less where, owing to Alcibiades's meddling, internal politics were concerned.

We are now in the beginning of the year 411 BCE. Alcibiades had been with Tissaphernes for only a few months. For the Athenian democracy, it will be a year of drama and near civil war.

Naturally, Alcibiades had friends in the army at Samos. He went to them, asking them to pass along a message to "the best men in the army," and his message was clear: "If only there were an oligarchy in place of the corrupt democracy that had banished him, he would be glad to return to his country and to make Tissaphernes their friend."[15] The drama had begun.

Once again, this is how Alcibiades operates, offering quite a deal. Here he is, a man condemned to death, with the gall to demand, without blinking, and on his own authority, a regime change.

Was he so fond of oligarchy? He had certainly had personal enemies in the camp of the radical democrats, such as Hyperbolus and Androcles; and he castigated them. In Sparta he had spoken out with rare vehemence about the folly of democracy. To reverse the democracy, therefore, would

15. "The best men" has a strong social-class connotation, in contrast to *poneroi*, "riff-raff," 8.47.

satisfy a genuine grievance; it would also help assure his future safety. For in fact, his old enemies would not let him return peacefully.

And yet . . . and yet, it is important to know that Alcibiades will in fact return to Athens, and as a friend of the democrats. Some scholars have suggested that he had always imagined making himself leader of the people against that oligarchy he endorsed so loudly.[16] But, intricate as it may be, that hypothesis rests on no evidence. Under the circumstances, Alcibiades was not solely responsible for the reversal of political positions. In democracy, everything happens, and can happen, when the conflicts between individuals are more important than the common good. As we will see, Alcibiades was not the only one guilty of this. In 411 there was an amazing back and forth, and numerous violent reversals followed. And Athens, just in time, found a superb solution.

Meanwhile, Alcibiades's secret message reached the Athenian leaders in Samos. They knew that he had full authority over Tissaphernes, and thus in Persia. Thus, given their personal leanings, "the captains and chief men in the armament at once embraced the idea of subverting the democracy." Some of them went to Alcibiades to discuss the matter. Alcibiades held before them the attractive possibility of securing the friendship of both Tissaphernes and the king, if the democracy were overthrown; and these men readily agreed. Once again, Thucydides shows the reader a range of motives that meshed well: "The most powerful citizens . . . now had great hopes of getting the government into their own hands and of triumphing over the enemy."[17] Their hopes strengthened, they returned to Samos. They formed a conspiracy, but they did not keep their plans secret. They told everyone that the king would offer friendship and money if Alcibiades were recalled and the democracy overthrown! The majority of the troops were hostile to the idea, but the offers were good. They did not resist. The small band had their hands free and the plot almost succeeded; they still had to consider the next steps and the way to start. They were not, after all, in Athens, but in Samos; and they had no authority to change the established regime back home.

---

16. See McGregor, in *Phoenix* (1965): 27.

17. 8.48.1 The passage omitted here said "the most powerful citizens, who also suffered most severely from the war." The wealthy citizens paid for the war, and they thought that, for paying more than others, they should have greater political power.

This led to arguments among them, and one of the generals, Phrynichus, suddenly declared himself opposed.

Phrynichus was a stubborn man. He had previously stood alone against his colleagues regarding a naval battle; he "flatly refused either to stay himself or to let them or anyone else do so if he could help it" (8.27.1). He won. And Thucydides says that, on that occasion and the following one, it appeared he did not lack real intelligence.

His reaction was the same to Alcibiades's proposals: one against all, he refused. He did so firmly and clearly, based on arguments that Thucydides relates point by point.

Thucydides says of Alcibiades that Phrynichus rightly "thought he cared no more for an oligarchy than for a democracy, and only sought to change the institutions in his country in order to get himself recalled by his associates; while for themselves their one purpose should be to avoid civil discord" (8.48.4).

The desire to avoid civil strife was and would remain the truest sign of civic-mindedness throughout this period. It was Phrynichus, ultimately, who saved Athens. It is interesting to note that the opposition to Alcibiades's plan came not from someone motivated by democratic zeal, but by someone with a longer view. If Phrynichus had stopped there, we would rightly give him credit . . .

He was equally skeptical about Alcibiades's promises. He knew that the king had no interest in allying himself with the Athenians, whom he mistrusted, whereas the Peloponnesians had always treated him well.

Last, there was talk about offering oligarchy to the allies. And he doubted that as well: "As the allies would never prefer servitude with an oligarchy or democracy to freedom with the constitution that they currently lived under, to whichever type it belonged" (8.48.6). He even analyzed the reasons the allies had for not favoring the Athenian oligarchs.

Such blunt analysis had, among other benefits, that of leaving no doubt: for Alcibiades, but also for the allies, it shows that a concern for internal politics is always secondary to the quests for power and for freedom. Everything else is pretext. Even in our own time, when ideology seems to determine everything and sometimes takes precedence over patriotic feelings, would anyone presume to say that Phrynichus's analysis is not just as valid? Is it possible to say that when a people choose democracy they do so out of an attachment to the regime, or from a desire to restore their independence? And can anyone say that any particular movement, toward communism for example, arises from an ideological choice or from practical interests—such as Alcibiades's sudden zeal for oligarchy?

Phrynichus, in any case, made a strong argument. It was not enough. The members of the group did not change their minds; they wanted to send a small delegation to Athens to prepare the city for these new decisions.

Phrynichus, beaten, told himself that Alcibiades would be recalled and would be informed of the position he had taken. He grew frightened. And the result was a series of steps and countersteps, plots and counterplots, that surpass belief.

The events, as reported by Thucydides, happened in the following way.

Phrynichus, seeing himself in danger, sent a secret message to the Lacedaemonian leader, revealing to him that Alcibiades was working now against Sparta and offering Athens friendship with Tissaphernes.

That is a betrayal if ever there was one. For he made these revelations to the military leader of the country against which he was at war. In his letter he justifies himself by explaining—Alcibiades could not have said it better!—that he was at war with Alcibiades, and that it was legitimate to destroy him, even at his country's expense. So even for him, a private quarrel gave legitimacy to a public betrayal. Athenian democracy really was, as we can see, in crisis.

What did the Lacedaemonian leader do on reading this missive? He went straight to Alcibiades and Tissaphernes, at Magnesia, near Ephesus, and told them everything, putting himself on their side.

Why? For the basest of reasons: remember that Tissaphernes had been careful to give money to different Peloponnesian leaders in order to gain their support for the cuts in pay.[18] This was one of those leaders, and some thought that he had been bought by Tissaphernes. Thucydides doesn't say so; but he reports that rumor, saying that the man had acted "out of personal profit, according to what was said."[19] Phrynichus the traitor was betrayed in turn, and for money!

18. 8.45.3; see above.
19. 50.3; cf. Delebecque, *Thucydide et Alcibiade*, 87–88, 110, as well as his review of the book by H. D. Westlake in *Revue des études anciennes* (1969): 475. Some scholars have found his charges to be without grounds.

He knew it, of course. At this point, something surprising occurs: appalled at the situation in which he found himself, Phrynichus wrote a new secret letter . . . to the same person! Curious obstinacy in a man who knew he had been betrayed. True, this time he offered much more and could hope that his offer equaled any other: he offered the Spartans the possibility of annihilating the whole Athenian army in Samos; and he showed how to do it. He knew that this was an even greater betrayal, but he thought he had to do anything he could: "Pleading that being in danger of his life on their account, he could not now be blamed for doing this or anything else to escape being destroyed by his mortal enemies" (8.50.5). It had come to a matter of life and death. However, no one—fortunately—would ever say such circumstances excused everything . . .

The most curious part of this is that, in writing the letter, he mistrusted, and with good reason, the one to whom he wrote. Also, in a reversal, he himself hastened to announce the danger of a Spartan landing in Samos and to argue for the construction of fortifications.

The letter Phrynichus feared as a result of these interactions arrived from Alcibiades: the Spartan leader had told him everything; and, addressing the Athenians of Samos, Alcibiades accused Phrynichus of treason.

Amazing: the one time Alcibiades told the truth, no one believed him! The Athenians thought that, in his usual way, he was not reliable (or *pistos),* and that he made up this story to destroy Phrynichus. If there was a plan for the enemy fleet disembarking at Samos, it would be normal for Alcibiades to know it . . . from the Peloponnesians themselves. So his letter only confirmed the rumors Phrynichus was repeating![20] We have to admire this eminently moral lesson: for having lied, Alcibiades was not believed, just as, after crying wolf, people stop listening. Added to this is the great irony of the game of lies and truth, for these plots cancelled each other out, thus maintaining the status quo.

Phrynichus was not so lucky with the Athenians: the messenger sent from Samos to Athens by the conspirators brought charges against him. He was stripped of his command. He had no choice: he had to join the side of the oligarchy, which, given how the situation had evolved, had now moved away from Alcibiades. Phrynichus would later be assassinated under the oligarchy.

---

20. Some scholars have noted that Phyrnichus had acted against Alcibiades during the scandals, and that fact may have led the Athenians to be suspicious.

The oligarchy did come. But before we follow the course of events in Athens, we must return to Thucydides's account of certain aspects of the extraordinary imbroglio pitting Phrynichus's betrayals against moves taken by Alcibiades. This account is both somewhat suspect and highly revealing.

Thucydides says that Phrynichus was an intelligent man. His first move toward the Lacedaemonians was imprudent, but the second was an unbelievable folly. Why would someone who knew he had been betrayed put his trust again in the person he knew had betrayed him, when his life was at stake?

Many modern historians have found that they could not believe the story as it is told here.

One extreme response is to adopt the view of the Athenians at Samos: Alcibiades is not trustworthy; he lies, and he made up the whole business to destroy Phrynichus. After all, this is a man perfectly capable of making up such a case, and Thucydides may have been, on this point, misled by his sources.[21] What proof was there? Still, it is hard to believe that this story involving major individuals (Alcibiades, Phrynichus, the Lacedaemonian leader), and that must have aroused debate, rests on nothing. The letters must have existed.

There is, though, another way to understand the text; a number of scholars have adopted it.[22] This view accepts the sequence of events, but believes that a man as shrewd as Phrynichus, having seen the result of his first betrayal, took the second step as a way of laying a trap. This was a fake deception: he knew that Alcibiades would use this letter against him and that, by taking all the necessary measures for the defense of Samos, he would render Alcibiades's charges useless. He subtly laid the groundwork for the Athenian defiance, as in fact occurred. Phrynichus, in this view, was no idiot but instead a master of deception.

That is one possible hypothesis. It does not fit perfectly with Thucydides's account, an inconsistency one might easily pass over if there were not a means of reconciling the two.

Phrynichus definitely sent a second letter to the Spartan. He may have hoped that by offering much more, he would attract more attention.[23] But

21. See Hatzfeld, 232–33.
22. Grote, Brunt, Westlake, and also E. Delebecque (*Thucydide et Alcibiade*, 87–88).
23. See Ellis, *Alcibiades*, 76.

he did not ignore the risk, and must have realized the extent of it after
the fact. Then, very quickly, he guarded against this risk by adopting the
only attitude that would defend him against Alcibiades's charges when
they came.[24] This explanation accords both with Thucydides's account
and with Phrynichus's reputation as an intelligent man.

We see how difficult this interpretation is, both unproven and controversial. How could it be otherwise, when everyone was lying, betraying,
and sacrificing all to private quarrels? How could anything be known for
sure, between versions that were perhaps bold fallacies? Alcibiades may
have invented the story about the letters. Phrynichus may have invented
a fake betrayal, in order to lay a trap (?). What detective story of our era
would contrive such a plot? We can see a time coming when it is impossible to believe anything. Even in the slightly crazy hypothesis about Phrynichus's letters, we cannot know either their authenticity or their sincerity.
Ultimately, these personal plots not only damage one's personal enemies:
they first destroy knowledge of the truth.

The most interesting aspect of this episode is its usefulness as a revealing signifier. It may, quite directly, have had the effect of raising Tissaphernes's doubts about his seductive adviser, apparently now flirting with the
Athenians.[25] However, beyond this direct influence on events, in a more
general way the episode helps us assess, despite the obscurity of methods,
the striking development of all these intrigues and betrayals.

We first saw Alcibiades as an isolated example of a citizen who put his
own interests above those of the state, because he indulged in the internal
quarrels between political leaders. That behavior seemed quite serious.
But now, in 411, we find that it was not an isolated incident. Alcibiades
does not get all the credit for the decline of civic-mindedness and he was
not the only one to manifest it: the same was true of his rivals, and of others on the opposing side. The evil spread; it was the sign of a new period
in the democracy. We should not fool ourselves; Thucydides, in judging
all the events described above, uses the plural. He did not say that such
personal ambition appeared in one of Pericles's successors, or in some of

24. This is largely what K. Dover says in the historical commentary on book 8, which includes references to other critical works.

25. In this, at least, Phrynichus may have achieved his aim, as Westlake says in the *Journal of Hellenic Studies* (1956): 99–104.

his successors; the phrase he used was more general: "With his successors it was different. More on a level with one another, and each grasping at supremacy, they ended by committing even the conduct of state affairs to the whims of the multitude." And later: "Nor did they finally succumb till they fell victims of their own internal disorders." These words are not about an individual; they apply to the spirit of the time.[26]

Why? Thucydides suggests the lack of an undisputed leader. But there are other reasons we might add.

First, perhaps, there was a contagion. It is obvious that, in this impassioned conflict, the anger of one man led the next one, out of fear, to take extreme measures, without a thought for the common good. Alcibiades's treachery arose when his enemies condemned him to death. Phrynichos betrayed because Alcibiades might have condemned him to die. The tactics became increasingly devious because everyone was caught up in a pitiless struggle. In a different sphere, it is the same: if one side resorts to financial irregularities, the other side tends to do the same. It is never by accident when scandals and suspicious deaths suddenly multiply on all sides. It is not a good sign; and the Athenian example is there to remind us.

It may also be—and Thucydides implies as much—that when a people are accustomed to being all-powerful, selfish ambitions arise. To please them, promises are made, and as soon as interest wanes, the normal reaction is to want to "change the constitution"—not for the good of the state, but for the good of those individuals or groups who are worried about maintaining their positions. Alcibiades called for an oligarchic revolution; it was the democrats who brought him back. And Phrynichus, who opposed him, became an active member of the oligarchy. What could be worse for a country than these abrupt shifts, especially when they occur in the middle of a war?

In fact, these personal conflicts and battles between political sides led, in the terrible year 411, to a revolution and almost civil war—all just when Athens was threatened from all sides. Who caused these conflicts, which were up to now latent and under control, to break out into the open? It wasn't the war and the disaster it caused. It was Alcibiades, driven by his demand for a regime change.

26. 2.65.10, 12; see above, chapter 3.

As so often in this story, this demand did not achieve what he wanted; but it did propel Athens into events for which, in the end, he bore responsibility.

And once more that devilish man, having sown the seeds of drama, emerged on top. His return to Athens loomed on the horizon.

8

With the Athenians on Samos

It is a curious paradox: Alcibiades had forced the adoption of oligarchy, ending nearly a century of democracy, and once under way, the plot grew and took shape. In the end, like a spark that is transmitted along the length of a wire before igniting a remote explosion, the oligarchy was firmly established without Alcibiades and in opposition to him. This was at no cost to him, however. Athens, under the oligarchy, opposed him, but the Athenians on Samos, who remained faithful to the democracy, trusted him.

This complete reversal of the situation cries out for explanation.

As we have noted,[1] the oligarchs of Samos had sent, against the advice of Phrynichus, a delegation to Athens to lay the groundwork for regime change and to recall Alcibiades. The leader of the delegation was one Pisander. Typical of the political mores of the time, Pisander had previously been a democrat; and he had been one of those investigating the

---

1. See above, chapter 7.

affair of the herms, facts that should have made him an unlikely advocate
of oligarchy or of Alcibiades! Nevertheless, an advocate he was, and an
eloquent one. Despite the various public hostilities that were breaking out
in Athens (coming sometimes from democrats, sometimes from religious
groups, and sometimes from people who simply did not trust Alcibiades),
Pisander went to the people and addressed each one of the main opponents individually:

> "In the face of the fact that the Peloponnesians had as many ships as their
> own confronting them at sea, more cities in alliance with them, and the King
> and Tissaphernes to supply them with money, of which the Athenians had
> none left, had he any hope of saving the state unless someone could induce
> the King to come over to their side?" Upon their replying that they had not,
> he then plainly said to them: "This we cannot have unless we have a more
> moderate form of government,[2] and put the offices into fewer hands, and so
> gain the King's confidence, and forthwith restore Alcibiades who is the only
> man living who can bring this about. The safety of the state, not the form of
> its government, is for the moment the most pressing question as we can al-
> ways change afterwards whatever we do not like."

There are two important points here.

The first, obviously, is the role as a man of destiny Alcibiades has managed to assume. This is because he is thought to direct Tissaphernes in all
things (he is, in fact, the king's favorite), the one holding the purse strings,
and the only one capable of assuring victory to one side or the other; he
was thus able to set a high price for his collaboration. The exile of yesterday has become Athens' only hope. He played his hand well.

The other point concerns the way Pisander glides smoothly along the
path to oligarchy. The word is never spoken. He refers to a "more moderate" politics, which is always the tone taken by a reactionary party; and
he speaks of putting responsibility in fewer hands, which was the agenda
of this particular group of Athenians. Such a program could cover a whole
range of outcomes.

Twice Athens would experience brief oligarchies. The one established
in 411, following the events we have just seen, was a true oligarchy. It

---

2. Meaning, of course, closer to oligarchy. The full quotation is from 8.53.2–3.

has been called the government of the Four Hundred because the democratic council, formed of five hundred individuals chosen at random, was, among other measures, replaced by a council of four hundred selected by vote of cooptation by the membership, starting with five of the presidents.[3]

The second oligarchy, established after the defeat of Athens and under enemy occupation, is called the regime of the Thirty, or the Thirty Tyrants, because power was placed in the hands of thirty individuals. In both cases, the regimes were harsh, allowing for arbitrary arrests and executions, with no legal recourse.

In both cases, however, an internal opposition appeared, in the name of "moderate democracy."

The supporters of this opposition called for an assembly. They acknowledged that this would be weaker than in the past, but would offer freedom of expression and discussion. They were successful for a time in 411, and Thucydides approved of the government of that time, as representing balance. The "more moderate" politics that Pisander had argued for could include either of these two regimes. And it is what allowed Pisander to convince the Athenians. Moreover, he left the door open, suggesting that the change could be provisional.

This is how reactionary governments are established: following a defeat in war, disguised as moderation, in the name of moral recovery. We have seen examples in the not too distant past.

Athens was thus persuaded to support this agenda of public safety. And it sent Pisander with ten other delegates to negotiate, in Asia Minor, with "Tissaphernes and Alcibiades."

Such deceit! Negotiations went badly. And Alcibiades was the first one responsible for the bad outcome.

Powerful he was: he spoke in the name of Tissaphernes. But his demands were catastrophic. During three successive meetings, he wanted for the king all of Ionia, then the neighboring islands, and then the right to build a fleet that would be free to act on the king's behalf on the entire coast of Asia Minor! These were demands that for decades Athenian

---

3. In addition, the serving magistrates were dismissed and their pay suppressed. These decisions were taken by an extraordinary assembly that met, not on the Pnyx, but at Colonus, outside the city (8.67.2–3).

traditions had refused as unacceptable and offensive.[4] Naturally, the Athenians refused and departed, convinced that Alcibiades had duped them.

Another bizarre story. What explains Alcibiades's attitude? True, he was simply the mouthpiece of Tissaphernes and had no choice about the conditions that were set. But he agreed to them, and Thucydides finds that he was partly responsible. The explanation is frankly complicated and not very convincing. Alcibiades would have realized that Tissaphernes, faithful to the policy of disruption that he himself had first espoused, would not accept the alliance with Athens; moreover, he wanted the refusal to come from Athens, in order to avoid looking bad: "While Alcibiades, who now saw that Tissaphernes was determined not to treat on any terms, wished the Athenians to think, not that he was unable to persuade Tissaphernes, but that after the latter had been persuaded and was willing to join them, they had not conceded enough to him" (8.56.3). That explanation might have been convincing if Alcibiades had actually maintained his credibility, if he had left the doors open and accommodation of perspectives possible. The account does not suggest any such thing.

So? Are we to think that in this business Alcibiades was a passive instrument in the hands of a Tissaphernes who was more stubborn than he had thought?

Perhaps we need not assume as much: after all, nothing had made Alcibiades put himself forward in that role. In fact, considering everything that followed the events, another explanation comes to mind—purely hypothetical, it is true, but that conforms with the thinking of the man and is able to fit nicely with Thucydides's explanation. Yes, Alcibiades had wanted the break to come from the Athenians (and had hoped it would come sooner); but he may also have been looking further, and, after launching the effort for oligarchy, wondered if it was not better to wait and see how things turned out. He was certainly aware that Pisander was an unreliable ally, and that he had had serious difficulties in Athens. He must have known as well that Samos, at the time zealous for the oligarchy, also included people on the other side. Using these problems as an opportunity to take a step back, it is possible he did not do everything he could to satisfy the Athenian delegates.

4. This is found in the discussions over the "peace of Callias" that was meant to protect the Greeks from the barbarians.

Actually, this man who was so adept at persuasion also knew something even more problematic, namely, how to use his ability to annoy others. Few politicians today can do it. But there have been a few, and famous ones.

In any case, whether the fault of Tissaphernes or his own, everything failed. And the results seemed as bad as they could possibly be for Alcibiades. Tissaphernes once again sided with the Peloponnesians; he concluded a new treaty with them, promising subsidies and ships. Moreover, Samos, welcoming Pisander, embraced the oligarchy and pushed Alcibiades aside. Pisander's delegation, returning to Athens, overthrew the democracy in the cities it passed, even before achieving the same result in Athens, where his friends were already working hard. They had even resorted to violence: Androcles, Alcibiades's old foe, was assassinated by the conspirators for being an enemy of Alcibiades; the conspirators did not yet know that Alcibiades would not be recalled! The oligarchy was established without him.

What hope was there for this new government except to make a treaty with Sparta?

"They also sent to Agis, the Spartan king at Decelea, to say that they desired to make peace, and that he might reasonably be more disposed to treat now that he had them to deal with instead of the inconstant People."[5] Agis, seeing the city subject to such chaos, declined to make a treaty. The Athenians insisted: their only hope was to stop the war. Without Alcibiades, they were forced to accept defeat, and end it.

That might have happened, but it did not: another reversal was at work. And Alcibiades, once again, was front and center.

The reversal began with Samos.

Samos had first embarked on oligarchy. There were attacks. Hyperbolus, the democrat whom Alcibiades had struck with ostracism, was assassinated. Androcles in Athens, Hyperbolus in Samos: Alcibiades's enemies fell, as though at random. But this disorder brought consequences. The generals, who were inclined to oppose oligarchy, were warned, as were those men known to be most opposed to the movement. These individuals in turn worked with the soldiers. On the appointed day, when the partisans of the oligarchy were going to attack on a larger scale, they

5. 8.70.2.

ran into an organized resistance and were beaten. The two sides made peace—under the democracy.

These supporters of democracy, while triumphant, were unaware of the situation in Athens. They wanted to inform the city of their victory and send delegates aboard the Paralus, an elite state ship that had contributed to their success. That was a mistake: some were arrested or killed. Their leader was able to escape and returned to Samos immediately. There, he brought news from Athens, "exaggerating everything," according to Thucydides. He painted a terrible picture of the tyranny reigning there; the outrage was so great that fighting was about to break out.

But order returned. Henceforth there were two Athens: the government in Athens, oligarchic, and that in Samos, democratic. It was settled: everyone in the army, whether oligarchic or democratic, swore "to accept a democratic government, to be united, to prosecute actively the war against the Peloponnesians, and to be enemies of the Four Hundred and to hold no communication with them."[6]

Henceforth Samos, or rather the Athenians on Samos, considered themselves independent. The true Athens was at Samos. And in order to say that the city of Athens was no longer with them, the Athenians on Samos said that she was "detached," using the word that was normal for designating allies who defected.[7]

We have known, in recent history, such schisms. France had a government in Vichy, and one in London. But differences spring to mind. Neither of the two Athens was occupied by an enemy or had fled abroad. The break was entirely among Athenians and Athenians alone. Moreover, it was much deeper than we can imagine, a time when everything that happened was due to distance and the time needed for communication. Today, events would have taken a very different course with the telephone, radio, television. There can be very few examples of a rupture affecting such a small city and installing two enemy factions so far apart.

The rupture was conceived by Alcibiades. It would change the course of his life.

Among the Athenian leaders on Samos committed to pursuing the war, some clearly wished to recall Alcibiades—among them, Thrasybulus, one

6. 8.75.2. Today we would say they broke off diplomatic relations.
7. 8.76.3. *Aphestēken.*

of the principal authors of the effort to support the democracy. At the time, he was trierarch. This powerful man would later be credited with the triumph of democracy after the second oligarchy, at the end of the war, and would then preside over the reunification of Athens.

Ultimately, he won the support of the army; when they came together in the assembly, all voted to recall Alcibiades and guaranteed his safety. Thrasybulus went to Tissaphernes to bring him back. Thrasybulus was, as Thucydides explains, "convinced that their only chance of salvation lay in [Alcibiades's] bringing over Tissaphernes from the Peloponnesians to themselves" (8.81.1).

Here is Alcibiades, brokering the deal, and finally returning, if not to Athens itself, at least to one of the two Athens, the democratic Athens on Samos. What he had proposed to the oligarchs, he accomplished with the democrats. This latest reversal deserves admiration. First, there had been the agreement tying the oligarchy to Alcibiades; after the break, there was the oligarchy without Alcibiades and on Samos, the democracy; there was oligarchy without Alcibiades at Athens, democracy with Alcibiades on Samos. One need not be a political genius to realize that the democracy with Alcibiades would be the stronger of the two, and that the government of the Four Hundred would soon be overturned.

And meanwhile, Alcibiades returns to Athenian politics with strength and confidence.

First, his initial communications: to appeal to the people, he evoked his exile; and then, of course, he made promises. Thucydides emphasizes all his promises:

> Alcibiades accordingly held out to the army such extravagant promises as the following: that Tissaphernes had solemnly assured him that if he could only trust the Athenians they should never want for supplies while he had anything left, no, not even if he should have to coin his own silver couch,[8] and that he would bring the Phoenician fleet now at Aspendus to the Athenians instead of to the Peloponnesians; but that he could only trust the Athenians if Alcibiades were recalled to be his security for them.[9]

---

8. In Xenophon, Cyrus the Younger uses an analogous expression (*Hellenica* 1.5.3: "He would demolish the very throne on which he sat, made of silver and gold"). As we would say, "He would give him the shirt off his back." His text uses the oriental expressions.

9. 8.81.3. Aspendus is in Pamphylia, in southern Asia Minor.

Given all this, is it surprising that the army made him general and put him in charge of their duties? They were happy and hopeful; they would be victorious. Alcibiades would take care of everything!

Thucydides rightly calls this boasting, as we have seen nothing in Tissaphernes's inclinations that backs up these exaggerated statements, these oaths, this conviction. But for Alcibiades, the time for persuasion was now or never. And the Athenians, beset with problems, slipped easily back into what was always their natural characteristic. The Corinthians noted it in book 1 of Thucydides, specifically optimism: this meant having "high hopes" or "cheerful hopes"—in Greek, *euelpides*, the name Aristophanes gave one of the characters in his comedy the *Birds*. "They are," according to the Corinthians, "adventurous beyond their power, and daring beyond their judgment, and in danger they are sanguine."[10] They were convinced that they would succeed easily in everything, with Tissaphernes's help.

Seen in this way, their enthusiasm was once again evidence of Alcibiades's charm, of his ability to persuade, and of the amazing *aura* surrounding this person who was otherwise so disturbing.

Alcibiades was not one of those demagogues who will say anything to please people. His first move was the mark of perceptive conviction.

In their newfound confidence, forgetting the dangers of warfare, the soldiers on Samos were ready to head for Piraeus and defeat the oligarchy. Despite their resolve, Alcibiades strongly opposed this. They had put him in charge of the war: he was going to take care of the war, and go straight to Tissaphernes. And so he did. Once again, his side avoided civil war as well as certain defeat in the war against Sparta.

That was not all. When, later, the delegates of the Four Hundred (always late!) arrived on Samos, appearing calm and peaceful, the soldiers of Samos grew enraged, seized once again with the desire to head for Athens, abandoning Ionia to the enemy. Once again, Alcibiades intervened, and with the same effect. Thucydides emphasizes that he did the state a great service:

> At that moment, when no other man would have been able to hold back the multitude, he put a stop to the intended expedition, and rebuked and turned aside the resentment felt, on personal grounds, against the envoys; he dismissed them with an answer from himself, to the effect that he did not object

10. 1.70.3.

to the government of the Five Thousand,[11] but insisted that the Four Hundred should be deposed and the Council of the Five Hundred reinstated in power. (8.86.5–6)

He ended the pursuit of hostilities and brought the two sides to an agreement.

By his actions, Alcibiades avoided disaster. He also brought nearer the outcome that would soon triumph over the Four Hundred: that is, a moderate democracy and balance of the two extremes. Above all, he was finally speaking as a leader.

One may find this sort of doublet in the history surprising, and surprising also to see Thucydides so much more emphatic on the second occasion than on the first. It should not concern us. The first case involved vague efforts; on the second occasion, the delegates of the Four Hundred were there, anger was at fever pitch. The crisis was much more serious. It was also the occasion of clear leadership and of a more specific policy. This is why Thucydides insists, in a phrase whose very words have been contested, writing: "Now it was that Alcibiades for the first time [or "the first one, at this moment"][12] did the state a great service, and one of the most outstanding kind."

According to the text one chooses, the emphasis of the judgment is different: if Thucydides is believed to have written that Alcibiades served the city of Athens "for the first time," the criticism of Alcibiades is strong; if, on the other hand, he wrote that at that time Alcibiades was "the first" to render service, the praise is unreserved. Whichever reading is chosen, Thucydides is emphatic about the role Alcibiades played on this occasion.

It is actually moving to see the return of a responsible leader, one adopting the tone of Pericles. Thucydides praised Pericles for knowing how to rein in a mob: "Whenever he saw them unseasonably and insolently elated, he would with a word reduce them to alarm." In short, he was reasonable when they were irrational. For once Alcibiades imitated Pericles's example.

---

11. These Five Thousand are the Assembly that the oligarchs had promised to install—an assembly smaller than in the past and based on census classes.

12. 8.86.4. Instead of *prōton* ("for the first time"), most manuscripts have *prōtos* ("the first"). Most recently, we have agreed with the reading *prōton*, with Classen, and against Schwartz, Hude, Delebecque. The distinction is not important for the issue here.

His attitude bore fruit.

It was particularly effective in Athens itself, where some resistance was growing, encouraged by "the power of Alcibiades at Samos, and their own conviction that the oligarchy was unstable" (8.89.4). Theramenes, the leader of the moderates, triumphed. There were riots, fears about an enemy action; a battle took place very near Euboea, and led to the loss of that island for Athens. However, despite some panic, the moderates were successful. The leaders of the oligarchy withdrew to Decelea. A moderate democracy was established. And without delay, there was a vote to recall Alcibiades!

The gamble had paid off—on the condition that the war also was won. Here it is worthwhile to consider how our hero managed to convey the sense that he brought a dowry in the form of an alliance with Tissaphernes.

There was much talk throughout this whole period about the famous fleet that Tissaphernes was building in Phoenicia and that would change the war between Sparta and Athens. In Thucydides's work, it was an issue from the moment Alcibiades went to live with the satrap: Alcibiades advised him against giving supremacy to Sparta by sending "the Phoenician fleet which he was equipping" (8.46.1). It is a simple reference, but it is apparent that the arrival of these ships must have been hoped for, promised, discussed, expected for a long time. It depended on Tissaphernes but also on the king, as Phoenicia did not belong to the satrapy of Tissaphernes.

When Alcibiades went to the Athenians on Samos, this fleet had still not arrived; but it seemed ready and to be already en route; without hesitation, Alcibiades promised that it would come to help, not the Peloponnesians, but the Athenians: "that he would bring the Phoenician fleet now at Aspendus to the Athenians" (8.81.3).

On this subject, however, Tissaphernes wanted to maintain equal balance, knowing that the Spartans were upset: he "prepared to go to the Phoenician fleet at Aspendus, and invited Lichas [the Spartan] to go with him" (8.87.1).

Will he give the fleet to Sparta? Does he want to? That would be bad for Alcibiades; but Thucydides acknowledges that this is not certain: "It is not easy to ascertain with what intention he went to Aspendus and did not bring the fleet after all." He says that there were exactly

147 ships.[13] They would have changed everything. But they never arrived. Did Tissaphernes wish to use the two camps without helping either? Was he just pretending, in order to please Sparta? Was money an issue? Thucydides leans toward the former and suggests that the satrap's long absence was bound to prolong the status quo and cause delay. It may also be that developing problems within the Persian Empire had been one more reason not to send the fleet.[14] In any case, the ships that were so long expected never appeared.

Tissaphernes made excuses: he did not bring the fleet because it wasn't as big as was expected . . . just words, nothing else.

Alcibiades knew how important all this was for him: he never hesitated! Learning that Tissaphernes was going to Aspendus, he set sail there as well, with thirteen ships. At this time, at the moment of departure, he makes the second promise to the Athenians on Samos: he says he will "do a great and certain service . . . as he would either bring the Phoenician fleet to the Athenians, or at all events prevent its joining the Peloponnesians" (8.88.1).

Well done, Alcibiades! His first promise had been to procure the Phoenecian fleet for Athens. But he must have known, or guessed, that it would not be easy and that he risked a confrontation with Tissaphernes, who had made up his mind. So? He would turn to his advantage what was, in fact, his failure: he would take credit for having prevented the fleet from joining the Spartan side. This would be an easier result to obtain. It might even help him with the Spartans: since Alcibades had followed Tissaphernes, Sparta would be inclined to think that Tissaphernes had listened to him, and was dealing with Athens. As Thucydides explains it, Alcibiades wanted to "compromise [Tissaphernes] as much as possible in the eyes of the Peloponnesians through his apparent friendship with himself and the Athenians, and thus in a manner to oblige him to join their side" (8.88.1). In all of this there was a great deal of plotting and calculation and pressure about a fleet that played a leading role by its absence! The consequences were not minor. Sparta began to doubt the ships would ever arrive and began dealing with the other satrap, Pharnabazus. The absence of the fleet was to Alcibiades's credit.

In fact, it is uncertain whether he ever went to Aspendus. Thucydides has him going to the southern part of Asia Minor, to Phaselis and to

13. Isocrates says 90, Plutarch says 150, and Diodorus says 300. These may reflect the difference between the number expected and the actual number; Thucydides's number is, in any case, the most precise.

14. Hatzfeld, 252–53.

Caunus, and later returning "from Phaselis and Caunus."[15] He may have done no more than shown himself, and watched from a distance. But it was enough. He returned to Samos, having prevented the ships from going to the Peloponnesians and obtaining this result: "He had made Tissaphernes more friendly to the Athenians than before" (8.108.1).

Pure legend? Or the most adroit intervention anyone could have expected? The art of personal propaganda began right here, with a dazzling success that has defied criticism ever since.

What we might call "the meeting at Aspendus" remains the greatest example of the art of making the most of the most difficult situations.

Alcibiades, however, was not satisfied with this savvy diplomatic move. While the other Athenian leaders on Samos had started fighting in the environs of Chios, here is Alcibiades, barely returned to Samos, departing with some twenty ships: he is going to Halicarnassus to demand money and then to fortify the island of Cos opposite it. The money was needed to meet the costs of the war. As for Cos, it needed to hold up against Caria. Once this business was taken care of, he too departed for northern Asia Minor, where the Peloponnesian fleet had preceded him and the Athenians of Samos. Soon Tissaphernes himself would return, first to his own territory and then to the Hellespont: the battle was moved to the straits.

The result was that the reinforcements Alcibiades brought contributed to a sizable victory. He served his recovered homeland well.

Is that the correct word? Recovered? The vote to recall Alcibiades had occurred while he was busy at Aspendus. He could go back. This is the summer of 411. Was he going to go back?

The dates surprise us. He did not return to Athens for four years, in the summer of 407.

Why the gap? Why the delay? Out of caution, apparently.

The situation was not yet stable anywhere.

It was not stable in Athens.[16] The city had just experienced the trauma of revolution. It was living under a mixed regime, brand new,

---

15. 8.88, 108.1.

16. His recall is surrounded by vagueness. Critias, the future member of the oligarchy of the Thirty, boasted of having proposed the decree (Plutarch 33.2). But the decision is attributed to the initiative of Theramenes (Diodorus 13.38), and many modern scholars have the effective date of the decree later, in 408.

and was soon to revert to democracy and a rebirth of the influence of demagogues—such as Cleophon, who represented radical democracy, the side of the old enemies of Alcibiades, Hyperbolus and Androcles. Alcibiades was still mistrusted by some democrats for having earlier offered to return to Athens only if there were oligarchy. In order to fight this faction, Alcibiades's friends would have to do some groundwork. Alcibiades, who was in command of a part of the Athenian army, could only return as an elected general, his position recognized. They were far from achieving that. He had gained enough experience and wisdom to know that perfectly well.

In addition, the war itself was far from settled. Alcibiades had helped; he had boasted of his importance. But he had not yet provided a single decisive victory. His relations with Tissaphernes were complex and not secure. Militarily, the war was not lost, but it was stalled. He was still largely responsible for the disaster in Sicily, as well as for the occupation of Decelea in Attica, and for the Peloponnesian successes in an Ionia where serious defections had occurred. It would require more than the absence of the Phoenician fleet for him to return as a savior.

In four years, four long years, he had to accomplish this transformation. But after all he had achieved, how could he fail?

The long-term goal was Athens. But it could only be achieved after much work from afar.

Before taking up that work, we should spend a moment on the story as portrayed in the theater. We have already referred to the treatment of the Sicilian expedition in Euripides's tragedies. At the very time Athens was watching these events unfold, Euripides presented *Phoenician Women*, a tragedy portraying the fratricidal struggles between the sons of Oedipus, Eteocles and Polynices. In it, Polynices was shown to be more sympathetic than he typically was, and he expressed the hardships of exile. There he was, an exile who waged war against his country in order to enable his return. Right away, this Polynices made people think of Alcibiades. It is even one of the reasons cited for mounting the play just after 411.

In fact, critics used anything and everything to make a connection between Polynices and Alcibiades! The mares on Polynices's shield; Alcibiades's stable of racehorses! And so on. I raised serious questions about these interpretations thirty years ago.[17] Possibly, in this or that detail, one can find a more or less deliberate connection; but that is not the meaning of the play. The meaning of the play is the clash of ambitions, and how these imperil the city. It is Polynices's desire for power that leads him to attack his country and leads Etiocles to declare that he is ready to sacrifice everything for that sovereignty. And in order to highlight the seriousness of such attitudes, Euripides contrasts both with the young Menoeceus, ready to die for his homeland.

Indeed, this had a ring of truth! And the recent events described here suffice to justify the necessity and urgency expressed by the speaker in Euripides's play. He agrees with Thucydides's verdict, explaining Athens' problems of personal ambition. Even better: Thucydides points above all to the role of personal ambitions in the years of crisis that Athens had just experienced. About the troubles of 411, he writes: "Most of them were driven by private ambitions" (8.89.3). If indeed Euripides's tragedy was about Alcibiades, it was not in the small external details comparing him with Polynices; rather it was in the degree to which he too had put the interests of the state after his own, like Oedipus's two sons.

Moreover, the verdict in the play is not only like that of Thucydides, but also like that of Plato in the *Gorgias*, where he describes another man of ambition, as direct and firm as Eteocles, Callicles. Callicles believes firmly that might makes right. He is obviously not Alcibiades, although men like Alcibiades help us picture him.[18] He is, however, the symbol of that crisis that Alcibiades helped spark, and of all the comparable crises that have ignited in history whenever a democracy went through moments of upheaval. Our own is no exception. The tragedy of *Phoenician Women*, born in such circumstances, is a plea for civic-mindedness, something we all need to exhibit.

Against the competition between ambitious men, it calls for reconciliation and agreement. Those are words for the order of the moderate democracy that followed the regime of the Four Hundred. But was there a complete return to peace? Alcibiades must have doubted it because when his goal—return to Athens—was finally within reach, he did not return, but, having grown prudent, waited.

17. "Les *Phéniciennes* d'Euripide ou l'actualité dans la tragédie grecque," a speech given at the Fourth International Congress of Classical Studies (Philadelphia, 1964) and published in *Revue de Philologie* (1965): 28–47.
18. See below, chapter 12.

Second Interlude

Alcibiades between Two Historians

The most recent events described here correspond to the final pages of Thucydides's work. That work was supposed to have continued to the end of the war, a fact to which Thucydides himself frequently alludes. However, the work ends abruptly in the fall of 411.

After that, Xenophon picks up the narrative. Although it is clear that Xenophon wished to continue the unfinished work, his account is quite different. He includes only that which directly concerns the war, without going into motives and calculation, without any effort to draw out or suggest political lessons. As a result, there is a disjunction, even in more modern accounts relating to this period.

The change in tone draws our attention to an important point: when Thucydides and Xenophon talk about Alcibiades, they are speaking about someone who was a contemporary, who came from the same milieu, both political and intellectual, someone with whom they were certainly acquainted.

Coming back to my preceding chapters, I need now to make this point: the question of Alcibiades's relationship to Thucydides is one that has drawn considerable attention, and for good reason; it bears quite directly on the structure of Thucydides's history.

Considering how well-informed Thucydides seems to be in regard to all those secret—and destined to remain secret—plots, many have speculated that there were personal contacts between Alcibiades and Thucydides.[1] Furthermore, some scholars have attempted to distinguish, in book 8, those passages that relayed information that came directly from Alcibiades and those that did not, as a way of tracing the history of the composition of the book by identifying which chapters preceded or followed a meeting between the two men, a meeting during which Alcibiades might have divulged detailed information.

We will not drag the reader into these scholarly debates. It seems impossible to say, even of secret meetings, that "only" Alcibiades could have revealed the tone of these discussions. There were then, as there always will be, leaks: well-informed friends, gossips, both dubious and reliable. In any case, Thucydides had, as he says, numerous and different sources of information. Reconstructing the development of book 8 from this is not easy to do. The book is unfinished. It is also imperfect. Unlike the other books, it includes no speeches. The composition is awkward: there are numerous flashbacks, some clearly consistent and others more or less obscure. Are these faults? He chose to narrate a war, in sequence, without addressing internal affairs. Then comes a phase of the war where key events took place far away, where internal affairs determined everything, where attention had to be given not only to Sparta and Athens but to Tissaphernes and Pharnabazus, and to the two opposing "cities" of Athens. A clear, linear account became impossible, especially for one who grasped all the intricacies connecting the various causes. The problem of evidence may have played a part. We have a sense of new evidence that may explain some of the details of the work. Some passages may have been written following more detailed information. Some of that came, possibly, straight from Alcibiades. There is just too much conjecture in all of this for me to lead the reader into the story of these relationships, of meetings between these two men,[2] and the reconstruction of his composition.

---

1. See E. Delebecque, *Thucydide et Alcibiade*, Faculté d'Aix-en-Provence (Ophrys, 1965), 245 pages; and P. A. Brunt, "Thucydides and Alcibiades," *Revue des études grecques* 65 (1952): 59–96.

2. This meeting would have occurred, according to E. Delebecque, in 406–405 in Thrace. Alcibiades would have started the whole affair: "The individual set out with a mission and found its author" (169).

This ongoing debate aside, it is important to remember two facts that are beyond question.

First, there may be debates about Thucydides's information, but we cannot determine the hypothetical influence of his personal contacts by the degree of sympathy found in the account.

Throughout his work, Thucydides marvels at the qualities of intelligence Alcibiades demonstrates. And he emphasizes throughout the work that the essential objective of his schemes is always self-interest. This level of lucidity and Thucydides's sense of the nuances preclude his being strictly dependent on privileged—and biased—information.

Moreover, the inconsistency of details that some have noticed, and that we have tried to explain by the nature of events, may be related to the evolution of politics itself. In Athenian politics, Alcibiades introduces an era of plots, betrayals, secret negotiations, and the lies of propaganda. He was not alone in these practices; they were widespread—and Thucydides says so. Certainly, if politics takes such a turn, the historian can no longer precisely follow; everything will depend on the quality of his information, on his ability to detect lies and fabrications. He can no longer report as clearly or as confidently. That is not Thucydides's fault. It is, quite simply, Alcibiades's fault.

Xenophon, too, was close to Alcibiades; he belonged to the group of Socrates's disciples, and he was interested in politics. However, he was not so curious to know why things happened. From him we have, above all, the facts—at times sharp and brilliant, but broken up with silences and, in some way, laid bare. Thucydides gave us his analysis, sometimes arguable. Xenophon left to the modern reader the work of analyzing, of explaining, of grasping the underlying reasons for events.

Moreover, the facts themselves, as we have said, contain silences. A simple detail will serve as an example: there is not a word in Xenophon's *Hellenica* about the death of Alcibiades, although it plays an important part in book 1 and at the beginning of book 2, and although his death was both dramatic and linked to the politics of several of the responsible parties at the time.

Because of this disparity in his account, it has sometimes been thought that documentation was its cause; and some have even thought that Xenophon was in possession of Thucydides's incomplete notes.[3] That, however, is strictly hypothetical, and there is no support for it.

3. E. Delebecque, *Vie de Xenophon*, 44.

For the most part, Xenophon does not appear eager to truly judge Alcibiades. His relationship to Socrates seems to have interested Xenophon less than his relationship to Plato. He is sometimes moved to present a version of the facts favorable to Alcibiades,[4] but he never speaks of him with any warmth or interest. He was most likely inclined to reject a man who, brilliant though he was, represented, along with the oligarch Critias, the bad disciple.[5] This point of view is still not as marked in the *Hellenica* as it will be later. It is clear, though, that between the virtuous military man Xenophon and the brilliant adventurer that Alcibiades always remained, there would not have been much sympathy.

Although, like Alcibiades, Xenophon would be exiled and welcomed in Sparta, that had not yet happened at the time he began writing the *Hellenica*. The differences in the manner of their exile and friendship with Sparta are an indication of their vast differences in temperament.

The reader of Thucydides is surprised that the historian knows so much; and it is difficult not to cite his enlightening and probing analyses. Reading Xenophon, however, one is surprised by how little he says; his account is like a bright light shone one moment on a scene before moving on the next moment, leaving all in darkness. It becomes necessary often to fill in the picture from other sources, often later ones.

This is when Diodorus Siculus emerges, the historian who offers scant analysis but who has read a great deal and consulted authors no longer available to us, such as Ephorus. Here, at the end of the work, we frequently find different versions; details will become vague. When we move from Thucydides to Xenophon, we must proceed with caution, feeling our way, even regarding factual details.

4. See below, for example, chapter 9.
5. Below, chapter 12.

A Triumphal Return

It took him four years to get back. Four years of fighting and winning.

The first endeavor, however, barely succeeded. Our bold hero, still hopeful about his standing with Tissaphernes, decided to go find him, as an Athenian leader and no longer an exile. He arrived proudly with a single ship, bearing gifts of hospitality, in the manner of someone ready to meet an equal. Tissaphernes did not adopt this tone toward him: he had Alcibiades arrested and imprisoned at Sardis, "saying that the king ordered him to make war upon the Athenians."[1] This was not for long: a month later Alcibiades escaped. Of his escape, Plutarch tells us that he "spread the lie that it was Tissaphernes himself who let him go." What a world! Either Alcibiades was once again telling lies to look good, or else Tissaphernes was playing both sides in order to attempt to reconcile with Sparta without completely breaking with Athens. Such were the methods.

---

1. Xenophon, *Hellenica* 1.1.9; Plutarch (27.7) says Tissaphernes thought that would satisfy the complaints of the Lacedaemonians.

They are exactly the unscrupulous methods of the oriental dictators that shocked the Greek mind. One thing was certain, however. Alcibiades could no longer claim to be the one who could bring the king's silver to Athens thanks to his privileged position with Tissaphernes. This episode would also delay his return to Athens; he would have to find other arguments, another way to press his case.

He found them in a series of victories, both taking place on the coast of the Hellespont and in the straits. The victories were not his alone, but he was on hand and he was the one most often taking the most active role.

We last saw the Peloponnesian and Athenian armies heading up to the Hellespont, with Alcibiades to join them soon. They are next found camped on the two banks of the straits of the Hellespont: the Peloponnesians on the southern side, bordering Phrygia, the Athenians on the north, bordering the Chersonese. The first are at Abydos, the second at Sestos.

We cannot go into the details of the military operations. We can, however, list the principal battles. Thucydides described the first one: the battle of Cynossema, a victory for the Athenians. Thucydides says that they would soon get over the feeling of inferiority they had following the disaster in Sicily and various other losses. They took more than twenty enemy ships, and their hopes were rising.

Alcibiades had at that time not yet arrived. But he came soon after with eighteen ships; and he arrived just as an even battle began between the two fleets. His intervention changed everything; the Peloponnesians had to retreat to Abydos. The Athenians took back the ships they had lost at Cynossema and, Xenophon says, seized thirty of the enemy ships.

Flush with this success—and with a momentary respite—the Athenian leaders prepared: each of them went off to neighboring cities and islands in search of money and ships, Alcibiades as well as the others.

There followed another battle, and then another victory, at Cyzicus, on the southern side of the Propontis. Xenophon says that this victory was largely the work of Alcibiades. We are told that the Peloponnesian leader Mindarus and the satrap Pharnabazus were both at Cyzicus. Alcibiades called the soldiers together and delivered a speech of courage and boldness recognized, in our own day, as Churchillian. He exhorted them to fight on the sea, on the land, and against the walls in front of them: "For we," he said, "have no money, but the enemy have an abundance of it from the king" (1.1.14). The severity of these statements is colored by the memory of only a few months earlier when Alcibiades was promising the Athenians that they would have, thanks to him, all the king's money. Alcibiades could always make a case even in failure . . .

Added to that, in the midst of battle, he had the qualities of a good general. He was able to maintain absolute secrecy. Then, when the time came, he attacked one morning despite a torrential downpour, punctuated by thunder, when there was almost no visibility. No time to go out, let alone wage battle! But this weather not only failed to stop him, it helped him: he was able to cut off passage to sixty enemy ships that were maneuvering far from port. These ships were heading for land. He followed them, ordered his men to disembark; they fought. The leader of the Peloponnesians was killed and all their ships either seized or burned. The next day, Alcibiades invaded the city. He stayed there three weeks and extorted a large payment. Cyzicus was on the south bank, the bank of the satrap. It was a clean strike. Alcibiades's boldness and speed had triumphed.

Diodorus Siculus, however, tells a slightly different story[2] in which Alcibiades's role was not so important. In his telling, Alcibiades had taken the initiative in launching the attack, but many decisions were attributed to other generals, and Alcibiades's success on land was due to their support. Is Diodorus drawing on a reliable source here?[3] Does Xenophon give Alcibiades too much credit? Possibly. However, that boldness was characteristic of him. And in any case, the question is simply one of degree. His participation and his resolution were undeniable.

The victory was an important one. Both Xenophon and Plutarch quote the message sent by the Lacedaemonians to the Spartan authorities. It was typically laconic, but brutally clear: "Ships lost; Mindarus killed; troops starving; no idea what to do."[4]

This is all true; the consequences followed quickly, and Alcibiades reaped the benefit. The people of Perinthus welcomed him inside their walls; those of Selymbria gave him money; the two cities are west of

2. Diodorus 13.51, with statements such as "Theramenes flew to the aid of Alcibiades, who was in danger."

3. Some scholars think it was Ephorus. Modern historians are split almost equally between the two versions (or are tempted to correct one as a function of the other). In addition to these different interpretations, there are differences in details as well, particularly regarding the number of vessels.

4. 1.1.23 = Plutarch 28.10; the translation is slightly altered.

Byzantium. He fortified another to the east that allowed the Athenians a crucial advantage—to levy a tax on all shipping through the Bosphorus.

These were important achievements. Alcibiades may have hoped that they would be sufficient to assure his return. In any case, he gained some breathing room. The victory at Cyzicus occurred in the winter of 411–410. We know nothing more before the summer of 409.

It is important to note that power in Athens during this time was held by the demagogue Cleophon, who was clearly an opponent.[5] Perhaps Alcibiades was waiting, in vain, for some encouragement. As this did not come, however, he went back to work. His winter quarters were at Lampsacus, from which he threatened Pharnabazus and even tried to attack Abydos. Then, the next spring, he was again found at the gates of Byzantium, which was attacking the surrounding barbarians. Then he turned against the great city of Chalcedon, opposite Byzantium, and surrounded by a wall extending from one sea to the other. There the enemy came out and attacked the Athenians, commanded by another leader. The battle dragged on . . . "until Alcibiades came to the rescue with a few hoplites and the cavalry" (*Hellenica* 1.3.6).[6] It was another victory, and the people of Chalcedon were once again loyal to Athens, once again paying tribute.

While the agreement ratifying this was being finalized, Alcibiades was absent: he had departed to the other end of the Hellespont in search of money.

Money again? In the past, the grandeur of Athens commanded payments that allies had paid more or less willingly. However, after the occupation of Decelea and the defections that followed the Sicilian disaster (for both of which Alcibiades was mostly to blame), with the heroic achievement of rebuilding a fleet, with the loss of Euboea, the need for money had become great. Alcibiades remembered what Pericles had said twenty years earlier: "Capital, it must be remembered, maintains a war more than forced contributions" (Thucydides 1.141.5). Alcibiades's bravery in battle had intensified in him a practical and realistic spirit.

---

5. For example, Hyperbolus or Androcles: see above, chapter 8. A cousin of Alcibiades, exiled at the same time, was taken prisoner by the Athenians and stoned: again, not very encouraging.

6. The translation is that of Carleton L. Brownson (repr., London: Heinemann, 1930), https://archive.org/details/xenophonwithengl01xenouoft.

On the way home, he laid siege to another city, Selymbria: he seized it and retook Byzantium with soldiers, both Greek and barbarian, and with cavalry.

Note the cavalry. Almost all battles in the Hellespont were naval battles. But Alcibiades liked to go ashore. He loved swift battles and sudden attacks. He wanted to take on the army of the satrap. So he insisted on the cavalry. As we just saw, it played a role under his command in the battle of Chalcedon.

As he was returning, strengthened with fresh troops and money, an important satisfaction awaited him. The agreement between the Athenians and the satrap regarding Chalcedon had been arranged and concluded in his absence by other Athenian leaders. The satrap, however, was not satisfied by this: "He needed for Alcibiades also to pledge to support the deal"; and he was awaiting Alcibiades's return.[7]

This demand represented a great honor. It recognized Alcibiades as the true leader of the Athenian forces, and the true victor. Alcibiades knew that, and he took advantage of it: he demanded a new agreement made specifically with him and he demanded an exchange of oaths between sovereigns. And it was done. The commitment was made in the name of the community. Not bad for an exile!

This agreement still exists in stone.[8] It is moving to imagine the ritual accompanying the ratification. It would have been the recognition of Alcibiades's new status. He had been pampered by Tissaphernes; he had advised and directed him. Later their relations grew strained. But now suddenly another satrap would recognize no one else. Moreover, and more important, he was recognized as the leader and representative of the city where, officially, he no longer existed.

The time had clearly come to make a change. In Athens, attention was on him. When Sophocles presented *Philoctetes* in 409, many people likely thought of Alcibiades. Philoctetes had been sent, alone, to an island; victory in the Trojan War depended on him. Alcibiades was in the same situation.[9] More and more people felt, increasingly, that the solution was at hand. There was no time to lose.

---

7. Similarly, and more briefly, see Plutarch, *Alcibiades* 31.2. This fact is not included in Diodorus's account (13.66).

8. IG I², 116.

9. See Glen Bowersock, *Fiction as History*, 57, who notes that a proverb cited twice by Aelius Aristides (once in connection with Philoctetes) is cited by Alcibiades in the *Symposium* 217e.

And throughout this time, another achievement, and not the least: the taking of Byzantium!

The city was occupied by the Peloponnesians and attacked by the Athenians. The Peloponnesian leader departed to ask for Pharnabazus's support. Following a secret negotiation, an agreement was sealed with some inhabitants, and Alcibiades was able to get his troops into the city through a gate that had been left open. Byzantium surrendered. The effort proved, once again, Alcibiades's unique abilities in scheming and persuasion.

To fully appreciate the situation, we have the picture drawn by Jean Hatzfeld, summarizing the achievements since the destruction of the Peloponnesian fleet at Cyzicus: "The straits were taken; communication re-established with the Black Sea and the wheat fields; customs installed at the entrance to the Bosphorus; the Athenian fleet supplied by the rich crops and pillage of enemy territory—and thus not suffering the problems of the city's finances; the cities of the region were again loyal, and once again paying tribute."[10] To which could be added the effective neutrality of Pharnabazus and the support of the Thracian barbarians . . .

All of that was important. And this time, it was enough. The following spring, Alcibiades's candidacy for the position of general was announced in Athens. The elections were delayed. Alcibiades was waiting on Samos, and then left to raise money in Caria before finally setting out, with some detours . . .

He was traveling when he received the news: he had been elected general—along with another individual who had also once been involved in the affair of the mysteries. Everything was swept away, relationships were repaired. He was returning in triumph.

In Athens, however, opinion was still divided. Xenophon, who was no doubt present at the time, writes about the debates and the rage they aroused. It was easy to blame Alcibiades; many recalled that he was the sole cause of all the problems of the past and could well bring on more in the future. There were arguments on both sides: the scandal of the mysteries had led to the Sicilian disaster, the occupation of Decelea, the defection of the colonies on the Ionian coast, the help given to Sparta by Tissaphernes . . . The other side recalled his talents and the intemperate decision

10. J. Hatzfeld, *Alcibiade,* 288.

that had precipitated his support of the enemy. Supporters argued that he had wanted to defend himself, but that he had been a victim "of the plot of those who were less powerful than he was and who made up for their weakness with this cruel plan," and who then "profited from his absence to prevent him from returning to his own country." They blamed the exile into which he had been forced, the dangers he had known, his powerlessness to help his homeland . . .

Rationales were found in various explanations in vogue at the time: his own circumstances, they said, would preclude Alcibiades's involvement in a regime change; only his less advantaged adversaries had anything to gain from that. That was a common argument, one that was to be developed at length in speech 25 of Lysias (*Defense against a Charge of Subverting the Democracy*), in sections 9–14. In short, both sides argued vehemently about Alcibiades's true leanings. Mostly, they were thinking about the future. By simply dismissing him, they had forced him to act against his country. If they gave him back his rights and put him in charge, he would be in a better position to help them.

Which is why his return was being followed with such intense interest.

There are several accounts. One is that of Xenophon, which may well be an eyewitness account; others were from a later period: they come to us from Plutarch and Diodorus.[11] Both, however, may have drawn on earlier, well-informed sources—the historian Ephorus, whose work has been lost, and Duris of Samos, who claimed to be a descendant of Alcibiades.

These works are important for two reasons.

The first reason is a literary one: the version that is most immediate and concrete, most apt to excite the imagination and emotions, is not the first-hand account by Xenophon but the one written five hundred years later by Plutarch. It is easy to see in it a work of literary genius. And it may be that the difference in the accounts is not accidental, that little by little, the original story may well have been enriched and embellished.

In Xenophon, Alcibiades returns alone.[12] With twenty triremes. Later accounts show him returning along with the generals and with an

---

11. See Xenophon, *Hellenica* 1.4.12–20; Plutarch, *Alcibiades* 32–33; Diodorus 13.69. We should add Cornelius Nepos 6.

12. Plutarch mentions other generals, without saying that they went ashore with him. Diodorus refers to the generals returning from the Hellespont together. Xenophon is not specific, but he mentions the separate returns.

enormous number of ships. Duris, as quoted by Plutarch, describes his ship as having a purple sail and a cortege of ecstatic supporters. At this point, even Plutarch expresses some reserve.

In fact, and considering whatever prudence Alcibiades might still have had, the reality must have been splendid.

The return took place on the day of the festival of Plynteria (the day when the robes of the statue of Athena were washed: from *pluno*, I wash). This seemed to be an auspicious date, as the statue of Athena remained veiled on that day, and no one would have chosen that moment for serious activity. But it was also a festival day. The whole city went down to the port: the crowd came from Piraeus and from Athens, thrilled by the occasion and wishing to see the famous man.

There he was. Twenty ships, says Xenophon. Plutarch paints a larger picture: "His own Attic triremes were decked from stem to stern with shields and other spoils of war, and had plenty of captured triremes in tow, as well as a cargo of an even larger number of figureheads from ships he had defeated and destroyed. The number of enemy triremes in both categories amounted to at least two hundred" (32.1). Why not add to the victorious little squadron the long display of insignia recalling all his victories? Alcibiades was not one to neglect such an opportunity or such a show.

We will indulge ourselves with some details, possibly imagined, from Duris. Plutarch continues: "Duris of Samos, who claims to be a descendant of Alcibiades, goes into more detail: He says that Chrysogonus, a victor of the Pythian Games, played the pipes for the rowers, and that the tragic actor Callipides called the time, both wearing their full competition costumes" (32.2). And why not, after all?[13] We will stop here, before the purple sail, in order to show some restraint. Obviously, this return had all the elements, even later, to stir the imagination, to start men dreaming.

All the while, Alcibiades was watching. He recognized his friends and relatives celebrating him, and he went ashore.

Once he was ashore, however, people hardly even noticed any of the other military commanders they met, but ran and crowded round him, calling out to him, greeting him and accompanying him on his way, and crowning him with garlands if they could get close to him, while those who could

---

13. Athenaeus 12.535.c–d provides the same information.

not watched him from a distance, and the older men pointed him out to the younger ones. (32. 3)

Alcibiades—in a strange position, having been made general but still under the decree of his prior conviction—went at once up into the city, surrounded by a security escort of friends, ready to repel any attempt against his person. He was welcomed to the Council, then to the Assembly, where he gave a promotional speech that no one dared to interrupt. And the people rewarded him with crowns and proclaimed him supreme leader with full authority!

Honors and reparations were to follow quickly. "They also voted to restore his property to him, and decreed that the Eumolpidae and the heralds were to revoke the curses they had spoken against him in accordance with the people's instructions" (33.3).[14] We even know that property was given to him in compensation for goods that had been confiscated.[15] In short, the people could not do enough to erase the memory of the past. A crown of gold, or several crowns of gold, was awarded (as Plutarch says, at 33.2). Later, there was much talk about the gifts that he received from the people.[16] A clear sign of the fragility of popularity, these gifts would once again be taken away; but that fact does nothing to diminish the fervor during these times of reunion. He could not have dreamed of a more glorious return.

He may well have had his doubts, his fears. Xenophon and Plutarch say he did. Xenophon writes that on arrival he was not eager to go ashore for fear of his enemies, and "mounting on the deck of his ship, he looked to see whether his friends were present" (1.4.18). He also says that those friends surrounded him to prevent any attack. For his part, Plutarch uses those fears as evidence of his accuracy: and he dismisses some of the details found in Duris as exaggerations: "Nor is it likely that he would have behaved in such a willful manner when he was returning from exile and after having been in so much trouble. In fact, he was very nervous as he came in to land" (32.2).

14. Plutarch 33.3, who states clearly: "All the other priests revoked their curses, except for Theodorus, the high priest, who said, 'No, I never prayed that he would suffer harm—provided he does no wrong to the city.'"
15. Isocrates 16.46.
16. Lysias 14.31.

Indeed, he was taking a risk. Those who had exiled him were still there. And his actions during the past few years would have been cause for even greater hostility. But timidity was hardly in his nature. It is pleasing to imagine the sharp eye of the leader, verifying that his allies were nearby. After that, self-confident man that he was, he would not have been surprised by the triumph he had so ardently prepared for and orchestrated. If it was necessary to show his fears, his great risk, it was only in order to make his success appear all the greater. No one moved. No one protested. In spite of everything, his return was an absolute and unqualified triumph.

The triumph itself was amazing.

It has impressed thinkers for centuries. Mably, for example, wrote with great effect in his *Observations sur l'histoire de la Grèce* (1766): "The people, not knowing whom to trust, flew before him and idolized him, because they had persecuted him."

True, in history there have been other glorious heroes who returned victorious. Everyone in France rushed out to see De Gaulle, if only from afar. We wept with emotion celebrating on the Champs-Élysées, French once again. We would have voted for everything to say thank you to the man who, just the day before, had been a rebel. But wait! The hero we celebrated had not been condemned by a popular tribunal. He had never betrayed his country. He had not gone to seek Hitler's help in defeating France. He had not gone to the United States to urge Americans to join the Germans . . . Surely there has never been a more stunning shift in popular opinion than was shown in the triumphal return of Alcibiades who, only five years earlier, was still fighting against Athens. The people must have been crazy! Alcibiades must have been a genius!

It must be added that while Alcibiades was received as a savior, Athens was in no way saved. Plutarch presents a whole scenario about the remorse the Athenians must have felt at the time of Alcibiades's return when they thought about all they had suffered as a result of sending him away; and they were delighted by all the benefits that already he had brought to them: "And yet now Alcibiades had taken these wretched, dejected remnants and resurrected the city to such an extent that not only had he restored its mastery of the seas, but on land he had also enabled it to conquer its enemies all over the world" (32.4).

This euphoric picture was far from accurate. Alcibiades had brought back some victories, on the coast of the Bosphorus, and brought some allies back to Athens' side. But the war was still going on. The Persians were still helping Sparta, and, in the middle of Attica, enemy forces continued to occupy Decelea, blockading everything and causing the Athenians serious economic hardship—yet another humiliation.

Then Alcibiades had a stroke of audacity and genius that amazes us today.

To understand the context, remember that the Mysteries of Eleusis are celebrated once a year, and that it was the custom for Athenians to go there in a ceremonial procession. It took place in September. It was a civic celebration, comparable to the Panathenaean or Dionysian festivals. But after the occupation of Decelea, the procession could not follow the usual route in safety. Eleusis was west of Athens, Decelea was north; but the enemy could invade and cut off the route. As a result, participants had been reaching Eleusis unceremoniously by sea. The new route meant forgoing certain rituals; it had been customary to stop en route and make sacrifices.

This affair involved Alcibiades in two ways: his condemnation had taken place precisely because he had mocked the mysteries; and the sanctions against him had been imposed by those who were responsible for protecting them. Moreover, the occupation of Decelea was his fault: it was he who had advised the Lacedaemonians to take it and everyone knew that.

Hence the idea for this act embodying all his bravado, his flair for the daring gesture, and above all his acute sense of how to please the crowd.

It was now May; the mysteries were to be celebrated in the fall. In the meantime, he was leading the war effort; he had to act, to fight, to win victories. No! He waited until September. He wanted to restore the procession under his personal protection.

Plutarch says:

> It therefore struck Alcibiades as a good idea, bearing in mind how it would enhance not only his piety in the eyes of the gods, but also his reputation among men, to restore the traditional form to the rites, by having his infantry escort and guard the ceremony past the enemy. This, he thought, would either thoroughly embarrass and humiliate Agis, if the king chose to do nothing, or would enable him to fight a sacred battle, with the approval of the gods, in a supremely holy and crucial cause, and to do so within sight of his native city, with all his fellow citizens there to witness his courage. (34.5)

Plutarch was a very religious man who lacked the words to express the emotion and admiration this effort inspired. The Athenians themselves were moved. Alcibiades had gone from desecrater to the most honored at the ceremonies. He who had been so loudly condemned for playing the hierophant was now the one who received the titles and highest honors at the celebration of the mysteries: he was named mystagogue and hierophant.

Meanwhile, the enemy never budged. People were afraid of him: he was invincible.

The success went almost too far: amidst all the joy and hopes that his return had aroused, some of the old political quarrels were beginning to appear: everyone wanted to talk to him, to use him. Diodorus tells us how the poor saw in him "their best friend and the man most capable of relieving their misery with a political revolution."[17] Plutarch even says that the men of the people would have proposed that he become tyrant "as a way of reaching a place where the envy of others could have no effect on him, where he could do away with decrees and laws and the idle chatterers who were ruining the city, and so act and administer the city's affairs without fear of the informers." Strange fate for a man who, only a few years earlier, had been attacked and exiled because he was suspected of aspiring to tyranny, to hear it suggested that he should now agree to it. In the enthusiasm of the moment, he might have done so. But he did not. The months that followed show that he governed as the ruler, but according to the rules of the democracy.[18]

Actually, all these different ideas were an indication of trouble in the political life of Athens: they show that political quarrels and passions were simmering beneath the appearance of a newfound unanimity.

But for the moment, these efforts were just flatteries; the ideas and suggestions were a testament to the huge success Alcibiades had made of his return. The hopes of everyone were on him: they saw only him, they depended on him alone. He was the man of destiny,

It can be risky to inherit such a role. History, even recent history, has seen a man of destiny end up in a withdrawal tainted with bitterness. It has also

---

17. Diodorus 13.68.
18. Taken from texts of decrees found in stone. These are official decrees, in which we see him proposing measures of tolerance toward those cities and peoples who return to the Athenian side (J. Hatzfeld cites IG I^2 116 and 117).

happened that unexpected returns that began with fanfare were cut short: the return from the island of Elba lasted one hundred days.

Alcibiades had everyone on his side: the people, religion and those who were connected to it, and patriots who were expecting victory. He was like a god, adored by all.

But he needed victories—at any cost and quickly. Triumphs follow victories; they also require them.

10

SLIGHTLY MORE THAN
ONE HUNDRED DAYS

He needed victories; but these would not be easily won.

There were, in particular, two new circumstances to be considered, and both were unfavorable.

The first was the presence of a new and remarkably able leader on the Lacedaemonian side, Lysander—the same one who had finally secured the Spartan victory and stopped Athens, an individual so significant that Plutarch ranked him among his great men and wrote a biography about him. Of all the different kings or leaders of the army that Sparta had during the war, he is the only one for whom this is true. He is ranked with the Roman Sulla. He was ambitious, authoritarian, and uncompromised. These two equally competent and powerful men, Lysander and Alcibiades, resembled each other in seeming to take up all the room. It was said of Lysander that Greece could not support two like him. The same had been said of Alcibiades. And Plutarch takes pains to distinguish between the harshness of Lysander and the arrogance of Alcibiades.[1] The fact is that these two

---

1. Plutarch, *Lysander* 19.5–6.

were worthy adversaries. One modern historian has written: "Lysander, the Alcibiades of the Eurotas."[2]

This is when they come face to face. Alcibiades returns to Athens in 407. In the spring of that year, Lysander is sent to lead the enemy fleet. It is a critical moment; he must stop the fleet commanded by Alcibiades.

Lysander, moreover, had money. The other new development was that Persia decided to support Sparta. All the procrastination and scheming of the satraps had ended: the king of Persia sent his own son, Cyrus (who is not to be confused with the great Cyrus, the founder of the Persian Empire and the hero of Xenophon's *Cyropaedia*).[3] His mission was clear: he carried a letter from the king, the text of which is preserved in Xenophon, naming him *caranus*, or absolute leader of all the forces of Asia Minor. His first move was to have Pharnabazus detain an Athenian ambassador; he had left before Alcibiades's return to Athens and did not return for three years.[4] This first move by Cyrus was one sign; the second was more serious. Lysander had scarcely assumed command when he sought out Cyrus and obtained from him very generous promises of support for the Peloponnesian soldiers. Cyrus responded that not only were these the instructions from his father, but that he himself, far from being of a different opinion, would do everything he could. He had come with five hundred talents, and if that did not suffice, he would use his own fortune, beyond what his father had given him; "and if this too should prove inadequate, he would go so far as to break up the throne whereon he sat, which was of silver and gold."[5] This sounds very much like the promises that Tissaphernes had made, according to what Alcibiades told the Athenians on Samos;[6] but this time the words were coming from Cyrus, and the promises would be kept. In addition, the money was going to Sparta and not Athens.

Lysander was in the same position with Cyrus that Alcibiades had been in with Tissaphernes: he flattered him, he charmed him. Plutarch writes, in the *Life of Lysander*, that by criticizing Tissaphernes, and by other means,

2. G. Glotz, *Histoire grecque*, 2nd ed., 3:113–14.
3. This is the Cyrus we meet in Xenophon's *Anabasis*, in events somewhat later.
4. Xenophon 1.4.3–7.
5. Xenophon 1.5.3.
6. See above, chapter 8.

"Lysander made himself agreeable, and by the submissive deference of his conversation, above all else, he won the heart of the young prince, and roused him to prosecute the war with vigor."[7]

It was just like Alcibiades's seduction of Tissaphernes. Even the role of the garden was repeated! Xenophon, in *Oeconomicus*, describes how the king brought Lysander into his garden at Sardis. And Lysander gushed with admiration: "Cyrus, I really do admire all these lovely things, but I am far more impressed with your agent's skill." His words delighted Cyrus, who replied: "Well, Lysander, the whole of the measurement and arrangement is my own work, and I did some of the planting myself."[8] Lysander was duly impressed by this. He quickly concluded that the king owed his happiness to his virtue! This edifying exchange apparently took place later. But it reveals the tone and underlines in a striking way the historical repetitions and reversals.

Nevertheless, while he waited, Lysander had his feet on the ground. He asked the young king for increased pay for his soldiers: he asked for one Attic drachma per man, which was double the Athenian salary. Cyrus answered that the norm was half a drachma. Lysander was quiet; then, needing to respond, he asked for one obol more[9] and got it. This amount was still greater than the Athenian rate: four obols to three. And Cyrus paid one month in advance.

This agreement was disastrous for Athens, which sent an embassy via Tissaphernes. This embassy, despite the support that Tissaphernes had apparently promised, was not even received.

A leader, and money: that changed everything, and did not make Alcibiades's task any easier.

These circumstances forced him to take a variety of steps that were not in his nature but that became necessary, such as pillaging and requisitions. At this point we are told that he had to leave for Caria "to levy money." Another source says he "sailed off to get money."[10]

One incident illustrating his action was the attack against the city of Cyme, despite its being an Athenian ally. His demands there enraged the

7. Plutarch, *Lysander* 4.3.
8. Xenophon, *Oeconomicus* 4.21–25.
9. One drachma equals six obols.
10. Plutarch 35.4.

inhabitants and unsettled his troops a bit.[11] Incidents like these were held against him; they represent legitimate complaints, and they would be exploited and used against him when the situation grew worse.

In addition, his troops, poorly paid, grew more and more undisciplined, the political upheavals having helped reduce the authority of their leaders. Alcibiades hardly had the time to change this.

However, he had to act. As usual, he was ready.

Having just returned from winning victories in the Hellespont, he chose now to attack in Ionia. He left Athens in October 407, with three hundred ships. Plutarch says that the most powerful citizens, worried once again about him, made every effort "to hurry him off on his expedition as quickly as possible" (35.1). The point of this is important, a reminder that the slightest failure risked reviving old animosities.

From the beginning, things did not go well. On the way to Ionia he stopped at Andros, which had defected from Athens and was being held by a very small occupying force. He disembarked and won a victory, but he did not take the town. He left twenty ships behind to continue the operation; he had not fully succeeded. Moreover, he had reduced the size of his own fleet.

Sailing on, he arrived at Samos, the large and secure Athenian base. He was joined there by his colleague Thrasybulus on his way back from Thrace, where he had won victories. Both had to act, and quickly.

The Peloponnesian fleet was just across from Samos, at Ephesus: it was being repaired thanks to the generosity of Cyrus. Would Alcibiades attack? He went by, with most of the fleet, to Notium, on the continent, a little north of Ephesus.[12] From there he could watch the Peloponnesian fleet. And it would be easy for Thrasybulus, who had gone north to attack Phocaea, to get to Notium. Alcibiades could safely join him in Phocaea. Everything seemed well planned. Alcibiades would not be going farther; he left his ships at Notium and put the fleet under the command of someone else.

At this point something paradoxical, almost unbelievable, happened: Alcibiades was not there, but he had given orders to avoid engaging the

---

11. The episode is squeezed into the account of Diodorus, who we know follows Ephorus, who was himself originally from Cyme. See also Cornelius Nepos 7.1–2. Regarding the sequence of Alcibiades's travels, the sources disagree.

12. Diodorus 13.71.

enemy. Despite this, there was a battle, a defeat. It was a defeat that would lead to his downfall once and for all.

Of course it was partly his own fault. As commander of the fleet he was authorized to designate a replacement. But he had made a choice that even today stuns us. He entrusted the fleet not to one of his senior officers but to his pilot, Antiochus, an old friend but someone of a lower rank and without experience.

Antiochus. We know him! Back when Alcibiades was in the Assembly and released his quail, it was Antiochus who, amid the commotion, caught it and brought it back.[13] That was the beginning of a close friendship between the two men. But he was not a very respectable individual. Plutarch calls him a common fool. And when Alcibiades was later accused of putting the command in the hands of foolish drunkards, the kind of men who had influence with him, they were no doubt thinking of Antiochus.[14] For him to have been chosen, Alcibiades must have greatly mistrusted the others, probably supporters of his enemies; or he simply could not resist his old fondness for provocation and wanted to show that the choice was his alone, without regard for rank or custom, that he was free to do as he pleased. And in fact, if Antiochus had obeyed his orders, the decision might have been inconsequential. Lysander was not going to attack while his fleet was undergoing repairs, and Alcibiades had left very clear orders—he told Antiochus not to engage the ships of Lysander. It was clear and direct.

Alas, Alcibiades put too much trust in his friend.

Once more, it is important to say it: in Athens, the city that in theory was so egalitarian, again and again we keep finding these "friends" and "enemies." We encounter these little cliques everywhere, each one hostile to the other, surrounding a leader, spying on each other!

Besides the organized groups, like the *hetaereiai*,[15] politics was run by connections stripped of any official character or ideological basis. In this case it appears that the same patterns had penetrated the military domain.

In any case, his friend was too zealous. He wanted to thank Alcibiades for his confidence by producing a surprise victory. Contrary to orders, he entered the port of Ephesus with the triremes!

---

13. The incident is described above, chapter 2.
14. Plutarch 36.2.
15. See above, chapter 3.

The accounts of the battle differ in Xenophon and Diodorus. Xenophon says that Antiochus sailed into the port with two triremes, which would have been an irrational provocation. Diodorus and the *Hellenica of Oxyrhynchus* mention ten of his best ships (13.71). Diodorus also says that Antiochus had warned the others to be ready. In both cases, the provocation was flagrant. Xenophon says Antiochus "sailed from Notium into the harbor of Ephesus and coasted along past the very prows of Lysander's ships" (1.5.12). Plutarch says that in addition to this he was "making coarse gestures and calling out rude comments to them" (35.6). In both cases, his intentions were obvious.

Naturally, a battle ensued. Lysander put only a small number of ships to sea, to follow Antiochus; the Athenian fleet came to Antiochus's aid in a more or less orderly fashion, and Lysander then attacked with his whole fleet in a line. He won a great victory, and the Athenians lost at least fifteen triremes as well as their crews[16]—possibly as many as twenty-two, according to Diodorus and the *Hellenica of Oxyrhynchus*.

Alcibiades returned to Samos and wanted to continue the battle. Lysander was too clear-sighted to risk that. He was satisfied with the battle he had won in Alcibiades's absence.

The battle at Notium was Alcibiades's downfall. His enemies emerged at once. And the wild confidence that had greeted his return was extinguished with this first defeat. Too much had been expected of him. As Plutarch wrote:

> Alcibiades seems to be a clear case of someone destroyed by his own reputation. His successes had made his daring and resourcefulness so well known that any failure prompted people to wonder whether he had really tried. They never doubted his ability; if he really tried, they thought, nothing would be impossible for him. So they expected to hear that Chios had fallen too, and the whole rest of Ionia, and were therefore irritated when they heard that he had not managed to accomplish everything as quickly or instantaneously as they wanted. (35.2–5)

There were other circumstances involved as well.

---

16. Fifteen triremes, according to Xenophon and Plutarch (*Lysander* 5.2).

We have referred to the incidents at Cyme that followed immediately after the defeat at Notium. To that we must add, if we are to believe Diodorus,[17] a bold move by the forces at Decelea against the walls of Athens itself. Alcibiades had nothing to do with it, but the attempt exposed the fragility of his rule: it was retaliation for his success during the procession of the mysteries.

The sense of betrayal was intense. It echoed even after his death. In a brief speech about Alcibiades's son, Lysias said of the father: "For if during his exile it was his power that enabled him to injure the city, how was it that, having obtained his return by deceiving you and being in command of many ships of war, he had not power enough to expel the enemy from our land or to regain for you the friendship of the Chians whom he had alienated,[18] or to do you any other useful service?"[19]

He had promised too much, as always. Only this time the deception was too great. Because of the defeat, the battle waged by a subordinate, the delay in responding to the situation, all the confidence that had been placed in him suddenly vanished.

After that, events happened quickly. In his absence, Athens reacted. Charges were brought. Someone came from the democratic side in Samos to describe the people's unhappiness and the chaos that was spreading in the army. There was talk of new scandals. Suspicions were raised about Alcibiades's actions in Thrace. Very quickly another representative of the democrats, the demagogue Cleophon, whose hostility toward Alcibiades was well known,[20] published an official charge. It was all starting again.

The Assembly immediately removed Alcibiades and the other generals who were held responsible for the defeat; in the elections that followed, at the beginning of 406, he was not reelected. The same fate befell the other general who had been compromised earlier: the faithful Thrasybulus himself was removed. As a result, confirmed democrats were elected.[21]

---

17. Diodorus 13.73. Xenophon does not mention this fact, but Diodorus gives many details, and there is no reason to doubt him (there are numerous omissions in Xenophon).

18. The accusation is valid. See above, chapter 7.

19. Lysias, *Against Alcibiades* 14.36.

20. See above, chapter 9.

21. Critias, the author of the decree recalling Alcibiades, was also banished, possibly around the same time. There are references to his time—and to conspiracies then—in Thessaly (Xenophon, *Hellenica* 2.3.36), and Aristotle (*Rhetoric* 1.1375b) states that he was attacked . . . by Cleophon!

A line was drawn. The triumph of one spring ended before the next spring, and concluded—with no major offense to blame—in a total collapse.

Past offenses and all the acrimony that accrued—these had not suddenly been erased by the noise of the cheering: they were always there.

It is overly simplistic to relate the event by itself without reference to the vacillation of the people. There is no doubt they were fickle; fifth-century authors wrote about it. Thucydides uses strong and compelling language to express his scorn for this capriciousness, adding "according to the way of the multitude." As an example, he cites the occasion when the Athenians, right after fining Pericles, forgot their anger and put him in charge of all their affairs.[22] Just a few years later Aristophanes used a clever phrase to describe the Athenians who are "quick to decide" and "quick to change their minds."[23] Closer in time to the events that concern this story (but still prior to the events involving Alcibiades), Euripides, in *Orestes*, uses more colorful language to describe this quality: in that play Menelaus says, "For when the people fall into a vigorous fury, they are as hard to quench as a raging fire." But if you don't oppose them, they may calm down. "They have pity, and a hot temper too, an invaluable quality if you watch it closely" (696–704). This fault was a familiar one, frequently lamented, and increasingly apparent.

Still, for the Athenians to reject Alcibiades a second time suggests that their attitude toward him had more specific causes.

It is clear that the weight of the past continued to be a burden for him. We should not forget how long it took Alcibiades before he was ready to return, nor the apprehension of many when he did return. After all, between the herms and the mysteries, after the small and large scandals of his youth, he had betrayed his country and caused it great harm. Then he had plotted with the oligarchs only to rejoin the democrats. He had toyed with Tissaphernes; he had exploited vulnerable people. How could Athenians have forgotten or forgiven? They had been led by his promises and ceded to the pressures of the time. But the financial problems had not been solved. The Persians had not come to the aid of Athens; just the opposite. How could they have trusted him? The slightest lapse of judgment (and we have seen an example!) should have made the incredible precariousness of the situation quite obvious.

22. Thucydides 2.65.3–4.
23. Aristophanes, *Acharnians* 632.

What, then, is the lesson from this? The past, when it is so strongly written into history, cannot be erased. And character does not change.

This time, where does he go? No city and no ruler could welcome Alcibiades.

He was neither condemned nor exiled. He could have returned to Athens and tried to explain himself. He must have known that that was hopeless. He must have grasped some time ago that this might happen, for he had made preparations for it, securing a distant refuge, in Thrace. As soon as he was demoted, stripped of his command, he abandoned the fleet, gave up on returning to Athens, and departed, without further delay,[24] for Thrace, initially for the Chersonese, on the Thracian border. Xenophon says: "So Alcibiades, who was in disfavor with the army as well, took a trireme and sailed away to his castle in the Chersonese" (1.5.17).

"Castle" is probably an imperfect translation: the Greek says he entered his walls. He had apparently foreseen the necessity and acquired several forts in the region.

These forts had belonged to him for two years. Their acquisition dates to the time of his victories on the shore beside the straits; they were never a purchase. Having led the negotiations with Thrace, he was able to obtain support for the war but also, apparently, some advantages for himself. (This is an aspect of politics found in every age). We know the locations of these forts. Cornelius Nepos is the only source for the names of all three places: Bisanthe, Ornoi, and Neon Teichos. Different sources name one or the other.[25]

Amazingly (and this is the second parallelism between these two individuals), the same fortresses were given to Xenophon, who refers to them in the *Anabasis*; his offhand reference in the *Hellenica* has led some scholars to think that the *Hellenica* was written before he was aware of them.[26]

Naturally all these dealings had become known and were used by the accusers of Alcibiades.

But that would not have prevented him, while waiting for things to get better, from living peacefully in the country where he had had successes, and where he was at home. Furthermore, it was not incriminating. And if

---

24. According to Diodorus he was awaiting the arrival of his replacement; but Xenophon is quite clear and closer to the truth: see Hatzfeld, 318, n. 1.

25. Cornelius Nepos, *Alcibiades* 8.4. See Plutarch, *Alcibiades* 36, citing a fortress built near Bysanthe. Lysias 14.25 mentions "Ornoi" but gives no details.

26. Hatzfeld, preface to the *Hellenica*, supported by E. Delebecque, *Essai sur la vie de Xénophon*, 33.

these fickle Athenians revoked their decision, he would have been available. Who can say whether or not Alcibiades was still hopeful?

This time, however, the people did not change their mind. We know from the literature of the time that opinion was divided. Evidence for this came just a year later, brought to us in the words of Aristophanes's play the *Frogs*.

This comedy was presented in January 405. The play suggests, or rather states, that despite his betrayals and his ambition, only one man could save Athens: Alcibiades. And it blames Cleophon, the infamous democrat, sole leader at the time, for all of Alcibiades's troubles. Was it simply coincidence that the play alludes to the chorus of the Mysteries of Eleusis,[27] for which Alcibiades had so proudly opened the way at the time of his return? Aristophanes even asks the question directly. As we know, the play presents a competition in the Underworld between Aeschylus and Euripides (Euripides had died in 406) in which the judge is Dionysus. Near the end of the poetry contest, Dionysus explains that he will bring back to life one of the two individuals most capable of giving good advice to the city: "On the subject of Alcibiades, what will we do with him? That's the first question" (1431–32).

So people were still talking about him. Thinking about him again, thinking about him always. The text is direct: "Alcibiades was like a baby who gave the state birthing pains."

It is actually difficult to know Aristophanes's own thoughts on the subject. Ultimately, the two tragedians are in agreement in offering harsh criticism of Alcibiades.

Euripides provides sharp condemnation, concurring with the judgment of Thucydides on the subject of corrupt politicians: "I hate the citizen who, by nature well endowed, / Is slow to help his city, swift to do her harm, / to himself useful, useless to the community" (*Frogs* 1427–29).[28] Aeschylus has his own style and turns to analogy. His advice: "We should not rear a lion's cub within the state. / But if we rear one, we must do as it desires" (*Frogs* 1431–32).

---

27. Aristophanes, *Frogs* 369–82.
28. *Four Comedies*, trans. Richmond Lattimore (University of Michigan Press, 1969).

This comparison with the lion is apt, recalling a passage in *Agamemnon* and the description of Helen, a passage so beautiful it merits quoting in full:

> A man reared a lion's offspring
> In his house, unsuckled, just as it was,
> In the beginnings of its life
> Gentle, dear to children,
> And a delight to the aged.
> And often he took it in his arms
> Like a newborn child
> Bright-eyed, and fawning on the hand
> As its belly's needs compelled it.
>
> But in time it showed the temper
> It had from its parents; for returning
> Kindness to those that reared it
> With horrid slaughter of their cattle
> It made a feast unbidden,
> And the house was befouled with blood
> Woe irresistible to the servants,
> A vast havoc of much slaughter.
>
> (*Agamemnon* 717–34)[29]

The comparison with the lion also evoked a king, an absolute ruler: Alcibiades, whether or not he was a tyrant, was inclined to such absolute power, power that was sown with risks for the future.

Some scholars[30] have taken this to suggest Aristophanes's endorsement of Alcibiades's return, knowing that he came with a certain style—in other words, as a dictator. But announcing it in the middle of the theater was tantamount to a rejection. Even the idea of a lion, in whatever fashion, only reinforced that impression. The play actually poses the problem more than a solution. We can say that ultimately the two tragedians are in agreement.

---

29. Translated by Hugh Lloyd-Jones (University of California Press, 1979).

30. See Hatzfeld, 330–31. On the comparison with the lion, see E. F.Bloedow, "On 'Nurturing Lions in the State': Alcibiades' Entry on the Political Stage in Athens," *Klio* 73 (1991): 49–63, which uses the image to condemn Alcibiades's beginnings.

After these observations, Aristophanes has Euripides and Aeschylus propose other measures for improving and strengthening the state.

The point is that the question was asked, and that, apparently, one year after his demotion, the city continued to ask itself if it shouldn't rely on Alcibiades once more.

This brings to mind the subject of the capriciousness of the populace. But it really goes beyond this, and Aristophanes's text encourages us to pursue the topic. Before replying to the question about Alcibiades, Euripides asks what opinion the city holds of him, and Dionysus answers by quoting a line from tragedy, slightly different versions of which have been used.[31] This verse describes the passion of a heart divided between love and hate. He says: "It loves him and hates him and wants to possess him."

The opinions of the two poets explain a lot about why Alcibiades was recalled. But they also explain all the different emotions this exceptional man aroused. More than the differences between friends and enemies, they portray Athens as a living person, ambivalent about what it wants, captivated by Alcibiades, bitterly resentful of the harm he has done, but incapable of doing without him.

This emotional ambivalence corresponds perfectly to the two sides of the man—his incomparable gifts and his unscrupulousness. In it there is sensitivity to the fact that this is characteristic of the people, and is also perfectly characteristic of all Alcibiades's relationships. His relationship with Socrates, remember, was marked by emotion and annoyance, tenderness and rejection. His relationships in Sparta or Sardis were equally emotional: people adored him, or wouldn't have him, or wanted him back.

Alcibiades offers an exemplary political model that lends itself quite well to the analysis of a historian like Thucydides; but also attached to him were the contradictions of his personality.

Athens did want "to possess him." But his situation remained unchanged. The scene in the *Frogs* provided an explanation for why: there had been too many problems, too much fear about his character and his ambition, too many dashed hopes, too much resentment. It was simply too late: Alcibiades never returned to Athens.

---

31. The scholiast says that this verse is borrowed from *Phrouroi* by Ion of Chios but has been somewhat revised. Since then, it has taken different forms in Latin.

11

A Final Appearance

Alcibiades was securely within his fortifications in Thrace, an independent operator.

He certainly kept his eye on Athens. And he was not without resources. He had built a personal army with Thracian mercenaries. With them, he was able to collect booty. And these resources would allow him to take action.

First, locally. For Thrace was experiencing problems and revolts: he could intervene and help the king win. Or he could look around and, as Plutarch said, "[make] things safe for the neighboring Greek settlements, so that they did not have to worry about being raided by the barbarian tribesmen" (36.5). That also meant watching the towns that he had recently restored to Athens' control. Could this have been a way to win back Athenian favor and perhaps engineer a second return?

The idea of a small, independent kingdom near the straits was not without precedent. The famous Miltiades, the victor at Marathon, drew his power from the government of the Chersonese, a government owing to the fact that his uncle, also called Miltiades, had been the tyrant of the Chersonese. Once again, we are forced to admire the speed with which Alcibiades, shaken by the recent events, instantly conceived a new political strategy, a bold one capable of correcting the situation. He set to work right away. He was already working on a plan.

But he had to wait.

Actually, he may have thought his chance had come with the battle of Arginusae. This was a naval battle begun under his successor, Conon, in the autumn of 406. The battle was a disaster: Athens lost twenty-five triremes, men, and equipment; worst of all, the leaders had failed in their sacred duty to retrieve the dead and dying. A gripping trial ensued. The generals who were involved in the battle were demoted. They in turn blamed the ships' officers, who had not carried out their orders, and those officers blamed the storm. There were bitter arguments about the process. At this time, Socrates appears and is the only one who refused any action or any form of judgment that did not conform to the law. The affair ended with a verdict of death for the eight generals charged, of whom six, who were in Athens, were executed. Athenians would come to regret this, as they always did in such cases.

While these events did not concern Alcibiades, they might have given him an opening, exposing as they did the complete disorder in Athens. And there must have been some efforts on his behalf: this is precisely the time of Aristophanes's comedy the *Frogs*, discussed in the previous chapter.

But nothing happened. Alcibiades would reappear in Athenian history only once, the following year. Under circumstances that were shocking and unforgettable.

It happened on the eve of the battle that would mark the final and definitive defeat of Athens, the defeat at Aegospotami. It took place near Alcibiades's fortress, at the entry of the straits that bordered the Chersonese.

Lysander, who had just finished repairing the fleet, suddenly set off from Rhodes for the Hellespont. He reached Abydos. Learning of that, the Athenians in turn headed north. While Lysander was taking back Lampsacus, very close by, the Athenians reached the Chersonese, wishing to take back Sestos on the northern coast. But they wished to be close to Lysander's fleet and moored at Aegospotami, a small, obscure village whose name means "the streams of the goats": a spot on the north side, but just across from Lysander in Lampsacus. This village would become famous in Greek history.

Between the two fleets was the Hellespont. Xenophon emphasizes that it was not wide at this point, only fifteen stadia, or less than three kilometers.

The two fleets have come face to face. Athens had 180 ships in a bad moorage. Lysander had a fleet in excellent shape (Cyrus had granted him additional subsidies) and a fine port. It was in his interest to wait.

He acted accordingly, appearing ready to engage but never leaving the port. He did this for four days.

And this is when Alcibiades, completely by surprise, showed up. He suddenly appeared in the Athenian camp, confident in his experience and what he had been observing. He offered himself as an adviser at the most critical moment, a moment of high drama, and proved once more his incomparable abilities.

From one of his forts he had seen and understood everything. He observed that the mooring of the Athenian fleet was vulnerable, just a simple beach with no nearby town. He knew that they would have to have all their provisions brought from Sestos. This is what he told the generals. He had also seen how things were going and Lysander's advantage. Each time the fleet returned to shore without Lysander engaging in combat, the Athenian crews felt confident, relaxed: Plutarch wrote that the crew would "disperse and roam around wherever they wanted when they were on land, while there was a sizable enemy fleet anchored nearby, which was trained to move silently into action without needing orders from more than one man" (36.6). Plutarch also said that Alcibiades could not see all this with indifference. He came, he analyzed, he advised.

A writer of fiction would have to search long and hard to create a more dramatic scene, one more fraught with symbolism. At the very moment of crisis, before the battle that would eclipse forever the glory of Athens, this exile, this solitary man rides in on a horse, from out of nowhere, offering the very best advice—and no one listened! True, the wise counselor who is ignored is a recurring theme in Greek history and in tragedy. In this case, he appears unexpected and at the most poignant moment. Alcibiades comes to the Athenians as a true apparition. It is the ultimate irony that this man who had always been able to persuade people, even when he was offering the worst advice, could persuade no longer. He gave a warning, but Athens was set on its path, to its peril.

We know why the generals were annoyed and suspicious. Why would they let the man Athens had rejected tell them what to do? Were they supposed to back off again and let him lead? All jealousy aside, they must have been horrified by his arrival, unsure of his intentions, shocked by his advice. All the terrible things he had done to Athens weighed on their judgment and ruined whatever chance he had of finally being able to be of service. The response, the insolence of it, revealed their feelings. Their names were Tydeus and Menandrus.[1] They ordered Alcibiades to leave, saying: "Others are in command now, not you," and, as Xenophon said: "We are the generals, not you."[2]

Alcibiades departed, suspecting, according to Plutarch, "that there was treachery afoot." In leaving, he made another of his provocative claims, saying that "if the commanders had not been so rude to him, he would within a few days have forced the Lacedaemonians either to have taken on the Athenian fleet despite their reluctance to do so or to have abandoned their ships."[3]

Could he have done that? It is not out of the question. Alcibiades had more than advice to offer. Diodorus (as well as Cornelius Nepos) suggests that he offered the generals the support of his connections to various Thracian kinglets. And this is what he meant by that final remark quoted above. Plutarch says it was possible, "if he had struck at the Lacedaemonians by land with a large force of Thracian javelineers and horsemen, and thrown their camp into confusion."[4] He offered not just the advice of a good general, but an alliance and the support of his long experience. All of which added to the accountability of the generals.

They would pay dearly for their attitude. Lysander fell upon the Athenian forces, which, as he knew, were (as they frequently were) imprudently dispersed; the triremes were empty or half staffed with rowers. Nine ships managed to escape: all the others were taken by the shore. Lysander captured most of the men who were ashore and took all—ships and men—to Lampsacus. A court ruled on the fate of the prisoners, and three thousand

1. Xenophon. Plutarch names only Tydeus.
2. Plutarch 37.1; Xenophon 2.1.26.
3. This would involve abandoning the ships to fight on the ground, as Alcibiades suggests below.
4. Texts cited are Diodorus 13.105; Cornelius Nepos, *Alc.* 8.3; Plutarch 37.

men were slaughtered.[5] The war was almost over. Lysander soon took Athens, burned the fleet, and destroyed the Long Walls that had guaranteed Athens safety and independence.

If the generals had listened to Alcibiades, would history would have been profoundly altered? Who knows?

Even Alcibiades was caught in the middle of the disaster and defeat. With Lysander ruling the entire region, he could not stay. With Athens defeated, Sparta established the regime of the Thirty Tyrants; many people were executed or banished. Alcibiades, feared by many, was exiled—along with his friend Thrasybulus. Even Alcibiades's son was banished. The Thirty hoped thereby to eliminate a possible rival leader and the possibility of any action against them. Alcibiades could not go over to Sparta or seek refuge with Tissaphernes. To whom would he go for safety? There was only one person left: this was the one man he had defeated without a personal quarrel, and that was the other satrap, Pharnabazus. We are reminded that this was the one who had shown him respect. And there was even some gossip about the personal deal made between the two men.[6]

Pharnabazus—that meant Bithynia. And that is where Alcibiades goes.

But could he stay there? Pharnabazus was allied with Sparta, and Sparta could pressure him. The noose was tightening, the angry mob growing, his death knell imminent.

Sparta, led by Lysander, ordered Pharnabazus to kill Alcibiades. This, at any rate, is what almost all sources say, beginning with Isocrates, but including Plutarch and Diodorus.[7] It was not at the satrap's court that Alcibiades would die. He was there for a number of weeks, after a journey full of hardship and having lost everything he owned. But when the order came to kill him, he was not there.

---

5. The war had reached a point of bitter cruelty. The Athenians voted to cut off the right hand of all prisoners if they were victorious in battle. This fact was well known to everyone, and it enraged their adversaries against them. Adeimantus, the only general who had voted against such cruelty, was spared by the Spartans but later accused of treason by Conon.

6. See above, chapter 9.

7. Isocrates 16.40; Plutarch 38.6 (in which he tells of the scytale—a type of secret message in use in Sparta—and adds to the other reasons a desire to please King Aegis, Alcibiades's old foe); last, Diodorus 14.11.

At this point, his movements are cloudy, disappear; the accounts of this period are contradictory. One thing, however, is certain: Alcibiades had left the court of the satrap. And death would take him in the fortified town of Melissa in Phrygia.[8]

Why was he there? And where was he going?

One answer, attributed to the historian Ephorus and recounted in Diodorus and Cornelius Nepos,[9] differs from the others and is complex and tinged with misleading orientalisms. In this version, Alcibiades is supposed to have discovered a plot against the king, would reveal it to Pharnabazus, and leave in search of a safe-conduct; but Pharnabazus, fearing that this compromised him (not having to do with Sparta or the Thirty), had him killed.

This version should be rejected. But it does give us a sense of the mysteriousness surrounding this story once Alcibiades's history is separate from that of Athens.

Plutarch attests to this in alluding to a version of the story that exonerates not just Sparta and Athens but Pharnabazus as well: in this version, Alcibiades was supposed to have seduced the daughter of a prominent family and kept her with him, angering the girl's brothers and leading them to set fire to his house. Plutarch is no more convinced of this telling than Diodorus was of Ephorus's; both authors simply recount them. Clearly, each is starting to embellish . . .

However, rejecting the account of Ephorus, the questions remain: What was Alcibiades doing in Phrygia, where was he going, what did he hope for?

There is another, stirring, possibility. It seems likely that Alcibiades was going back to the king, hoping once more to return to the master, seduce him, and offer to advise him in return for sparing his life.

We will never know. But there was a precedent for this, and we know that Alcibiades was highly conscious of Athenian history. The precedent here was Themistocles, who, accused of treason, had been banished from Athens in an ostracism. Finally, after numerous detours, he wrote a letter to Artaxerxes requesting asylum. The king was moved and after a year, after Themistocles had learned the Persian language and the customs of the country, he was accorded a position with the king more important

---

8. For the location, see L. Robert, *À travers l'Asie Mineure* (1980), 257ff.
9. Diodurus 14.11; Cornelius Nepos, *Alcibiades* 9.10.

than any Greek had ever held. Looking back in time, Thucydides recounts this at the end of book 1, providing numerous details about Themistocles's arrival at the court of the one he had defeated at Salamis.

How could Alcibiades, now being hunted down like his forerunner, not have nurtured the hope of ending up like Themistocles? Themistocles was the example that Socrates had held up to him, and whom the young Alcibiades thought he could never equal. We find the example of Themistocles in relation to Alcibiades mentioned in Plato's *Alcibiades* and later in the work of Aeschines of Sphettus. In the *Gorgias*, Plato cites Themistocles as first among the men who stuffed the city with harbors and arsenals and walls, leaving it the victim of an illness, for which someday, says Socrates, Callicles will have to pay, "or my friend Alcibiades" (519a). All these connections cannot be random. Besides, the destinies of the two men bear many clear resemblances. Themistocles was the victor in the Persian Wars, the man who had built the foundation of the powerful Athenian navy, and ended in exile. His life lends itself in many respects to comparison. The comparisons arise naturally all the time. Athenaus notes that Alcibiades had learned Persian "like Themistocles." In short, we are tempted to have Alcibiades say, as he does in the play about him by Jean Galbert de Campistron: "Themistocles is always in my thoughts," a line in the tragedy that is followed by ten more drawing the comparison.[10]

Of course, Campistron is not a source. However, this passage demonstrates how easily the parallels between the two men were made.

Returning to our sources, elsewhere Plutarch offers an explanation. Speaking of Alcibiades, he wrote:

> He decided to go up to the court of Artaxerxes. He thought he would prove himself to be just as useful to the king as Themistocles had been, if the king was prepared to put him to the test, while having a better excuse for being there. For he was not going to offer his services to the king and ask him for resources so that he could attack his fellow citizens, as Themistocles had, but so that he could defend his country against its enemies. (37.7)

10. Jean Galbert de Campistron, *Alcibiade* (a play written in 1685), act 1, scene 2. The theme begins by recalling Themistocles in Persia: "That persecuted Greek who sought refuge in the same climate where I am today." The parallel continues later in the play when Alcibiades shares the same dilemma that Plutarch ascribes to Themistocles (*Them.* 31.6): to command the Persian army against Greece or refuse and anger the king.

There it is, popping up in the middle of the crisis, the old competition with Themistocles spoken of in the Socratic texts.

Some modern scholars are skeptical: they think that Plutarch, and all those who followed, were the ones seeing Themistocles as a model for Alcibiades.[11] Hence the resemblances were the result of literary projections.

How would we know? That is possible. But the two explanations can be joined. How can anyone deny that the thought might have crossed the mind of Alcibiades? His welcome by Tissaphernes could hardly fail to have caused him to reflect. And it is difficult, knowing his character, to think that this precedent did not feed his imagination and his dreams. It is natural and it is pleasing to think that in this moment of turmoil there was a glimmer of hope for a heroic outcome in one who was about to die.

For in spite of all this, he was going to die.

Unlike his life, the death of Alcibiades was obscure and miserable. It was so full of pathos that no melodrama would ever dare to go so far.

Perhaps historians who cannot know have once again invented and embellished.[12] But almost everyone relates a tale that is striking in the contrast between a brilliant life and a sorry end.

Pharnabazus sent two men close to him to carry out the assassination: his brother Bagaeus and his uncle Susamithras. The scene took place far away, in a village in Asia. There were only two characters:[13] Alcibiades and a woman, a devoted prostitute. Everything began, as it does in a tragedy, with a prophetic dream. This is what Plutarch writes, and it deserves to be quoted in full:

> So Lysander sent a message to Pharnabazus ordering him to do the deed, and Pharnabazus gave the job to his brother Bagaeus and his uncle Susamithras. Now at the time Alcibiades was living in a village in Phrygia, and he had Timandra the courtesan with him. One night he had a dream in which he was dressed in Timandra's clothes, and she was cradling his head in her arms while she made up his face like a woman's with eyeliner and white lead.

11. See B. Perrin Bernadotte, "The Death of Alcibiades," *Transactions and Proceedings of the American Philological Association* (1906): 23–37.

12. Xenophon does not tell of the death of Alcibiades, as it did not pertain to his subject (see above, "Second Interlude").

13. Cornelius Nepos adds another person, an Arcadian, faithful to the end (Athenaus 13.574e–f).

> Others say that in his dream he saw Bagaeus cutting off his head and his body burning, but they agree that the dream happened not long before his death. (39.1–7)

The first part of the dream obviously foresaw the cares that the courtesan would take with the corpse of Alcibiades. But the assassins were already at work.

"The men sent to kill him did not dare to enter the house, but surrounded it and set it on fire."

He was caught in his lair like an evil beast.

But he continued to fight.

> When Alcibiades noticed the fire, he picked up nearly all his clothes and bedding, threw them onto the flames, and then, wrapping his cloak around his left arm and holding his drawn dagger in his right hand, he dashed out of the house before the clothing caught fire. He was unharmed by the fire, and when the foreign assassins saw him, they scattered. Not one of them stood his ground against him or came up to fight him hand to hand; they kept their distance and hurled javelins and fired arrows at him instead.

He fell finally, mortally wounded. The cowardice of his assassins in sharp contrast with the faithfulness of the woman with whom he lived: "After the assassins had left, Timandra collected his body for burial. She wrapped her own clothes around the body to cover it, and gave him the most splendid and ambitious funeral she could under the circumstances." Plutarch says that Timandra was the mother of Laïs the Corinthian, whom he describes in the *Dialogue on Love* (767f) as the one whom poets sang about and greatly loved: "You know that she enflamed Greece with desire and was fought over from sea to sea." He may have been the victim of assassination in a town in Phrygia, but Alcibiades, with the panache of the brave, retained an elegance in his choice of lovers, and died in the presence of a passionate woman.

Plutarch's account agrees with that of other historians. All of them described the burning house. There is some discrepancy about the presence of Timandra and a man, or about Timandra and another woman: skeptical modern scholars suppose that these different accounts were invented to add authenticity to the story. Let's keep Timandra, at least. Knowing

Alcibiades as we do, how could we even think he was alone? Another discrepancy concerns the handling of the corpse, and relates to the two premonitory dreams. Either the corpse was prepared by Timandra, or it was decapitated by the two assassins. Cornelius Nepos clearly says that they took the head of Alcibiades back to Pharnabazus.

We will never know for sure. But two impressions emerge from all of these accounts.

What strikes us first in this whole episode is the combination of treachery and cruelty. It is a combination that, to a great extent, is the sign of barbarians. There are frequent allusions made by Greek authors to these two faults in the people of Asia, so offensive to Greek ideals. We have already seen the cruelty of another satrap, Tissaphernes, whom Plutarch described as having no integrity but great wickedness and perversity, and we encountered the cruelty of one of his lieutenants whose treachery caused the deaths of Greeks on Delos.[14] Barbarians were generally viewed by Greeks as bloodthirsty and deceitful, in contrast with themselves.[15] This explains the meaning that the modern word "barbarian" retains, signifying "cruel."

In one sense, the contrast between the assassins hiding in the shadows and the man who goes out alone, unprotected, into the flames and forces them to flee symbolizes perfectly the cultural differences of which Greeks were highly conscious. Pharnabazus's treachery and the approach at night were signs of barbarism.

However, the picture is not so black and white; it was marked with nuances as well.

We should not forget that Pharnabazus was in this instance carrying out the orders or the wishes of Lysander, and Lysander was Greek. Adding to this point, even Plutarch had faulted him for the severity he had shown throughout his life; that had been apparent after the battle of Aegospotami. True, but Athenians had shown themselves capable of great cruelty, at least of cruel intentions, at that time. Alcibiades's exile by the Thirty, ordered without a valid rationale, doomed him to what would

---

14. See above, chapter 7.
15. On barbarian cruelty, see our two recent studies: "Les barbares dans la pensée de la Grèce antique," *Phoenix* (1993): 283–92; and "Cruauté barbare et cruautés grecques," *Wiener Studien*, Festschrift H. Schwabl (1994–95): 187–96.

follow.[16] To the contrast between Greeks and barbarians we must allow
for an additional element: the moral hardening that was increasingly part
of this period. This hardening was no doubt a function of the intensity of
the battles that were causing rage in Greece and also in the cities. Was not
the narrative of Alcibiades's life riddled with condemnations and assas-
sinations and from one chapter to the next?

Still, this hardening did not pass without a reaction among the Greeks.
Unlike barbarians, or at least those known to them, the Greeks were
shocked by their own behavior. Thus we find, penetrating the works of
some authors, the softer values like indulgence, tolerance, humanity, and
these burst out everywhere at the end of the war.[17]

Alcibiades was crushed by these conflicts, which the century that followed would work hard to cover up with a renewed idealism.

In this way, Alcibiades's death assumes meaning in the history of moral
ideas. But it does not need such commentary to have a strong impact and
to take on a tragic quality, obvious to everyone.

Naturally the details of it are uncertain. How could there be any cer-
tainty? Alcibiades's end came in a faraway place, with almost no witnesses. Contemporary authors never speak of it. The first source we have
was an author who lived five long centuries after the event, and the old-
est sources they cited wrote at least fifty years after the event. Literary
taste and imagination may have played a part in the account. The fact is,
though, that the end it describes was one worthy of his life. It has all the
elements necessary to move us and to encourage us to reflect on the highs
and lows of human destiny.

It moves us because this man, whose plots and subterfuges we have
seen, suddenly reveals the full strength of his spirit. It makes us think
of the lovely portrayal of him by Jean-Jacques Barthélemy in *Travels of
Anacharsis the Younger in Greece:* "One could not look into his heart to
find the stature virtue produces; but one found there the boldness that a
sense of superiority produces. No obstacle, no suffering could overcome
or discourage him; he seemed to be convinced that those who lack the will

16. In the tragedy by Campistron cited above, the threat came from a Greek delegation
that took credit for Alicibiades's death; no one else wished to do him harm. At times the play
contains a trace of historical truth.

17. On the emergence of this, see my book *La douceur dans la pensée grecque* (Les Belles
Lettres, 1979).

to do everything they want to do are those who do not dare to do everything they are capable of doing." His action in confronting death gave to Alcibiades the stature of a hero.

Even his death was that of a tragic hero. Like Sophocles's Oedipus,[18] Alcibiades plunged from the height of glory to deepest disaster. The most talented of Athenians, the man with the greatest intellect, beauty, and courage, who led first Athens' government and then Sparta's, and then that of a Persian satrap, the man given the most sumptuous homecoming Athens could provide, was finally assassinated, by order of a barbarian; a solitary figure rejected by everyone except perhaps a woman. He had experienced everything. He was not yet fifty years old.

Athenaeus wrote, in the third century CE, that Alcibiades's tomb could still be seen in the small town where he died. The emperor Hadrian erected a statue to Alcibiades, and he made an annual sacrifice there.[19]

There were other statues of Alcibiades—five or six centuries after his death—whereas the name of Pharnabazus has been forgotten by everyone and Lysander is very little known. Death is not the end for a man like Alcibiades.

18. See above, chapter 5.
19. Cornelius Nepos 13.574c.

12

Repercussions

Alcibiades was dead. His story, however, was not over. On the contrary, after his death and the end of the war, all the Athenians were fascinated by him. He became the center of intense literary activity. Historians studied his career and attempted to assess it. First Thucydides, and shortly after, Xenophon's *Hellenica*. Questions about Alcibiades and opinions of him preoccupied many others. Alcibiades's son underwent trials. Socrates was tried and condemned to death at this time, an event that provided an opportunity to inquire into the role he had played in the life of Alcibiades. Plato, Xenophon, all or almost all the Socratic philosophers started writing about Alcibiades, drawing inspiration from the lessons of his life. His personal history created a barrage of analysis extending to our own day.

First, though, we return to the quarrelling in Athens, particularly about Alcibiades, beginning with the trials of his son.

The son was an unfortunate substitute: he had resented his father, and Alcibiades had hardly cared for him.[1] Whether he was being attacked or defended, the real object of every action was his father.

We described previously the business of the chariot that Alcibiades had used in the Olympic Games of 416.[2] The case was retried more than fifteen years later, and we have the second part of a speech written by Isocrates on that occasion, between 398 and 395, for Alcibiades's son. It is speech 16, entitled *On the Team of Horses*. More than a defense of his son, this is a eulogy of the father. Isocrates recalls that the same men who destroyed the democracy had exiled Alcibiades (the second time); he retells the whole story of the mysteries as a coup mounted by people who were actually enemies of the democracy. He mentions the obstinacy of the enemies of Alcibiades, his condemnation, and declares that Alcibiades had thus been "compelled" to seek refuge in Sparta (9). Next, he accuses the enemies of Alcibiades of bad faith; it is then that he compares Alcibiades's actions in exile with the actions of the democrats of 404.[3] Finally, the speech praises his action at the time of his return, his efforts with Tissaphernes, his victories, and claims that under his command "never did the enemy erect a trophy of victory over you" (21). Beyond this, Isocrates goes over his ancestry, his youth, his victories at Olympus: in short, the whole of Alcibiades's life is recalled, twelve pages of defense and praise, and not a single fault. The text is one of unqualified ebullience. And all that, I repeat, less than ten years after the death of Alcibiades and in a newly democratic Athens.

It seems, moreover, that this is not simply the speech of a lawyer. Fifty years later, Isocrates returned to the subject of Alcibiades the man, without the need to do so. He did this in a treatise entitled *Ad Philippum*. And while in this work he recognizes all the harm that Alcibiades did to Athens by helping Sparta, the orator offers him to Philip as the prime example of a man's power.[4]

---

1. He had given up one of his father's forts; on the latter's feelings about him, see Lysias 14.27.

2. See above, chapter 2.

3. See above, chapter 6.

4. Isocrates, *Philip* 58–61. Consistent with his great idea, Isocrates shows how Alcibiades harmed Sparta insofar as he made it acquire a maritime empire.

In contrast to these eulogies, we have the accusations. Alcibiades's son was prosecuted primarily because he had failed in his duties to the state; he claimed to have served in the cavalry without undergoing an exam. This legal affair comes a few years later than the one for which Isocrates had written his speech. The speeches *Against Alcibiades* have come down to us under the name of Lysias: their authenticity has been challenged but not by everyone. In any event, this case should not have been about the father. Yet there is Alcibiades again at the center of the debate.

Certainly, it is in these speeches that we discover all the scandals involving the son (25–28). Questionable morals, dinners with courtesans, prison time, massacres, incest, it is all there, with names. It is easy to recognize the paternal habit of doing whatever he pleased. But besides these attacks on the son, there were others, many of them, against the father—either to show that he offered no defense of the conduct of his son, or to affirm that the latter had a lot to account for. Alcibiades should have been executed as a young man. He moved against Athens; he enabled the Lacedaemonians to occupy Decelea. He stirred the islands to revolt. And the author responded to Isocrates's argument that compared Alcibiades in exile to the democrats of 404; he refuted it. He even denied the competence of the man: betrayal is easy, and once he came back, Alcibiades actually failed in everything (36–37).[5] The speech goes so far as to accuse Alcibiades of having handed over the Athenian fleet to Lysander (38). The political attacks knew no limits.

In some ways, these speeches by Isocrates and Lysias provide a passionate postwar enactment of the trial of Alcibiades. And these speeches oppose one another: the speech in favor recognized nothing wrong; the one opposed found nothing right. Alcibiades's friends and enemies were still confronting each other, as they had during his lifetime.[6]

There was something more serious than the trials: there was the question of Socrates. Here the repercussions were enormous.

Socrates had never hidden his interest in the young Alcibiades. Now, the democracy restored, some people were beginning to think that Socrates had actually had some dubious characters in his circle. This suspicion was no doubt in the minds of those who attacked him.

---

5. Cf. above, chapter 10.

6. Lysias's speech was delivered against important figures who were coming out in favor of the young Alcibiades, urging that they be ignored; the city was still just as passionately divided as it had been during the life of the great man.

Socrates's trial took place in 399, five years after Alcibiades's death. There were two charges foremost in the accusation: Socrates was guilty of failing to recognize the city's gods as gods and introducing new ones; and he was guilty of corrupting the youth. The crimes were punishable by death.

We can put aside the accusation about the gods and Socrates's famous "daemon." But how are we to understand the charge of corrupting the youth?

It was not simply a matter of talking with them about his so-called impiety.[7] It may have been about taking the place of their fathers and leading them away from practical pursuits. Xenophon's *Apology of Socrates* suggests that this was the case for at least one of his accusers, Anytus: Socrates had turned his son away from working as a tanner as his family wished (29).

That alone, however, would not have warranted death. Anytus had other reasons for complaint. At this time, at least, he was a confirmed democrat, among those who had returned by force after the tyranny of the Thirty. Some of the people around Socrates (as well as Plato) were seriously compromised, among them Critias, the most important and committed of the Thirty. In Socrates's trial, was there a political aspect? Yes, probably.[8] In letter 7, Plato contrasts the trial with the moderation shown in general by the victorious democrats.[9] It is difficult, however, to separate the political from the moral. Even today, who can say what part each of these aspects plays when accusing someone of having "collaborated"? Corrupting the youth meant taking away their respect for democratic institutions, making them enemies of the people, or men without principles.

In any case, Alcibiades could be cited on both accounts: Alcibiades, who had spent time with Socrates and later acted out of unscrupulous ambition, to the great regret of Athens; and who had been accused of aspiring to tyranny and who had at one time plotted with the oligarchs of 411.

---

7. The order of these two charges differs in Plato and Xenophon: in the *Apology* 24b, Plato puts the corruption of the youth first.

8. Paul Cloché refuses to see in the trial any attack on the oaths of reconciliation (*La restauration démocratique à Athènes en 403 av. J-C.* [Paris, 1915]). For a more political point of view, see J. Luccioni, *Les idées politiques et sociales de Xénophon* (Orphrys, 1918); and Delebecque, *Essai*, 87.

9. Plato, letter 7, 325c–d.

Alcibiades and Critias were dead, one in 404, the other in 403; but both names were recalled with dread and counted, in every way, as compromised disciples of Socrates.

We can assume that the speeches made at the trial were specifically aimed at these two men. Perhaps Polycrates's pamphlet against Socrates, published a few years after the trial, was even clearer. Nevertheless, it is Xenophon who is the clearest. The day he wished to defend the memory of his teacher by writing the *Memorabilia*, he began with two chapters responding directly to the two main charges: the gods and the corruption of the youth. The second part of his response is formal: "Among the associates of Socrates were Critias and Alcibiades; and none wrought so many evils to the state. For Critias, in the days of the oligarchy, bore the palm for greed and violence; Alcibiades, for his part, exceeded all in licentiousness and insolence under the democracy" (1.2.12).

This is why Alcibiades became a grievance against Socrates, how he contributed to his death, and how the defense of Socrates will always involve ruling on the case of Alcibiades.

This may seem unjust and simplistic: no one today would dream of incriminating a teacher (much less condemn him to death) simply because some of his students turned out to be bad people. But there are several things to remember: first of all, the fundamental importance of the city at that time; second, that it was not simply a matter of the lessons but of the deep, personal bond involving adults, and even more that Alcibiades had been a beloved student, a fact seen and known by everyone. Finally, and most important, in Socrates's teachings, which were heard by many or heard about, he had frequently attacked the leaders of democratic Athens, talked about the dangers of incompetent voters, and said other things that seemed a threat to Athenian democracy. It is enough to recall the play Aristophanes devoted to Socrates in 423, the *Clouds*, and all the injustices included in it, to imagine the shape that words like these could take when delivered, correctly for the most part, into the political realm. In his own way, Socrates did teach politics since he taught about justice: it was easy to think that this teaching involved partisan ideas.

In all of this there was something to fear, and reason to think Socrates capable of inspiring a Critias and an Alcibiades, to the great misfortune of Athens.

According to the sources, we sometimes find the two names, sometimes only that of Critias.[10] However, there is no doubt about the basis for the accusation of corrupting the youth.

Xenophon's response is simple and insistent. He said that both Critias and Alcibiades were ambitious men; they wished to associate with Socrates only to prepare themselves for success, and then went their own way; they never wanted to live like Socrates. People change during their lives. If Socrates had had a bad influence on them, they would have been at their worst during the time they were around him. What happened was just the opposite. Both of them were drunk with self-importance, ceded to temptations, and turned away from Socrates, who, moreover, had never approved of their inclinations. Nevertheless, Alcibiades had developed a taste for political discussions at a young age. Politics turned him away from Socrates (47). To address this issue, Xenophon named a whole list of good disciples of Socrates, those who followed his teaching in pursuit of the good and who were above reproach.

This straightforward text deserves to be cited first. But it is far from being an isolated case and far from being the earliest. It is actually less directly about Alcibiades than many others. Besides the works of Xenophon himself that deal with Socrates's case without speaking of Alcibiades by name—for example, his short *Apology of Socrates* and his *Symposium*—we confront, beginning with the trial of Socrates, a series of impressive works, as if suddenly everyone wanted to have a say about Alcibiades.

In fact, who did not? It is enough to enumerate the titles. For most of these works, there is *only* a title. But that testimony suffices.

Alcibiades of Plato.

A second *Alcibiades,* also attributed to Plato, the authenticity of which is dubious.

Alcibiades by a friend of Socrates named Aeschines of Sphettus (not to be confused with the orator Aeschines): the text is lost, but a rhetor of the second century CE preserved extracts from it.[11]

---

10. See Aeschines, *Against Timarchus* 173: "Did you put to death Socrates the sophist, fellow citizens, because he was shown to have been the teacher of Critias, one of the Thirty who put down the democracy?"

11. About Aeschines of Sphettus, see H. Ditmar's article in *Philologische Untersuchungen* 21 (1912): 65–173, which, for the titles cited here, challenges the authenticity of various texts.

Axiochus by the same Aeschines of Sphettus, concerning an uncle of Alcibiades and mentioning Alcibiades only in passing; we know about this work thanks to Athenaeus, an author of the third century CE.

Alcibiades by Antisthenes, fragments of which relating to Alcibiades are also in Athenaeus.

Alcibiades by Phaedo, the same Phaedo who gave his name to a dialogue by Plato; the entire text has disappeared and is simply mentioned in Diogenes Laertius.

Alcibiades by Euclid of Megara, another Socratic and not to be confused with the mathematician; this work, like the previous one, is lost.

That is quite a list: and no doubt incomplete. The vague fragments that have survived indicate that a legend is being born. For a good example of the kind cited above regarding Socrates,[12] we find gratuitous accusations like those of Antisthenes who accused Alcibiades of incest with his mother, daughter, and sister!

As we can tell, Socrates's disciples were not always kind to someone whose life had brought shame on their master. Still, we should not try to make too much of these long-lost texts, except to note that they testify to unprecedented interest in a single individual.

It is, however, worth considering just what Alcibiades signified in Plato's work.

First of all, it is possible, from the standpoint of this book, to recognize a number of those traits I described earlier that now find full justification.

At the moment when Alcibiades entered politics, the choice put before him had been clearly indicated in Plato's *Alcibiades*.[13] This dialogue now joins a series and assumes its true meaning, that of a defense.

Of course, there is Plato's famous *Apology of Socrates*. But it does not name Alcibiades.

If, like me (and others, including Maurice Croiset),[14] you believe the *Alcibiades* is a work by Plato, you will agree that it was written very early,

---

12. Above, chapter 2.
13. Above, "First Interlude."
14. Also Friedländer; but many others are opposed. Dittmar believes that this dialogue was inspired by some passages in Socratic texts, among those that are enumerated here. See R. S. Bluck, *Classical Quarterly*, n.s., 3 (1953): 46–52.

no doubt during Plato's time in Megara (and thus before the *Apology*). In that case, it constituted a separate response, entirely focused on the question of Alcibiades.

In fact, Plato here portrays Alcibiades as a man of unbounded ambition. But Socrates makes clear that Alcibiades was not ready to pursue his ambitions because he knew too little: first, he would need to understand justice. Alcibiades agrees to that. But Socrates remains doubtful—which Plato's knowledge of the ending clearly reflects: "I fear, not because I distrust anything in your nature, but because I see the power of this city, that it will overcome me and you."

There could be no better defense of Socrates than to show the intention of all his efforts and the nature of Alcibiades's ambition and of the popular will that would prevent those efforts from succeeding.

We can also now understand why all these texts emphasized the extreme youth of Alcibiades. We saw it in the *Symposium*.[15] Naturally, this was even more evident in the *Alcibiades*, a dialogue in which we hear almost the entire exchange between Socrates and Alcibiades and in which the latter is preparing to address the people "very soon."[16]

In addition, the young man is naive and compliant. It is the very lack of boldness that has misled some critics. But in the series of texts we have just surveyed, the meaning of this extreme youth is very clear: it brings out the fact that Alcibiades was close to Socrates only long before his political career, and that his subsequent faults did not correspond to the teaching of Socrates but rather to his rejection of that teaching.

And why did he reject it? It is important to note that, from Socrates's very first words, the main question was ambition, and in the next dialogue, Socrates contrasts that with justice. This central theme of Platonism starts right here, in relation to Alcibiades.

Finally, we see emerging the idea that a life led in ignorance and in pursuit only of material wealth is a life of misery. This eminently Socratic idea suggests, indirectly, that ambition can be the ruin of a man or of a state. In the case of Alcibiades, who did not listen to Socrates, these miseries, his own and that of the state, were in fact realized with great potency.

15. See above, chapter 1.
16. Plato, *Alcibiades* 106c. See also 123d: "before he was even twenty years old." On the fact that previously Socrates had followed Alcibiades "in silence," see 106a.

Plato avoids all allusion: he adheres to the ideal and would not rely on arguments of a practical interest; he offers only at the end a shining image of the man and the city that would choose not absolute power, but virtue.

If I am insisting on this point, it is because many of the writings and teachings of Plato will later depend on it: everything happens as if the case of Alcibiades had haunted him and then had, from near or far, nourished this perception.

I know that the *Alcibiades* may not be authentic. In that case, encounters with a variety of Platonic dialogues would have been the inspiration for the author of the *Alcibiades*. Even in such a case, however, the suggestion made here remains valid. That is the important point. Because in the end, we can remove the *Alcibiades* the way one might remove the tracing paper that fixes the place names on a geographical map, while the map is silent; still, the names remain useful for reading the map, giving it meaning and precision. In the same way, we can remove the suspect dialogue. There remains Alcibiades the personage, clearly named in the dialogue, with all the problems raised by his association with Socrates, who provides a line of argument that holds up and—is surprisingly satisfying. It would still be about Alcibiades even in a text where he is not named.

This is most of all true in the *Gorgias*.

The links are obvious. In this—a dialogue whose authenticity is not in doubt—can be found all the various questions and themes found in the *Alcibiades*: the great men, like Pericles, never transmitted to their sons their political powers. And the city had no need of walls, navies, roads, or greatness, only virtue. These themes are renewed, filled out, vividly portrayed in the *Gorgias*.

But in particular, these reprises evince a similarity in their general inspiration. The *Gorgias*, as we know, is about rhetoric, but also, besides rhetoric, about practical success obtained in defiance of justice. The dialogue takes place over three periods and with three interlocutors, each increasingly forceful. The last one, Callicles, is not familiar from any other work and is neither a sophist nor a teacher of rhetoric: he is an ambitious man, ambitious without limits, without scruples, who defends the right of the strongest. This quality alone suggests that the memory of Alcibiades is not far away.

Naturally, I am not claiming that Callicles is Alcibiades: that is not the point. I explained elsewhere that Callicles seems to me to be a fictional figure meant to express outwardly what is hidden at the heart of the teaching of the sophists as some disciples understood it.[17] This is unchecked ambition, the same ambition that Euripides portrayed in high relief in 410 in the character of Eteocles,[18] and which was denounced by Thucydides in the same period, the period of the most disgraceful plots. We have to think that Plato too, more than anyone else, was making a connection to the most ambitious of all, Alcibiades. Callicles is not Alcibiades, but there is a lot of Alcibiades in him. More to the point, Socrates uses the occasion to condemn the same behavior as it relates to states, and the error of those who try to acquire power through force. Everyone knew that he was talking about the empire of Athens, the imperial tyranny that expanded and then sank of its own weight. Could Plato not have been thinking of the man who was the author of the great plan, who had wanted to conquer not just Sicily but the entire Greek world for Athens, and who in the end left the city without its allies, its fleet, or its walls? Alcibiades was included in that condemnation as well.

Moreover, toward the end of the dialogue, Socrates, criticizing the political leaders of Athens who had pursued power at the expense of justice, says that the city, having grown fat on advantages, and feeling itself slip into the weakness that naturally follows, will begin to blame their successors: "And if you are not on your guard, they may perhaps lay hands on you and on my friend Alcibiades, when they have lost what they once owned in addition to what they have since acquired, though you are not the authors of their troubles, but perhaps the collaborators in, them" (519a–b).

Alcibiades's name, and the allusion to future disappointments, seems to be both a confirmation and an admission: the example of Alcibiades fostered Plato's thinking and led him to transform the virtuous principles of the teacher, to which Alcibiades did not adhere, into a deepened political theory about politics and its aims.

All of this does not end here: besides the *Gorgias,* there is the *Republic,* an analysis of what justice ought to be in a state. The work emphasizes the

---

17. *Les grands sophistes dans l'Athènes de Périclès* (Fallois, 1988), 210–17. Nor do I accept the absence of Alcibiades's scruples on the teaching of the sophists, as Bloedow does: *Klio* (1991): 64–65. In both cases, the connection is an indirect one.

18. See above, chapter 8.

necessity of subordinating everything to the good of the whole. Alcibiades has been forgotten, but his life gave rise to questions that would continue to grow at the heart of Platonism. We could say, finally, that what might seem excessive in the rigor of Plato's city can be explained by a fear of seeing the rebirth in a city of an Alcibiades or a Callicles.

Before we leave Plato, the analysis of these ideas allows us to pause briefly at Plato's conclusions and to compare them to Thucydides's conclusions.

Both authors blame ambition and see in it the cause of the final disaster. But Plato and Thucydides identify a different point at which ambition goes too far.

Thucydides thought the government of Pericles was excellent, that his policy was a wise one, and that if Athens had just listened to him, it would have triumphed in the war and held the empire. Thucydides describes how the empire became harsh and more and more ambitious; and that led to a growing number of hostilities and to poor decisions that caused it to fall. But for Thucydides, there had been a time when Athens was great, a time he extols through the words of Pericles, in brilliant terms. He talks forcefully about the city's principles, its irresistible character, and its beauty. He links Athens to virtue itself: "Feast your eyes on her from day to day, till love of her fills your hearts; and then when all her greatness will break upon you, you must reflect that it was by courage, sense of duty, and a keen feeling of honor in action that men were enabled to win all this" (2.43.1). Thucydides makes a clear distinction between Pericles and his successors, between the time of civic responsibility and that of personal ambitions.

Plato, on the other hand, includes all the great men of the past—Themistocles, Cimon, Miltiades, Pericles—in his censure. He blames the very principle of empire, of political power itself. He makes a connection between Alcibiades and his predecessors. And for this reason we must return to the ideal state—ideal and unreal. The divorce between the political thought of the historian and political philosophy is right here: Alcibiades's troubles are etched in these two diverging categories.

All of that would make a strongly coherent logic were it not for the dialogue with which this book opens, namely the *Symposium*. Now, at the end of our journey, we must return to it.

Why was the disciple who came to ruin chosen as the most brilliant figure in this dialogue? Why bestow on him, of all people, Socrates's ringing praise, praise that is found nowhere else in this work? Why here, this open, perceptive Alcibiades, so close to Socrates? Is this not inconsistent with the later reaction and condemnation that we have just seen?

We should first note that, even in these texts about his life and the political role that Alcibiades ultimately adopted, Plato's tone, or at least the tone he has Socrates express, always contains a trace of affectionate indulgence. In the *Alcibiades*, he has no difficulty perceiving the potential of the adolescent Alcibiades. The skepticism he shows in acknowledging this potential is a nice way of showing that though he does not doubt Alcibiades, he doubts those forces that will weigh "on you and on me." In the *Gorgias*, at the moment of the most dire predictions about the future, he again refers to "my friend Alcibiades." This phrase reflects a charming reluctance to call him guilty; instead, he is "just a little complicit."

In the *Symposium,* the subject of the dialogue is not ambition or politics; it is love. Just as the prophetess Diotima, whom Socrates quotes, presents the benefits of love as giving birth to the beautiful, just as the love she describes inspires in the one who loves the most beautiful thoughts in order to share them with the beloved, thoughts that lead each one to the contemplation of the Beautiful, so the teaching of Socrates, inspired by love and inspiring love, may lead souls to the other type of love, lead them to the Good. This is no longer a time for rigorous dialectic, nor for arguments about the just. Now another quality is introduced, one that links Socrates's teaching to a kind of religious initiation, and that evolves from love in the ordinary sense of the word to love of the Good.

To suggest this novel quality, Socrates could only be invoked by a man inspired—even intoxicated—by a man with whom Socrates had a close and affectionate friendship; by a man above all capable of discovering that the kind of love Socrates bore for him was different from what he expected, from the kind with which he was familiar.

The text then unfolds on two planes, as we mentioned earlier without trying to explain the reason for it:[19] first, a portrait of Socrates as seen by someone with enough self-confidence to speak freely, but also sensitive enough to admit to feeling confused, moved, troubled, by the revelations Socrates reveals to him; and second, a simple account, but one full of

---

19. Above, chapter 2.

self-conscious irony—the account of an amorous overture that ends with a lofty lesson about pure love and pure beauty.

At the end of this episode, Alcibiades is both vexed and full of respect. He understands how exceptional Socrates is. He grasps the wonder of teaching by intimation, and of this sacred discourse, "approaching all that should be kept in mind if one is to become a man of honor."

Alcibiades concludes with these words. The admission that he expresses in this passage is the best possible illustration of this transposition of love, placing at the heart of Platonism a warmth and an intensity that the dialectic too often causes us to forget.

There is, then, no contradiction between the texts that we have seen and this one: one may regret the choices Alcibiades made in his life and take from them a moral lesson, and at the same time recognize in him, better than in anyone else, the interpreter of the miracle associated with the figure of Socrates, a miracle by which love is elevated to the Good and makes one want it.

We have no hesitation recognizing at the end of this book what we saw at the beginning—the image of a seductive and provocative young man, wearing an ivy and violet crown, who arrives late at a banquet, already drunk. We can forget the adventures that will come, the plots and betrayals, the glory and the death. We can, in spite of everything, love Alcibiades, the beautiful Alcibiades. And we can imagine that the extraordinary turmoil of his life can be appreciated in scale and substance only in juxtaposition with the portrait drawn by a writer of an imagined dialogue, with which Alcibiades had nothing to do.

What remains, as always, is literary art.

CONCLUSION

Alcibiades has come down to us by the dual path of historical and literary texts. The story of his life requires consulting both kinds of sources. The honors bestowed on his tomb by the emperor Hadrian have served as the epilogue of Alcibiades's death. This is not surprising since Hadrian was known to be an admirer of Greek culture. Nor is it surprising that cultivated Romans knew about Alcibiades. They read Plato, the Greek historians, and later Plutarch. Cicero often quoted our hero. And in addition to the biography written by Cornelius Nepos, cited frequently in this work, we encounter Alcibiades in all the scholars of the imperial age: Valerius Maximus, Frontinus, Justin.

After that? A heavy veil of silence fell. There is no mention of Alcibiades through the Middle Ages until the reappearance of Greek texts.

In the fifteenth century we find, in an odd source, an indication of just how unfamiliar these facts and names had become. It was Villon actually, whose *Ballade des dames du temps jadis* added to the names of famous courtesans the name of one Archepiada, in whom some scholars found (*horresco referens!*) an echo, distorted in both name and gender, of that individual who figures among the famous men of Plutarch and Cornelius Nepos![1] Are the scholars correct? Could they be? The fact that they even considered such a hypothesis is a measure of how far there was to go before Alcibiades would again be known. That distance, however, was soon to be covered during the Renaissance. Just one century later, Montaigne cited Alcibiades in his *Essais* some fifteen times, with details. He knew the anecdotes and scandals recounted in Plato. He took an interest in Alcibiades's beauty, in the affectation of his lisp. Montaigne was familiar with the references in Plato's *Symposium*, and with other sources on Socrates.[2] On the whole the persona appealed to him and aroused his sympathy. One is even a bit surprised to see how far that sympathy sometimes went: in *Essai* 2.36, in which he refers to important men, he goes so far as to write: "For a man who was no saint, but, as we say, a gentleman, of civilian and ordinary manners, and of moderate ambition, the richest life that I know, and full of the richest and most desirable parts, all things considered, is, in my opinion, that of Alcibiades." What? This man who betrayed his country, was twice exiled, and died by assassination with no one to defend him? The validation is almost as confusing as the strange metamorphosis granted by some scholars to Villon and his Archepiada! Was Montaigne guided by Plato's dazzling texts? Was he seduced by Plutarch's testimony? He was not, in any case, guided by a sound knowledge of history or by the analysis of Thucydides.

Equally surprising was the emergence, in the next century, of the figure of Alcibiades in Campistron's tragedy of 1685. The play bears Alcibiades's name and portrays his death, not in a lonely fort in upper Phrygia, but at the Persian court, in the presence of the king and satrap, as well as of two women, both in love with him. Alcibiades is himself also in love. Since this was the end of the seventeenth century, how could it be otherwise? He is secretly in love with the king's daughter. Furthermore, he is no traitor; rather, he has refused to lead the Persian army out of loyalty to Greece! He is, to be sure, endowed with that familiar boldness and seductive charm. And he is an exile. But that is all. All the rest arises out of the imagination

---

1. And isn't this metamorphosis as surprising to us as finding, among the martyrs of Lyon in 177, a Saint Alcibiades?
2. One or two of the allusions are still somewhat mysterious and could be mistakes.

of the author, informed by his reading of Plutarch and by the memory of Themistocles.

History was moving forward, however. In the following century, authors like Mably, l'abbé Barthélemy, and Rollin readily cite Alcibiades in the context of Greek history. Scholarship became more rigorous; sources were categorized, facts better established. That is not to say that everyone knew about Alcibiades. If we examine the random references in textbooks, we find that Alcibiades is often little known and hastily condemned. These manuals mention only his guilt in the affair of the herms, largely based on a misunderstanding, or the incident of the dog with its tail cut off, with no sense of the alarming significance of the incident. Those with more knowledge knew how exceptional an individual he was, one who had known highs and lows, great glory and great suffering. They did not, however, fully understand how these extremes related to each other and why.

The linkages between these aspects of Alcibiades's story and the reasons for them take on greater meaning for us today and deserve our thoughtful consideration. These are the relationships I have sought to emphasize, and the ones with which I want to conclude.

Like everyone else, I am affected by the exceptional quality of this individual and by his fate. I admit that I would have experienced less pleasure in writing this book if the wild adventures of the man, his successes, his boldness, and the dramatic vicissitudes of his life had not amazed me and left me breathless—even knowing in advance the trajectory and the outcome. A contemporary of Alcibiades said that Greece could not have endured two Alcibiades.[3] At his best and at his worst he had no equal; nor did his life's story.

I am above all, however, a reader of Thucydides, and constrained by the strength of his analyses. Moreover, I have written this book at a time when we are living in a democracy and when, as we face daily crises and problems, we feel an urgent need to understand them and to work to resolve them. Given my scholarly and intellectual ambience, I could not have continued with the portrayal of Alcibiades's exceptional life without being sensitive to the associations and reflections his life inspires in us today.

3. Plutarch 16.8.

In this respect, I have been well served: on every page, there seemed to be a detail that signaled something for me, more or less clearly, about our own time; and from page to page, in light of Thucydides's commentary, I gained a perspective that sheds light on us today.

At other times, even recent times, these similarities and perspectives would no doubt have presented a different order of importance.

I am certain, for example, that fifty years ago, when I was writing a book on *Thucydides and Athenian Imperialism*, and with the war against Hitler raging throughout Europe and beyond, the most striking thing to me about the life of Alcibiades would have been the way in which he identified with imperialism in Athens, and, thanks to Thucydides, with imperialism in general. I would have been struck by his desire to take on the Peloponnesians, then by the audacity of the Sicilian expedition and the grand design that was lurking behind this initial desire for conquest. I would have admired the way in which all those forces that impel the powerful to new conquests are revealed in him as he makes more and more enemies. And I would have appreciated the example of that expedition that constituted the beginning of the end; for finally everyone united against the conqueror. Consequently, I would have been keenly aware of the way in which Thucydides marked the differences between the imperialism of Alcibiades and the more moderate, more prudent imperialism that Pericles embodied. I would also have stressed the way in which, as Thucydides's analyses foreshadowed, the alliance against Athens quickly formed, first in Sicily, then in Ionia, and in almost the entire Greek world. And I would have marveled to observe how, across the years, Hitler's forces overextended themselves in the same way and ended with a similar disaster.

Of course, Alcibiades and Hitler have nothing in common; but the lesson that the Greeks themselves read in the history of Alcibiades would have meaning when applied to altogether different circumstances.

More generally, I would no doubt have recognized in these events what linked *hubris* to *nemesis*. And in particular I would have delighted to see the birth, in terms of imperialism and Alcibiades, of the concept that public opinion can be highly significant.

This concept emerges, negatively, from the work of Thucydides. Some of his speakers dared to say to the Athenians: "Aren't you going to alienate the goodwill of the cities by behaving like this?" Others noted that they would have to rely on what remained of that goodwill. The Greek word is *eunoia*. Isocrates, at the beginning of the following century, constructed a theory of *eunoia*, of the need to know how to achieve reconciliation, in external and internal politics, and in the work of the orator.[4]

In his imperialist politics, Alcibiades contributed to Athens' loss of this important asset; and the conduct of the cities of Sicily provides proof of that. But at the same time, Alcibiades, through his insolence and his provocations, lost the support of a whole sector of Athens. He made enemies, and those enemies were his undoing.

Thucydides put it simply: his insolence in private life impacted his political career: "His habits gave offense to everyone, and caused them to commit affairs to other hands, and thus before long to ruin the city" (6.15.4).

Alcibiades, who could be persuasive whenever he wished, was unable to inspire confidence in those on whom, ultimately, his fate would depend. According to Isocrates, this was the way a sense of morality could prove beneficial.

Today, in that same domain of foreign relations, perhaps we might be more sensitive to the drama of the quarrels between Greek cities, quarrels that the gold of rich Asians crudely settled.

There, too, experience was painful for the Greeks. As was often the case for them, however, it soon bore good fruit. They grasped the folly of all these quarrels dividing cities so close in culture. Alcibiades had been part of these quarrels, had encouraged and exacerbated them; to them he owed, indirectly, his downfall. Even during his lifetime we encounter Greek opposition to these deals with barbarians. And some years later, at the beginning of the fourth century, there were calls for unity and the creation of a Greek bloc to oppose the most powerful barbarians: Gorgias, Lysias, Isocrates supported this effort and fought for it. The Greeks established federations and confederations. Can we not, in building Europe, recognize in the scandal of Alcibiades's final years and his plots with the satraps a call to rally and to do better?

The lesson is that we must not follow either path: that of the imperialist Alcibiades in the beginning or that of the beggar at barbarian courts playing one city-state off the other. Alcibiades's actions are a wake-up call, one that has meaning right now.

---

4. See my article "*Eunoia* in Isocrates, or the Political Importance of Creating Good Will," *Journal of Hellenic Studies* 78 (1958): 92–101.

But this analogy with the unification of Europe is, in the case of Alcibiades, indirect and superficial; when we look back at his life, the crisis in democracy is what is most striking and moving today. Here the parallels come into full view and constantly astonish us.

First, there were the personal rivalries that ultimately paralyzed the state. It was Nicias against Alcibiades. Though there was almost no difference in their external policies, the people trusted only one or the other. The first result of this dichotomy was that it ensured the failure of every effort. The second problem was that it led to tensions, ruses, and futile attacks. Even ostracism, created, at least in part, to avoid these conflicts, was manipulated by various efforts and shifting alliances. Ambition, when it wants something, overcomes every obstacle, regardless of the means.

And that is precisely what it was: personal ambition, the desire of a single person to exercise power. Athenians distrusted Alcibiades for what they thought was his aspiring to tyranny. But ambition, as everyone knows, can also leave its mark in democratic institutions and cause just as much harm as tyranny would.

These selfish ambitions lead not only to demagoguery, but, when pushed to the extreme, to political provocation and retaliation of the worst kind.

And that brings us to the "affairs," something we see in our own day.

The scandals involving Alcibiades were of all types.

His taste for luxury, closely linked to the appetite for power, led him to spend money for athletic glory, and that brought him the attention of everyone. But the expenses he incurred for this purpose were suspicious and led to a long trial. Such things happen when ambition, tied to boldness, knows no limits or scruples. They are not the signs of a healthy democracy.

There are times when one scandal or another arises, and the "problems" multiply. There are accusations and denunciations. There is an arrest. Careers are wrecked by a wave of panic. Alcibiades was such a victim. This man, who had so much to be held to account for, was probably brought down by accusations that he could have successfully countered.

And emotions are so much stronger in a democracy. Conspiracy theories arise easily: "He aspires to tyranny," said the enemies of Alcibiades, the way we would today say "to fascism." In both cases, there is talk of a plot against the state. Fear turns contention into drama.

After that, the domains of justice and politics become intermingled. In Athens, this tangle was common and almost constant: the same people were voting in the Assembly and in the courts of justice. Sometimes the Assembly had the power of a court. In our country, however, justice is a separate domain, and everyone insists that it must remain so. The press, however, links justice to shifts in public opinion. People are not so insistent on the independent judiciary when troublesome facts interfere. Among individuals today who are under scrutiny, how many feel themselves caught in a trap like Alcibiades?

Clearly, it is not necessary to force the comparison. The two eras in this comparison are not alone in scandals. Cicero's Rome was rife with trials dealing with embezzlement and criminality. In Europe today, our country is not alone in its scandals.

And yet how can we help feeling startled by such connections? And how can we avoid the questions they raise?

For example, whether in ancient Greece or France today, one cannot escape the impression that scandalous behavior among leaders is getting worse.

Thucydides says clearly that rival ambitions arose after Pericles's death; and he explains that this happened because no paramount leader of the people emerged. Is that true today as well? There have been other times in the history of democracy in France when there were enormous scandals, but we are unlikely to find another period in which the habit of pursuing and imprisoning politicians for corruption flourished as it does today, in full view of everyone. Is this because, as in Athens, the power struggle between political leaders leaves no clear winner? That explanation does not seem to fit, at least not very tightly. But the fighting between parties, or between individuals, officially recognized, is expensive and leads to carelessness. Isn't this, cast in terms of groups and economics, the same principle?

Could this be a weakness inherent in democracy? The Athenian example suggests not. In desperation, the Athenians renounced the democracy in 411, but there was no change in individual passions or in the policies of the cities. In fact, if there was a real danger inherent in competition within the democracy, that problem existed only in the character of the citizens themselves, in the power of leading men, and in civic pride.

Everyone knew that Athens, having entered the war with confidence, had lost its vigor and its faith. Everyone knew that the sophists had managed to encourage realism and skepticism in the youth. And everyone knew that morality had been undermined by the war. Thucydides analyzed all these moral effects of the war and of civil war. Is it any different today? Do people today, as in Athens, not talk endlessly about our moral crisis? Democracy cannot survive the debasement of values. That is why the quality of education, the formation of future leaders, must be the primary concern of politicians who care about democracy—and this is clearly not the case today.

In some ways, the Athenian experience can also be reassuring: a U-turn is always possible. There was one in Athens, following the defeat and the occupation, and after the Athenians had overthrown the government of the Thirty. The first great decision of the restored democracy was to end, once and for all, the political quarreling. For us as well, defeat and occupation were the occasion for a comparable reversal around newfound values capable of inspiring heroic acts. There may be other occasions as well, and, if we are clear-eyed, they might not come at such great cost.

These thoughts have led us far from Alcibiades. And they exceed the experiences of his lifetime: the reconciliation of the parties and the desire for unity among the cities came only as a reaction, after him and without him. He had experienced years of crisis, contributing valuable talents to the fray, but they were all quickly lost in intrigues, quarrels, and revolutions. He added to this chaos both casually and boldly, both thoughtlessly and with imagination. He was also a victim of it. He could have done great things for Athens and for Greece. Reviewing his life we see how much he did, ultimately, to harm his city and country, not to mention the ruin he brought to himself. This amazing man is a model for all time—one to study, but not to imitate.

In the final analysis, will I have simply offered an example of a Greek historian of dazzling lucidity and an example of a Greek hero whose life provides only negative lessons? That would mean forgetting all the beautiful images of Alcibiades we have seen. That would mean forgetting his charm as well as his sharp intelligence, his way with words, and his courage in facing enemies and adversity. When we remove the political evaluation, his abilities and talents come to the fore. Alcibiades is like a hero in Greek tragedy who outshines the average man, but who is brought down by a fatal flaw. He is an Agamemnon who sacrificed his own daughter, an Ajax who once insulted Athena, an Eteocles who could not escape his paternal curse, a Hercules foolishly in love with a young captive. Alcibiades was as magnificent as they were and ended just as badly.

We should not fool ourselves. This story is about the fact that admirable heroes are destroyed by a flaw or an indiscretion, and that they illustrate the contrast, eminently tragic, between glory and ruin, something that is characteristic of both Alcibiades and tragedy. It is not about any particular resemblance to one of those tragic heroes. And yet I have pointed out the parallels throughout this book. Some would recognize Alcibiades's ambition in Euripides's hero Eteocles and his desire for power; others would find a resemblance to Philoctetes, Socrates's hero, who, far from home, was indispensable for future success, and on whom the sacking of Troy depended. The parallels in these situations are not the point here—though the impact of such a strong personality makes comparison quite easy.

In any case, there was an undeniable tragic element in Alcibiades's life.

Perhaps he himself was caught in a vise, not the vise of fate, but of political necessity. The trap we referred to before closed on him, as did those set by the gods for the tragic heroes.

Obstinately he stood his ground against everything. Never beaten, he fought with bravery in every battle. Socrates obtained for him an award for bravery. Alcibiades's bravery never faltered in an attempt to escape disaster. He faced everything with clarity and obstinacy, with skill and boldness. The picture we have of his death illustrates this quality perfectly. Like the Homeric heroes who, knowing they were about to die, cried out, "So what? I will fight!" he fought, alone. This, at least, is a positive lesson.

In one edition of Thucydides, I found it distracting that the publisher had chosen for the cover of the book a picture of Leonidas, nude, holding a sword. Leonidas was the Spartan hero of the Persian Wars, at the beginning of the fifth century. He was also a legendary hero, one whose style of combat was very different from the strategic maneuvers described by Thucydides at the end of that same century. Now here I am today, imagining Alcibiades leaving his burning house just like that cover picture of Leonidas. We have to expect this with Greece. Even when describing dark times and events that, as told by the harshest critics, are comparable to the most sordid events in our modern experience, we can expect to see them all in a heroic light, one that transfigures man, wrenching him from his sad context to cast him outside of time, into a universal beauty where we can look on him with pride.

INDEX

www.ingramcontent.com/pod-product-compliance
Ingram Content Group UK Ltd.
Pitfield, Milton Keynes, MK11 3LW, UK
UKHW040805060425
457000UK00013B/92/J